NATIONAL SECURITY LAWS
In Indian Scenario

NATIONAL SECURITY LAWS

In Indian Scenario

DR. SHAILESH K. SINGH
LL.M., M. Phil., Ph.D.
(Asst. Professor)
Shri Ji Institute of
Legal Vocational Education and Research, Bareilly (U.P.)
(MJP Rohilkhand University, Bareilly)

and

DR. SANJEEV K. CHADHA
LL.M., M.Phil., Ph.D.
Asstt. Prof. Law
HNB Garhwal Central University
Campus Badshahithaul, Tehri Garhwal
Uttarakhand

Foreword by :

JUSTICE K.D. SHAHI
Director, IMS-School of Law
Dehradun, Uttarakhand

REGAL PUBLICATIONS
New Delhi - 110 027

NATIONAL SECURITY LAWS
In Indian Scenario

ISBN 978-81-8484-136-7

Typeset by
RAHUL COMPOSERS
358, Pocket-B, Phase-2, Sector-16 B, Dwarka, New Delhi - 110 075

Printed in India at
MAYUR ENTERPRISES
WZ Plot No. 3, Gujjar Market, Tihar Village, New Delhi - 110 018

Published by
REGAL PUBLICATIONS
F-159, Rajouri Garden, New Delhi - 110 027 • Phone : 45546396
E-mail : regalbookspub@yahoo.com

Contents

Message

The subject matter of this book is relevant in present context as most developing nations of the post-1945 period have been facing internal security problems. Terrorism has now acquired global dimensions and has become the challenge for the whole world. The reach and methods adopted by terrorist groups and organizations take advantage of modern means of communication and technology using high-tech facilities available in the form of communication system, transport, sophisticated arms and various other means. This has enabled them to strike and create terror among people at will. The criminal justice system was not designed to deal with such type of heinous crimes. In view of this situation it is necessary to enact legislation for dealing with terrorist activities and preventing them. I congratulate Dr. Sanjeev K. Chadha and Dr. Shailesh K. Singh for writing an educative and interesting book.

I hope that the book will be useful for the students and teachers, I bestow my good wishes to the writers for compiling an issue which is so untouched. The book will surely nurture lawyers, academicians, politicians and other interested persons in the subjects.

PROF. S.K. SINGH
Vice Chancellor
Hemwati Nandan Bahuguna Garhwal University
Srinagar, Garhwal (Uttarakhand)

Foreword

The subject matter "National Security Laws" is relevant in present Indian context, as India is facing multifarious challenges in the management of it's internal security. There is an upsurge of terrorist activities, intensification of cross border terrorist activities and insurgent groups in different parts of the country. Terrorism has now acquired global dimensions and has become the challenges for the whole world.

I congratulate Dr. Sanjeev K. Chadha and Dr. Shailesh K. Singh for writing an educative book. I bestow my good wishes to the writers for compiling an issue which is so common but so untouched.

This book will surely nurture, politicians, academicians, aspirants and can be proved as an accepted yardstick of knowledge. The compilation is very conherent and is recommended for the appreciation.

JUSTICE K.D. SHAHI
Director, IMS-School of Law
Dehradun, Uttarakhand

Preface

Worldwide terrorism has created problem and compelled the countries to pass anti-terrorist laws. India is also one of them has passed many laws to combat terrorism but has to amend them frequently to keep pace with time.

An attempt has been made through this book to compiled maximum Anti-terrorist Act at one place analyse them in today scenario with suggestion "How to combat this unlawful activity".

This book will help all the law students who are pursuing post-graduation and research in law. In presenting the book we acknowledge with gratitude the various works of great jurists. Judges legal professionals, defence analyst without whose help it would not have been possible to complete the work.

We are also thankful to the publisher for printing and publishing the book and also those who have helped us in making our dream come true.

DR. SHAILESH K. SINGH
DR. SANJEEV K. CHADHA

Acronyms

ABCNY	Association of the Bar of the City of New York
AFSPA	Armed Forces (Special Powers) Act, 1958
AIR	All India Reporter
BJP	Bharatiya Janata Party
CBI	Central Bureau of Investigation
Cri. L.J.	Criminal Law Journal
CTC U.N.	Security Council Counter-Terrorism Committee
FBI	Federal Bureau of Investigation
HC	High Court
ICCPR	International Covenant on Civil and Political Rights
IPS	Indian Police Service
LTTE	Liberation Tigers of Tamil Eelam
MDMK	Marumalarchi Dravida Munnetra Kazhagam
MHA	Ministry of Home Affairs
MISA	Maintenance of Internal Security Act, 1971
NHRC	National Human Rights Commission
NIA	National Investigation Agency
NPC	National Police Commission
NSA	National Security Act, 1980
OHCHR	U.N. Office of the High Commissioner for Human Rights

PDA	Preventive Detention Act, 1950
PHRA	Protection of Human Rights Act, 1993
POTA	Prevention of Terrorism Act, 2002
POTO	Prevention of Terrorism Ordinance, 2001
SARs	Suspicious Activity Reports
SC	Supreme Court
SCC	Supreme Court Cases
SIMI	Students Islamic Movement of India
TAAA	Terrorist Affected Areas (Special Courts) Act, 1984
TADA	Terrorist and Disruptive Activities (Prevention) Act, 1985
TNM	Tamil Nationalist Movement
UAPA	Unlawful Activities (Prevention) Act, 1967
UDHR	Universal Declaration of Human Rights

पापी जनों को दण्ड देना चाहिये समुचित सदा।
वर वीर क्षत्रिय–वंश का कर्तव्य है यह सर्वदा।।

–जयद्रथवध (प्रथमसर्ग)

1

Introduction

GENERAL

Most developing nations of the post 1945 period have been facing with internal security problems. Internal sources of the national security problem often come up to uncontrollable degrees in these new nations, hampering the developmental activities and even putting the regimes to a stage of destabilization and ineffectiveness to the highest level. Strangely, national security threat perception in these nations has been, more or less, one sided and even conservative with a preconceived notion that national security means 'external defence' only.

Many of the third world nations seem to have ignored the fact that against the backdrop of socio-cultural, economic and political realities and also because of their being in the category of developing status in many sectors, perception of national security has to be assessed from various dimensions, i.e. from internal and external exigencies. It can be recalled that in most of the third-world nations, a variety of group or sub-group violence (which can be termed as internal war situation) have been witnessed from time to time. It is surprising that such a phenomenon are taken almost as a part of life without given a thought that such a conflict acts, may, within a short time, translate into a chronic national security problem. There is a general tendency on the part of the regimes in many third world nations to identify a conflict act only when it has become a violent and somewhat, an uncontrollable national issues. It seems that the authorities in these new nations have not been able to examine the evolutionary process of conflict behaviour within the nation in terms of the possibility of the conflict acts converting into an organized violence in the near future in the form of rebellion, sessionist, and insurgency movements or activities.

India's decades-long struggle to combat politicized violence has created what one observer has termed a "chronic crisis of national security" that has become part of the very "essence of India's being." Thousands have been killed and injured in this violence, whether terrorist, insurgent, or communal, and in the subsequent responses of security forces. Terrorism, in particular, has affected India more than most countries. By some accounts, India has faced more significant terrorist incidents than any other country in recent years, and as the recent attacks on the Mumbai commuter rail system make clear, the threat of terrorism persists. Like other countries, India has responded by enacting special antiterrorism laws, part of a broader array of emergency and security laws that periodically have been enacted in India since the British colonial period.

First in Varanasi then in Delhi then in Mumbai local trains and I do not think there is even a need to mention the continuing terrorist's barbaric activities in Kashmir. The bomb blasts have outraged every patriotic Indian. No civilized nation can allow this kind of barbaric inhumanity to be partly or fully supported or sponsored by any neighbor or domestic insurgents. The only way we can combat it is to minimize, if not eliminate, such occurrences. Prevention is crucial; and laws like POTA can prevent such occurrences. Acquittals even in a case like Parliament attack occurred because of poor prosecution rather then because of POTA.

After the 9/11 attacks on the world trade center the world's outlook towards the terrorist and terrorist organization has changed the laws have become much more stringent to curb such activities. The Indian outlook also changed specially after the 13 December attack on the Indian parliament which is seen as a symbol of our democracy then it became necessary to enforce a law which would be more stringent so that the terrorist can not go Scot free because after the lapse of TADA in 1995 following the wide spread complaint that it was being abused there was no law which could be used as a weapon against the rising terrorist activities in India.

India is facing multifarious challenges in the management of its internal security. There is an upsurge of terrorist activities, intensification of cross border terrorist activities and insurgent groups in different parts of the country. Terrorism has now acquired global dimensions and has become the challenge for the whole world. The reach and methods adopted by terrorist groups and organization take advantage of modern means of communication and technology using high tech facilities available in the form of communication system, transport, sophisticated arms and various other means. This has enabled them to strike and create terror among people at will. The criminal justice system was not designed to deal with such type of heinous crimes. In view of this situation it was felt necessary to enact legislation for the prevention of and for dealing with terrorist activities.

MEANING

> "...........A nation has security when it does not have to sacrifice its legitimate interest to avoide war and is able, if challenge, to maintain them by war"
>
> —*Walter Lippman : U.S. Foreign Policy : Shield of Republic p. 51*

> "...........Security in objective sence, measures the absence of threats to acquired values, in a sence (subjective), The absence of fear that such values will be attacked".
>
> — *Arnold Wolfers*

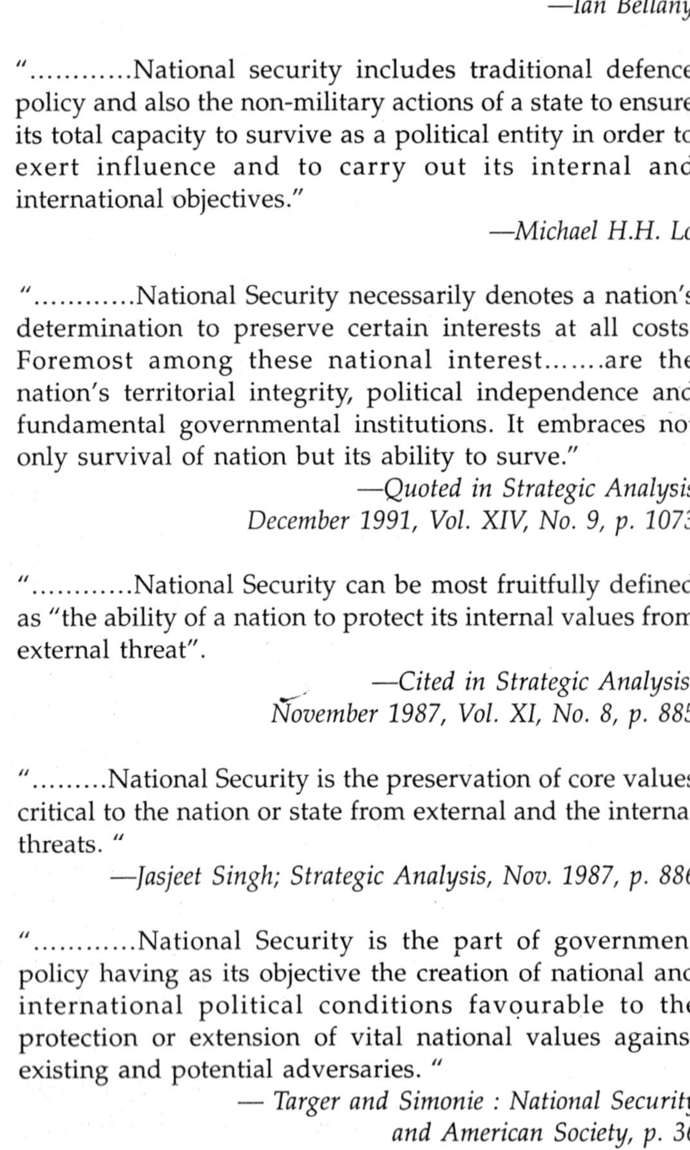

"...........Security itself is a relative freedom from war, coupled with a relatively high expectation that defeat will not be a consequence of any war that should occur."

—Ian Bellany

"...........National security includes traditional defence policy and also the non-military actions of a state to ensure its total capacity to survive as a political entity in order to exert influence and to carry out its internal and international objectives."

—Michael H.H. Lo

"...........National Security necessarily denotes a nation's determination to preserve certain interests at all costs. Foremost among these national interest.......are the nation's territorial integrity, political independence and fundamental governmental institutions. It embraces not only survival of nation but its ability to surve."

—Quoted in Strategic Analysis December 1991, Vol. XIV, No. 9, p. 1073

"...........National Security can be most fruitfully defined as "the ability of a nation to protect its internal values from external threat".

—Cited in Strategic Analysis, November 1987, Vol. XI, No. 8, p. 885

"........National Security is the preservation of core values critical to the nation or state from external and the internal threats. "

—Jasjeet Singh; Strategic Analysis, Nov. 1987, p. 886

"...........National Security is the part of government policy having as its objective the creation of national and international political conditions favourable to the protection or extension of vital national values against existing and potential adversaries. "

— Targer and Simonie : National Security and American Society, p. 36

"...........Security is the relative freedom from harmful threats."

—*John E. Morz; Beyond Security: Private Perception Among Arabs and Israelis, p. 105*

HISTORICAL CONTEXT

I. Pre-Independence (Pre Constitution)

Laws authorizing the use of extraordinary powers by the executive during formally declared periods of emergency have existed in India from the earliest days of direct British rule[1]. Following the 1857 Indian uprising and the consolidation of British control, the Indian Council Act of 1861, which was the statute establishing the overall governance framework for British India, authorized the Governor-General to legislate outside the ordinary lawmaking process in emergency situations by unilaterally issuing ordinances to ensure "the peace and good government" of India.[2] Such ordinances frequently were used to authorize administrative detention and to establish special tribunals to adjudicate cases relating to law and order, especially during wartime.[3] Two subsequent framework statutes, the Government of India Acts of 1919 and 1935, also granted the Governor-General emergency ordinance-making authority based on similar criteria.[4] In addition to this general emergency ordinance-making authority, the British enacted special emergency legislation during the two world wars. During World War I, the British enacted the Defence of India Act of 1915, which adapted the wartime "emergency code" from Britain for use in India.The Act authorized civil and military authorities to detain individuals or impose other

1. Venkat Iyer, States of Emergency: The Indian Experience 67 (2000).
2. Indian Councils Act of 1861, 24 and 25 Victoria, c. 67, § 23.
3. *Id*. at 68. While this ordinance-making power was used only seven times before 1914, it was exercised 27 times during World War I, and included the authorization of preventive detention. Id. at 68 and nn.6-7.
4. Government of India Act of 1919, 9 and 10 Geo. 5, c., Government of India Act of 1935, 26 Geo. 5 and 1 Edw. 8 c. 2.

restraints on personal liberty if they had "reasonable grounds" to suspect a person's conduct was "prejudicial to public safety."[5]

A second Defence of India Act was enacted in 1939, at the outset of World War II, authorizing the government to preventively detain anyone whose conduct was likely "prejudicial to the defence of British India, the public safety, the maintenance of public order, His Majesty's relations with foreign powers or Indian states, the maintenance of peaceful conditions in tribal areas or the efficient prosecution of the war."[6] Special tribunals were established to adjudicate violations of the Act's wartime rules, which remained in effect until they lapsed in October 1946.[7] But the British never limited their use of such extraordinary powers in India to formally declared periods of emergency. During non-emergency periods, the British also relied extensively upon sweeping laws

Authorizing preventive detention and criminalizing substantive offenses against the state.[8] As early as 1818, a regulation in Bengal granted the executive general authority to place individuals "under personal restraint" –notwithstanding the absence of "sufficient ground to institute any judicial proceeding" whenever justified to maintain British alliances with foreign governments, preserve tranquility in the princely states, or preserve the security of the state from "foreign hostility" or "internal commotion."[9] Detainees had no right to learn or contest the basis for their detention, and detention

---

5. British emergency code and wartime legislation, see A.W.B. Simpson, Round Up The Usual Suspects: The Legacy of British Colonialism and the European Convention on Human Rights, 41 LOY. L.REV. 629, 639-42, 646 (1996); Rachel Vorspan, Law and War: Individual Rights, Executive Authority,and Judicial Power in England During World War I, 38 VAND. J. Transnat'L L. 261 (2005).
6. Pursuant to the Act, approximately 800 such orders were issued in Bengal alone. SIMPSON, at 647.
7. *Id*. at 73-74 and n. 39; Mohammed Iqbal, Law of Preventive Detention In England, India And Pakistan 6 (1955); Jinks,
8. Indeed, given the extent of the government's preexisting, non-emergency powers, measures taken during the formally recognized emergency of World War I merely "topped up" those existing powers.BROWN,
9. SIMPSON, at 637-38; Pannalal Dhar, Preventive Detention Under Indian Constitution 72-73 (1986).

orders were not subject to time limits or independenoversight.[10] The 1818 regulation ultimately was extended throughout India.

The British also sought to extend the extraordinary powers initially justified on the basis of wartime emergency into non-emergency periods. Before the end of World War I, the British began to explore ways to preserve during peacetime the wartime emergency powers authorized by the Defence of India Act. A government committee recommended that several wartime powers be maintained during peacetime, and in response, the government in 1919 enacted the Anarchical and Revolutionary Crimes Act, known as the "Rowlatt Act" for the chair of the committee recommending its enactment.[11]

Both the substantive provisions of the Rowlatt Act and the circumstances surrounding its enactment and ultimate lapse three years later foreshadowed issues that have arisen in recent years under TADA and POTA.[12] The Act conferred broad power upon the government to combat "anarchical and revolutionary movements," a term the law did not define. Despite the lapse of the Defense of India Act and the end of the war, the Act preserved detention orders and other restraints on freedom of movement entered under that law's wartime authority.

In addition to authorizing preventive detention and other restraints on free movement, the Rowlatt Act defined particular substantive criminal offenses and set forth special procedures to adjudicate those offenses if the government determined that (1) anarchical and revolutionary movements were being promoted in all or part of India, and (2) the specified offenses were related to those movements and sufficiently prevalent to justify special, expedited procedures. Special courts were established to try such offenses, and ordinary procedural protections did not apply—the Act authorized in camera trial proceedings and eliminated the right to appeal. However, the law did ensure

10. DHAR, supra note 122, at 72-73. As a practical matter, detainees could obtain permission to make representations against their detention.
11. Iqbal, at 123 and n. 1, 126; Dhar, at 72-73; Granville Austin, the Indian Constitution: Cornerstone of a Nation 107 (1966).
12. D. Gopalakrishna Sastri, The Law of Sedition in India, Indian Law Institute Study No. 6, at 9-37(1964). the Punjab Sub-Committee of the Indian National Congress (Mar. 25, 1920), in 20 The Collected Works of Mahatma Gandhi 1; A.P. Muddiman.

some judicial oversight over the exercise of prosecutorial discretion, requiring the government to provide its allegations to the chief justice of the High Court, who had discretion to seek additional facts before deciding whether to constitute a special court to adjudicate the alleged violation.[13] With its extension of draconian wartime powers into an ordinary, non-emergency period, the Rowlatt Act became a focal point of the noncooperation campaign led by Mahatma Gandhi in the early 1920s.[14] In the face of this intense popular opposition, the government tempered its policies and permitted the Rowlatt Act to lapse in 1922.[15] However, the British did not refrain from exercising emergency-like powers during peacetime.

To the contrary, the government continued to exercise preventive detention authority throughout the 1920s under the preexisting 1818 regulation and to rely on what British Prime Minister Ramsay MacDonald termed "government by ordinance."[16]

II. Post-Independence (Post Constitution)

From 1947 to 1975, independent India followed the same basic pattern established by the British in its use of emergency and security laws. While India's post-independence constitution includes an extensive array of fundamental rights protections, its emergency and security provisions incorporate a number of

13. *Id.* at 127; IYER, at 69; Vijay Nagaraj, India: The Politics of Anti-Terror Legislation,Commonwealth Human Rights Initiative Seminar, Human Rights and Anti-Terrorism Legislation in the Commonwealth, at 1 (June 2003), available at http://www.humanrightsinitiative , British India: Acts of the Indian Legislative Council, 3 J. COMP. LEGISL. & INT'L L. 125, 126-28 (1919). org/new/papers/vijay_nagaraj.pdf.
14. Sarkar, at 187-95.
15. Simpson, at 647; Brown, at 203; see D.A. Low, 'Civil Martial Law' The Government of India and the Civil Disobedience Movements, 1930-34, in Congress and the Raj:Facets of the Indian Struggle, 1917-47, at 165, 165 (D.A. Low ed., 1977) (in immediate wake of anti-Rowlatt campaign, government "changed its policy towards nationalist agitation" and decided "so far as possible [to] avoid repressive measures, since these seemed to do more harm than good").
16. Low, (quoting MacDonald); see A. Fenner Brockway, Government by Ordinance in India, THE NATION, Feb. 24, 1932, at 226, 226; SIMPSON, at 647(discussing reinstatement of emergency powers under Bengal Ordinance of 1924 and Bengal Criminal Law Amendment Act of 1925).

the same basic principles found in the Government of India Act of 1935: extraordinary powers that may be exercised during declared periods of emergency, but supplemented by several layers of preventive detention and other security laws that readily afford the government multiple options to exercise similar powers even outside of formally declared periods of emergency.

(a) Formal Emergency Powers

The Constitution created several sources of formal emergency power similar to those used by the British. As originally written, the Constitution authorized the President to declare a national emergency in circumstances involving a grave threat to the security of India or any part of its territory on account of (1) war, (2) external aggression, or (3) internal disturbance or imminent danger of internal disturbance.[17] Upon proclaiming an emergency, the central government could exercise a broad range of special powers.

Perhaps most significantly, fundamental rights under article 19 of the Constitution would automatically be suspended by the declaration of emergency, and the executive was conferred with the power to suspend judicial enforcement of any other fundamental rights.[18] Between 1950 and 1975, the central government exercised its authority to declare a formal state of emergency twice—in 1962, when Chinese and Indian armed forces clashed along India's northern border, and in 1971, when war broke out between India and Pakistan.[19] Each of the two wartime proclamations of emergency was followed by parliamentary action conferring sweeping powers upon the executive. The Defence of India Act of 1962, for example,

17. India Const. art. 352; Gopal Subramanium, Emergency Provisions Under the Indian Constitution, in Supreme but not Infallible, at 134, 136.
18. India Const. art. 358-59; see Subramanium, supra note 147, at 143; IYER, at 141. In addition, the declaration of emergency empowered the central government executive to assume the power to direct state governments concerning the manner in which their own executive authority should be exercised. Parliament also could assume the power to legislate concerning matters that otherwise would be within the exclusive jurisdiction of the states.
19. Iyer, at 141.

authorized the central and state governments to engage in preventive detention extending well beyond the length of time permitted under ordinary preventive detention laws.[20] While the rules established a system of administrative supervision and review, they set no maximum period of detention, and detainees were not entitled to learn the grounds for detention or to challenge the detention in any forum. The rules also authorized restrictions on freedom of movement and freedom of assembly; conferred broad search, seizure, and warrantless arrest powers upon magistrates and the police; increased penalties for a number of criminal offenses; and, to adjudicate violations, authorized the creation of special tribunals in which many ordinary criminal procedural protections were not available.[21] The government also suspended judicial enforcement of rights that may have been violated under the emergency proclamation.[22] While the formal ground for invoking the Constitution's emergency authority in each instance was war and external aggression, in each case the government maintained the state of emergency long after armed conflict had ceased, echoing efforts by the British to extend into peacetime the sweeping emergency powers authorized on account of war. Although the conflict with China was over within days, the 1962 emergency proclamation remained in effect until 1968.[23] Similarly, the 1971 war with Pakistan ended within weeks, and relations between India and Pakistan were soon normalized, yet the 1971 emergency proclamation remained in effect, along with a concurrent state of emergency declared by Indira Gandhi in 1975 in response to threats allegedly posed by "internal disturbance,"[24] through 1977.

20. The rules authorized preventive detention of anyone for the purpose of "preventing him from acting in a manner prejudicial to the defence of Indian civil defence, the public safety, the maintenance of public order, India's relations with foreign powers, the maintenance of peaceful conditions in any part of India, or the efficient conduct of military operations." IYER, at 109.

21. *Id.* at 109-14.

22. *Id.* at 105.

23. While efforts to terminate the 1962 emergency were dampened by the onset of war between India and Pakistan in 1965, that conflict, too, was over within weeks. *Id.* at 125.

24. See infra section III.C. India Const. art. 123(1); IYER, at 79-80.

Finally, the Constitution preserved a version of the power held by the British Governor-General to legislate by ordinance and supersede state governments. When both houses of Parliament are out of session, the President, at the direction of the cabinet, may promulgate an ordinance if satisfied "that circumstances exist which render it necessary . . . to take immediate action."[25] Such ordinances have the force of law, but must be ratified by an act of Parliament within six weeks after the end of its recess.

(b) Non-Emergency Preventive Detention Laws

Like the colonial legal framework, the Indian Constitution explicitly authorizes preventive detention during ordinary, non-emergency periods. Subject to limited procedural safeguards, the Constitution explicitly grants both the central and state governments power to enact laws authorizing preventive detention. [25] Within weeks after the Constitution went into force, Parliament enacted the Preventive Detention Act of 1950, which authorized detention for up to 12 months by both the central and state governments if necessary to prevent an individual from acting in a manner prejudicial to the defense or security of India, India's relations with foreign powers, state security or maintenance of public order, or maintenance of essential supplies andservices.[26] The act also implemented the limited procedural protections required by the Constitution.[27]

The PDA was originally set to expire after one year. Indeed, the Home Minister explicitly stated that the bill was meant as a temporary expedient, intended only to address exigent circumstances in the aftermath of independence and partition, and that any decision to make it permanent demanded closer study.[28] However, as with the use of formal emergency

25. India Const. art. 22(4)-(6). Id. art. 22(7). Id. art. 22(3).
26. Bayley, at 99-100.
27. For example, the Act required the government to provide the detainee with the grounds for detention within five days and required Advisory Board review of all detention orders. Id. at 102.
28. The Home Minister even confessed to having lost sleep for two nights before introducing the bill. A.G. Noorani, Preventive Detention in India, Econ. and Pol. Weekly, Nov. 16, 1991, at 2608 (quoting Vallabhbhai Patel); see also Jinks, at 341-42 (quoting statements by PDA supporters that preventive detention was a "necessary evil").

authority, this "temporary expedient" was routinely reenacted each year for almost 20 years. While it finally lapsed in 1969, preventive detention authority returned less than two years later under the Maintenance of Internal Security Act, which largely restored the provisions of the PDA.[29]

TERRORISM

Origin of Word 'Terrorism'

The term "terrorism" comes from the French word terrorisme, which is based on the Latin verb terrere (to cause to tremble). It dates back to 1795 when it was used to describe the actions of the Jacobin Club in their rule of post-Revolutionary France, the so-called "Reign of Terror". Jacobins are rumored to have coined the term "terrorists" to refer to themselves.

Various Definitions of 'Terrorism'

Terrorism refers to a strategy of using violence, social threats, or coordinated attacks, in order to generate fear, cause disruption, and ultimately, brings about compliance with specified political, religious, or ideological demands.

Terrorism refers to extortion, Kidnapping and pilling to attract wider attention to a particular cause and thus to force a targeted authority to conceded demands of the perpetrators of terror. Terror tactics are generally adopted by isolated groups or ethnic minorities who are despaired of getting a sympathetic authence for their real or perceived grievances. They generally get moral or financial support from the group or community on whose behalf they take up arms to challenge the authorities. Most Terrorist movements derive their motive force from sections of population who nurse strong feeling of being wronged, deprived or deride of their just rights by the people wielding political power. Terrorists remain men's to the governments as long as they enjoy a measure of overt or covert support from some sections of the people. They begin to lose grounds as their activities start dislocating the lives of the people in whose name they claim to fight gradually, their

29. Maintenance of Internal Security Act, No. 26 of 1971 [hereinafter MISA]; see Iyer.

erstwhile supporters turn against them for indiscriminate use of terror.

When a group or community feels that the preservation of its identity or way of life is threatened by a stronger group, community or state and no normal or usual methods of redressing its grievance will be effective, it takes resort to violence or Terrorism to achieve its cherished objectives.

Since time immemorial, terrorist acts have included assassination, seizing hostages and a variety of atrocities that only fiendish minds could devise. Terrorists give innumerable, explanation for their violence. They declare that society is sick and cannot be cured by half measures of reform and that, as the state itself uses the violence, it can overcome only by violence. They also assert that the righteousness of their cause justifies any action they may take-contemporary terrorism involves a group of individuals who are from affluent industrialized society. They seek to destroy this society in the name of some revolutionary concept. Examples of such groups would include The Italian Red Brigade, German Border, The Indian Naxalite Movement, etc.

Another group of terrorists comprises those espousing more traditional political causes- The Unification of Ireland.

Acts of international terrorism are committed to terrorize nations and governments into compliance. International terrorism is distinguished by three characteristics. First, it embodies a criminal act. Second, it is a politically motivated and their violence is directed against innocent people. Finally, international terrorism transcends national boundaries through the choice of a foreign target, the commission of the act in a foreign country and an effort to influence the policies of a foreign government.

The European Union includes in its 2002 definition of "terrorism" the aim of "destabilising or destroying the fundamental political, constitutional, economic or social structures of a country". Terrorism is defined in the U.S. by the Code of Federal Bureau of Investigation as: "the unlawful use of force and violence against persons or property to intimidate or coerce a government, the civilian population, or any segment thereof, in furtherance of political or social objectives". The FBI further describes terrorism as either domestic or international, depending on the origin, base, and objectives of the terrorists.

Although conditions for rise of Terrorism exist in many parts of the country, it finds favourable environment to grow in states located near the international border. For one thin, Terrorists can hit the targets and then escape into a forgiven country without an, apprehension of being chased or arrested in that country. Secondly, they get arms, training, strategic and financial support from the bordering country which will always like to see it neighbour in trouble. Thus, most Terrorist groups in Punjab and Jammu and Kashmir receive and over support from the bordering Pakistan while the insurgents of north-east have their sanctuaries and training camps across the borders in Bangladesh and Myanmar. The L.T.T.E. (Liberation Tigers of Tamil Elam) could emerge as a menacing group in Sri Lanka with the support of people of Tamil origin not only in the boring India but also from Tamils living in other countries of the world including Great Britain. But Sri Lankan's Commando destroy the LTTE Main yet.

Types and Reasons of Terrorism

Terrorism is one of the greatest problems and it is a burning question why Terrorism is spreading just like fire in a Jungle. Some people who don't have any fear of death and fear of being destroyed by anyone. According to types and Reasons of Terrorism, it can be classified as per below:

- (A) Domestic Terrorism
    - (a) Religious
    - (b) Revolutionary
- (B) International Terrorism
    - (a) To Destroy Resources
    - (b) To Outshine

(A) Domestic Terrorism

(a) Religious

Religion has been one of must common reason of many

type of fights, terror, horror for e.g. At the time, why English rule over India they accepted the policy, i.e. Divide and Rule. They divide the people by using religious base, i.e. Hindu and Muslim religion. They fire the hearts of those people and pros surge them be dead for their own religion till now. Young people are generally the victim of this Terrorism. At the cost of their own life, they attack on difference type of temples and Gurdwaras.

Just fire Akshardham, as this Swaminarain temple is Architectural manel make of pink sandstone. It is the seat of the Bochasanwasi Shri Akshar Purshttam Sanstha the largest of the multiple sects who fallow the 19th century guru Swaminarain. It's sprawling campus is a tourist spot with thousands of people from ale faiths visiting it every day. It is in a VIP area near the CM's house. We can hit you wherever we want.

The deadly attack on the Swaminarain temple shows that Terrorists have shifted focus to soft targets. Their attempt to trigger communal tensions was thwarted this time but the tactic has emerged as the newest threat.

(b) Revolutionary

Terrorists give innumerable, explanation for their violence. They declare that society is sick and cannot be cured by half measures of reform and that, as the state itself uses the violence, it can overcome only by violence. They also assert that the righteousness of their cause justifies any action they may take-contemporary terrorism involves a group of individuals who are from affluent industrialized society. They seek to destroy this society in the name of some revolutionary concept. Examples of such groups would include The Italian Red Brigade, German Border, The Indian Naxalite Movement, etc.

(B) International Terrorism

(a) To Destroy Resources

The main reason and main and important factor of Terrorism is that every country events to destroy others resources and wants to inerrage their space as it can be elastic just like is main Terrorists Laden always attack on Kashmir with it's own reasons.

(b) To Outshine

To outshine other countries terrorism is considered on the strategy of Pakistan which always tries to outshine others, most of time the victim became India. India and Pakistan are the old enemies; mainly after English people adopted the policy of Dorado conquer. Pakistan always wants to others countries like it attacked on America's one wonder of the world.

The new attack of 26/11, i.e. 26-11-2008 in Mumbai is the latest terror attack. And Sri Lankan Team in Pakistan attack by terrorist is the open challenge by the terrorist to all worlds. World trade centre was one of the wonder of the seven wonders of the world 11th September was the dangerous day for America. 19 students hijacked four U.S.A. planes. At 9:00 A.M. First plane attacked the first tower of world trade centre. 9:15 AM second airplane attacked the second tower of world trade centre. Some minute's later third plane attacked pentagon. One pentagon side was damaged. Some minutes later fourth plane damage in alone. An emergency was announced and suddenly white house was also became empties. It was a big Terrorist situation. There was only smoke and snoke at the place of world trade centre. People were falling from windows like hurtle pigeons. It was a catastrophic scene. According type terms many people are also ruined their life. 50000 people injured in this attack the attacker was Osama Bin Laden.

Root of the Mayhem

The word terrorism never sounded as grievous as it seems to be. At times brains gobble pertaining to the origin of the bloody form of holocaust, which is terrorism. But have we ever tried to analyze within our so-called intelligent brains that where from this word terrorism crept into our society. Is this a result of day today honing of some mischievous brains or it popped up suddenly on one fine day out of nowhere. If we recapitulate the past we can surely get our answers that how this form of mayhem actually evolved. In the aftermath of September 11, 2001, a consensus quickly emerged that poverty and lack of education were major causes of terrorist acts and support for terrorism. Subscribing to that theory are politicians, journalists, and many scholars, as well as officials responsible for administering aid to poor countries.

Defining terrorism is difficult. Some definitions, emphasize the "subnational," "clandestine" character of "politically motivated violence," while others include the state as a perpetrator. What's common to most definitions is the inclusion of terrorists' goal of inducing fear in a target audience that transcends the physical harm caused to immediate victims, the ultimate purpose being persuasion. A large body of evidence exists on hate crimes, a close cousin to terrorism. These are crimes against members of a religious, racial, or ethnic group selected solely because they are part of that group. Hate crimes are usually less orchestrated than terrorist acts. The effect of both terrorism and hate crimes is to wreak terror in a greater number of people than those directly affected by the violence.

The economic theory about participation in terrorism considers the supply side first - that is, why do people commit terrorist acts. As is conventional in economics, involvement in terrorism is viewed as a rational decision that depends on the benefits, costs, and risks involved, compared with those of other activities. Public opinion polls can provide information on which segments of the population support terrorist or militant activities.

News reports often create the impression that Islam is a source of terrorism. Note, though, that suicide attacks are a relatively new, alien element in the history of mainstream Islam. But suicide attacks and other forms of terrorism have been carried out by people belonging to other established religions, too, and by individuals professing no religious faith at all.

The root cause of manmade disaster and terror is very complex and don't mean to trivialize the importance of what has recently occurred or the need for developing creative solutions to the global problem of terrorism. Somewhere along the line, we can chance a guess to say that, a solution was possible before the need for radical terrorism and ultimately war.

As we move ever closer to war, we should keep in mind that terror comes from many sources and is not a central Asian problem. It has occurred in Canada, the United Kingdom, Mexico and the United States. Terrorism in these countries has been both international and domestic in nature.

This should not be a war on Muslim terrorists; it should be a war on global terrorism, as the potential problem exists in all nations of the world. If the fight is to be credible, it is incumbent upon all nations of any coalition to begin the fight at home by eliminating the structures that allow terrorist cells to operate and fund international and domestic terror.

Root Cause of Terrorism in India

It is a bit unfortunate that we as a country are facing hostilities from our neighboring countries since independence. Pakistan since its creation has always harbored terrorist elements against India with an intention to destabilize our country. China the Big Brother supports Pakistan in their endeavor to divide India. We face threats from Bangladesh and from Sri Lanka in the South. Since we have open borders with Nepal, terrorists use Nepal as easy entry and exit points. Our borders with Pakistan and Bangladesh are porous and not fully sealed. We face trouble on the North -East side with China claiming Arunachal Pradesh. These countries hobnob with these terrorists and have helped them to establish their bases from where they can carry out their evil acts. So all the expertise for planting Bombs on soft targets come from these countries. But not everything can be done from these foreign bases. So they take advantage of the unemployed youth and others who fall easy prey to their indoctrination and create local groups who ferment trouble in all cities across India. They take help from some political class and the corrupt officials provide fodder for their entry and exit from India.

So Terrorism is not about Muslims only and their quest for Jihad. Not all Muslims are terrorists and not all terrorists are Muslims. India's 140 million Muslims are a salutary negation of the facile thesis about Islam's incompatibility with democracy. The terrorists that we encounter today are not men who commit evil acts out of revenge. For these men indoctrinated by outfits like the Al Qaeda and the Dawood gangs, terrorism is a full fledged profession. Only few Muslims believe that these phonies are fighting for any cause but their own. Hindus have stopped fulminating against terror despite the heavy toll it takes each time. For these terrorists who are invisible, they have no Agenda. They do it in the name of Jihad or some linguistic or religious cause, which a common man does not identify himself with.

India earned its reputation as a soft state that can be intimidated into meeting terrorists' demands. Our then foreign minister in the year 1999 in the month of December personally escorted three terrorists freed by India in order to secure the release of passengers of a hijacked Indian Airlines flight to Tliban controlled Afghanistan. This act led to the 9/11 attack in New York as one of these very terrorists was later implicated in the 9/11 attacks.

Democratic politics, political freedoms, civil liberties and religious tolerance must be protected at all costs. The corruption and politicisation of the police forces must be minimised. We need a dedicated and an unbiased police force. Criminalisation of politics must stop. Instead, we have number of parliamentarians with pending criminal cases. Some jailed parliamentarians also cast their vote on important National issues which is alarming! Terrorism prospers and thrives in such conditions. In a way, Poverty is an incubator of terrorism and a root cause of corruption. It breeds the Naxalites and the local terrorist groups. The government needs to be tough in implementing reforms to maintain rapid economic growth and uplift the status of its downtrodden people.

More importantly, India's terrorism problem is largely specific to Kashmir. There is a difference between terrorists and freedom fighters and one should not equate them. India must muster International support in this issue and put pressure on Pakistan to stop supporting these terrorists. India habitually points fingers at Pakistan which is the hotbed and the epicentre of terrorism all around the world. But merely pointing fingers will not help matters. For a small country like Pakistan to be able to infiltrate groups of Indians and recruit them to the terrorist's cause indicates failures of the intelligence on the other hand. We have to look into this fact. There is no co-ordination between the central intelligence agencies and the states. Each points a finger at others each time a bomb blast takes place. This is matched by the flaws of the criminal justice system, which is rudimentary by the standards of mature democracies. Whether it is the Bombay bomb blasts of 1992 or the Gujarat riots in 2002, justice takes many years to deliver. Justice has neither been done, nor seen to be done. India needs to be tough but not reactionary to the causes of terrorism.

Ontology of Terrorism

Terrorism has become the systematic weapon of a war that knows no borders or seldom has a face.

People experiencing circumstances of relative deprivation will protect their self-esteem and identity by attributing these circumstances to powerful enemies that unfairly impose such situation on them. They tend to develop an autistic and biased system for processing of information that allow people to see themselves as victims, and therefore to justify an attack on the attributed source of their deprivation and humiliation. This form of self-empowerment helps to protect their individual and group's identity and to exercise social pressure towards group unity. It can be argued that Hitler's rise to power was a direct result of the humiliations and deprivations suffered by Germans during the 1920's. Nazi propaganda manipulated German's sense of grievance by stressing and glorifying. The conditions of relative deprivation, collective humiliation and perceived injuries created an identity crisis in Germany that was fertile soil for fascism to flourish. The sufferings of Germany during were the ultimate source of the deprivations and humiliations artfully manipulated by Hitler. The current circumstances of Muslims around the world have similarities with pre-Nazi Germany, including a situation of relative deprivation and deep feelings of vulnerability. This beaten and vulnerable identity is not an attractive one. It is rejected, initially by an extremist minority that resorts to powerful images of a glorified past and a supposedly intrinsic superiority over their enemies to create an attractive alternative identity. Needless to say, this alternative identity is very difficult to resist in particular for young members of society. Extremists that find self-serving explanations for the deprivations, humiliations and sense of vulnerability in real or imaginary but always powerful enemies that unjustly have imposed these circumstances upon them manipulate the new identity. The sense of humiliation is transformed into anger and a sense of historical injustice, which creates longing for the reconstruction of a glorious past.

In the case of Muslims, a longing for a return to the past when the present situation seems hopeless is understandable. Muslims have seen their participation reduced to a secondary, subordinate role as a result of the partition of the Ottoman Empire at the end of WWI. Rampant levels of poverty and oppression in many Muslim countries add to the sense of humiliation and grievance to create an identity crisis that is exploited by religious and political extremists to gain influence. Although deeply unrepresentative of Islam's long history of tolerance and despite the fact that a war against civilians is a gross violation of Islamic law, the force of the reasoning contained in this declaration comes from the fact that it provides a more appealing explanation to the deprivations and humiliations of Muslims around the world. It translated the responsibility to an evil and powerful enemy that purposefully victimizes Muslims. This account, although biased and self-serving, provides a more appealing explanation that is highly appealing. As mentioned before, identity is a powerful ontological force that guides our perception and behavior. It would be naive to think that the current crisis is limited to any terrorist group. Thus is the reason why terrorists have become a symbol of defiance. The terrorist groups manipulate this to impose a self-serving, extremist, but highly appealing identity.

Impact of Terrorism

Terrorism, like viruses, is everywhere. There is a global perfusion of terrorism, which accompanies any system of domination as though it were its shadow, ready to activate itself anywhere, like a double agent.

Though there is nothing new about terrorism and religious fundamentalism in the history of humanity, the present day scenario in the world at large, and in the Indian subcontinent in particular are undoubtedly very alarming.

In recent times, religious fundamentalism and terrorist activities have become extremely well organized with local, national and international network involving a huge number of personnel at all levels and an enormous amount of resources.

The September 11 senseless attack on mass civilian targets and the resulting heavy loss to human life and property has catapulted terrorism as the foremost threat to national and global security. These incidents lulled us into thinking that this evil is endemic to only a few regions of the world, and can be curtailed either by strong police or military action, or by bringing the perpetrators of such crimes and their masterminds to justice. The 9/11 was indeed a turning point in this regard. It was an event that deeply shook the equilibrium of the social fabric of the entire world. Human relationship became profoundly distorted. Warmongers are finding pretexts of all kinds, not the least religious Fundamentalism and terrorism, to justify their blatantly unjustifiable position.

Consequently, over the centuries India has developed a culture of harmony that acknowledges unity and promotes diversity in religious pursuits and cultural expressions. It is because of this noble heritage that India has become the homeland of many religions guaranteeing for centuries their peaceful coexistence here. But every coin has two sides, so is this. Since its independence in 1947, India has been facing the problem of insurgency and terrorism in different parts of the country. The insurgency has been taken to mean an armed violent movement, directed mainly against security forces and other government targets, to seek territorial control; terrorism has been taken to mean an armed violent movement directed against government as well as non-government targets, involving pre-meditated attacks with arms, ammunition and explosives against civilians, and resorting to intimidation tactics such as hostage-taking and hijacking, but not seeking territorial control. India has faced exclusively terrorist movements in Punjab and Jammu and Kashmir, bordering Pakistan, and part insurgent-part terrorist movements in the northeast, bordering Myanmar and Bangladesh; in Bihar, bordering Nepal; and in certain interior states like Andhra Pradesh, Madhya Pradesh, etc defying international borders. Terrorism has become the systematic weapon of a war that knows no borders or seldom has a face.

India has also faced terrorism of an ephemeral nature, which sprang suddenly due religious anger against either the government or the majority Hindu community or both and petered out subsequently. So it can be derived to some extent that it would be wrong to target only Muslim because there have been evidences of even Hindus and Christians involving in such heinous act.

In incidents like Madrid Commuter Train Bombing, Oklahoma City Bombing, and Lockerbie Disaster: The Crash of Pan Am Flight 103, Subway Attack in Japan rates of distress and posttraumatic symptoms have been found to be high in individuals studied following terrorist events.

We are not in a position to affirm that the steps we propose are adequate to root out terrorism. We still argue that these are important steps, worth taking.

The terrible thing about terrorism is that ultimately it destroys those who practice it, slowly but surely, as they try to extinguish life of others, the light within them dies.

Major Terrorist Groups of India

TABLE 1
Terrorist Groups of ASSAM

Sl. No.	*Name of Group*	*Short Name*
(1)	(2)	(3)
1.	United Liberation Front of Asom	(ULFA)
2.	National Democratic Front of Bodoland	(NDFB)
3.	United People's Democratic Solidarity	(UPDS)
4.	Kamtapur Liberation Organisation	(KLO)
5.	Bodo Liberation Tiger Force	(BLTF)
6.	Dima Halim Daogah	(DHD)
7.	Karbi National Volunteers	(KNV)
8.	Rabha National Security Force	(RNSF)
9.	Koch-Rajbongshi Liberation Organisation	(KRLO)

(Contd.)

TABLE 1 (*Contd.*)

(1)	*(2)*	*(3)*
10.	Hmar People's Convention-Democracy	(HPC-D)
11.	Karbi People's Front	(KPF)
12.	Tiwa National Revolutionary Force	(TNRF
13.	Bircha Commando Force	(BCF)
14.	Bengali Tiger Force	(BTF)
15.	Adivasi Security Force	(ASF)
16.	All Assam Adivasi Suraksha Samiti	(AAASS)
17.	Gorkha Tiger Force	(GTF)
18.	Barak Valley Youth Liberation Front	(BVYLF)
19.	Muslim United Liberation Tigers of Assam	(MULTA)
20.	United Liberation Front of Barak Valley	(ULFBV)
21.	Muslim United Liberation Front of Assam	(MULFA)
22.	Muslim Security Council of Assam	(MSCA)
23.	United Liberation Militia of Assam	(ULMA)
24.	Islamic Liberation Army of Assam	(ILAA)
25.	Muslim Volunteer Force	(MVF)
26.	Muslim Liberation Army	(MLA)
27.	Muslim Security Force	(MSF)
28.	Islamic Sevak Sangh	(ISS)
29.	Islamic United Reformation Protest of India	(IURPI)
30.	United Muslim Liberation Front of Assam	(UMLFA)
31.	Revolutionary Muslim Commandos	(RMC)
32.	Muslim Tiger Force	(MTF)
33.	People's United Liberation Front	(PULF)
34.	Adam Sena	(AS)
35.	Harkat-ul-Mujahideen	HuM
36.	Harkat-ul-Jehad	HuJ

TABLE 2
Terrorist Groups of Punjab

Sl. No.	*Name of Group*	*Short Name*
1.	Babbar Khalsa International	(BKI)
2.	Khalistan Zindabad Force	(KZF)
3.	International Sikh Youth Federation	(ISYF)
4.	Khalistan Commando	(KC)
5.	All-India Sikh Students Federation	(AISSF)
6.	Bhindrawala Tigers Force of Khalistan	(BTFK)
7.	Khalistan Liberation Army	(KLA)
8.	Khalistan Liberation Front	(KLF)
9.	Khalistan Armed Force	(KAF)
10.	Dashmesh Regiment	
11.	Khalistan Liberation Organisation	(KLO)
12.	Khalistan National Army	(KNA)

TABLE 3
Terrorist Groups of Jammu and Kashmir

Sl. No.	*Terrorist Outfits*		*Other Extremist and Secessionist Groups*
(1)	*(2)*		*(3)*
1. 2. 3.	Lashkar-e-Omar (LeO) Hizb-ul-Mujahideen (HM) Harkat-ul-Ansar (HuA, presently known as Harkat-ul Mujahideen)	1.	Mutahida Jehad Council (MJC)—A Pakistan based coordination body of terrorist outfits active in Jammu and Kashmir
4. 5. 6. 7.	Lashkar-e-Toiba (LeT) Jaish-e-Mohammed (JeM) Harkat-ul Mujahideen (HuM, previously known as Harkat-ul-Ansar) Al Badr	2.	Jammu and Kashmir Liberation Front (JKLF)—The dominant faction of this outfit declared a ceasefire in 1994 which still holds and the outfit restricts itself to a political struggle.

(Contd.)

TABLE 3 (*Contd.*)

(1)	(2)		(3)
8.	Jamait-ul-Mujahideen (JuM)	3.	All Parties Hurriyat Conference (APHC)—an alliance engineered by Pakistan's Inter Services Intelligence (ISI) of 26 diverse political and socio-religious outfits amalgamated to provide a political face for the terrorists in the State.
9.	Lashkar-e-Jabbar (LeJ)		
10.	Harkat-ul-Jehad-i-Islami		
11.	Al Barq		
12.	Tehrik-ul-Mujahideen		
13.	Al Jehad	4.	Dukhtaran-e-Millat (DeM) - an outfit run by women which uses community pressure to further the social norms dictated by Islamic fundamental groups.
14.	Jammu and Kashir National Liberation Army		
15.	People's League		
16.	Muslim Janbaz Force		
17.	Kashmir Jehad Force		
18.	'Al Jehad Force (combines Muslim Janbaz Force and Kashmir Jehad Force)		
19.	Al Umar Mujahideen		
20.	Mahaz-e-Azadi		
21.	Islami Jamaat-e-Tulba		
22.	Jammu and Kashmir Students Liberation Front		
23.	Ikhwan-ul-Mujahideen		
24.	Islamic Students League		
25.	Tehrik-e-Hurriat-e-Kashmir		
26.	Tehrik-e-Nifaz-e-Fiqar Jafaria		
27.	Al Mustafa Liberation Fighters		
28.	Tehrik-e-Jehad-e-Islami		
29.	Muslim Mujahideen		
30.	Al Mujahid Force		
31.	Tehrik-e-Jehad		
32.	Islami Inquilabi Mahaz		

Table 4
Terrorist Groups of Manipur

Sl. No.	*Name of Group*	*Short Name*
(1)	*(2)*	*(3)*
1.	United National Liberation Front	(UNLF)
2.	People's Liberation Army	(PLA)
3.	People's Revolutionary Party of Kangleipak	(PREPAK)
	(The above mentioned three groups = Manipur People's Liberation Front)	(MPLF)
4.	United Islamic Liberation Army	(UILA)
5.	United Islamic Revolutionary Army	(UIRA)
6.	Chin Kuki Revolutionary Front	(CKRF)
7.	Kangleipak Communist Party	(KCP)
8.	Kanglei Yawol Kanna Lup	(KYKL)
9.	Manipur Liberation Tiger Army	(MLTA)
10.	Iripak Kanba Lup	(IKL)
11.	People's Republican Army	(PRA)
12.	Kangleipak Kanba Kanglup	(KKK)
13.	Kangleipak Liberation Organisation	(KLO)
14.	Revolutionary Joint Committee	(RJC)
15.	National Socialist Council of Nagaland—Isak-Muivah	(NSCN-IM)
16.	People's United Liberation Front	(PULF)
17.	North East Minority Front	(NEMF)
18.	Islamic National Front	(INF)
19.	Islamic Revolutionary Front	(IRF)
20.	Kom Rem People's Convention	(KRPC)
21.	Kuki National Front	(KNF)
22.	Kuki National Army	(KNA)

(Contd.)

TABLE 4 (Contd.)

(1)	(2)	(3)
23.	Kuki Revolutionary Army	(KRA)
24.	Kuki National Organisation	(KNO)
25.	Kuki Independent Army	(KIA)
26.	Kuki Defence Force	(KDF)
27.	Kuki International Force	(KIF)
28.	Kuki National Volunteers	(KNV)
29.	Kuki Liberation Front	(KLF)
30.	Kuki Security Force	(KSF)
31.	Kuki Liberation Army	(KLA)
32.	Kuki Revolutionary Front	(KRF)
33.	United Kuki Liberation Front	(UKLF)
34.	Hmar People's Convention	(HPC)
35.	Hmar People's Convention-Democracy	(HPC-D)
36.	Hmar Revolutionary Front	(HRF)
37.	Zomi Revolutionary Army	(ZRA)
38.	Zomi Revolutionary Volunteers	(ZRV)
39.	Indigenous People's Revolutionary Alliance	(IRPA)

TABLE 5
Terrorist Groups of Meghalaya

Sl. No.	*Name of Group*	*Short Name*
1.	Hynniewtrep National Liberation Council	(HNLC)
2.	Achik National Volunteer Council	(ANVC)
3.	People's Liberation Front of Meghalaya	(PLF-M)
4.	Hajong United Liberation Army	(HULA)

TABLE 6
Terrorist Groups of Tripura

Sl. No.	*Name of Group*	*Short Name*
(1)	*(2)*	*(3)*
1.	National Liberation Front of Tripura	(NLFT)
2.	All Tripura Tiger Force	(ATTF)
3.	Tripura Liberation Organisation Front	(TLOF)
4.	United Bengali Liberation Front	(UBLF)
5.	Tripura Tribal Volunteer Force	(TTVF)
6.	Tripura Armed Tribal Commando Force	(TATCF)
7.	Tripura Tribal Democratic Force	(TTDF)
8.	Tripura Tribal Youth Force	(TTYF)
9.	Tripura Liberation Force	(TLF)
10.	Tripura Defence Force	(TDF)
11.	All Tripura Volunteer Force	(ATVF)
12.	Tribal Commando Force	(TCF)
13.	Tripura Tribal Youth Force	(TTYF)
14.	All Tripura Bharat Suraksha Force	(ATBSF)
15.	Tripura Tribal Action Committee Force	(TTACF)
16.	Socialist Democratic Front of Tripura	(SDFT)
17.	All Tripura National Force	(ATNF)
18.	Tripura Tribal Sengkrak Force	(TTSF)
19.	Tiger Commando Force	(TCF)
20.	Tripura Mukti Police	(TMP)
21	Tripura Rajya Raksha Bahini	(TRRB)
22.	Tripura State Volunteers	(TSV)
23.	Tripura National Democratic Tribal Force	(TNDTF)
24.	National Militia of Tripura	(NMT)
25.	All Tripura Bengali Regiment	(ATBR)
26.	Bangla Mukti Sena	(BMS)
27.	All Tripura Liberation Organisation	(ATLO)
28.	Tripura National Army	(TNA)
29.	Tripura State Volunteers	(TSV)
30.	Borok National Council of Tripura	(BNCT)

Table 7
Terrorist Groups of Nagaland

Sl. No.	Name of Group	Short Name
1.	National Socialist Council of Nagaland (Isak-Muivah)	NSCN(IM)
2.	National Socialist Council of Nagaland (Khaplang)	NSCN (K)
3.	Naga National Council (Adino)	NNC (Adino)

Table 8
Terrorist Groups of Mizoram

Sl. No.	Name of Group
1.	Bru National Liberation Front
2.	Hmar People's Convention- Democracy (HPC-D)

Table 9
Terrorist Groups of Arunachal Pardesh

Sl. No.	Name of Group
1.	Arunachal Dragon Force (ADF)

Table 10
Left-wing Extremist Groups

Sl. No.	Name of Group
1.	Communist Party of India-Maoist (CPI-Maoist)
2.	People's War Group
3.	Maoist Communist Centre
4.	People's Guerrilla Army
5.	Communist Party of India (Marxist Leninist) Janashakti
6.	Tritiya Prastuti Committee (TPC)

Table 11
Other Extremist Groups

Sl. No.	Name of Group
1.	Tamil National Retrieval Troops (TNRT)
2.	Akhil Bharat Nepali Ekta Samaj (ABNES)
3.	Tamil Nadu Liberation Army (TNLA)
4.	Deendar Anjuman
5.	Students Islamic Movement of India (SIMI)
6.	Asif Reza Commando Force
7.	Liberation Tigers of Tamil Eelam (LTTE)
8.	Kamatapur Liberation Organisation (KLO)
9.	Ranvir Sena

List of Anti-terrorism Laws

Sl. No.	Acts/Ordinance/Bills (Chronologically)	Familiar Short Names/Comment
(1)	(2)	(3)
1.	The Bihar Maintenance of Public Order Act, 1947	
2.	The Bombay Public Safety Act, 1947	
3.	The Madras Suppression of Disturbances Act, 1948	
4.	The Assam Maintenance of Public Order (Autonomous District) Act, 1952	
5.	The Assam Disturbed Areas Act, 1955	
6.	The Armed Forces (Assam And Manipur) Special Powers Act, 1958	
7.	The Nagaland Security Regulation Act, 1962	
8.	The Unlawful Activities (Prevention) Act, 1967	(UAPA)
9.	The Uttar Pradesh Control of Goondas Act, 1970 and Uttar Pradesh Control of Goondas Rules, 1970	

(Contd.)

TABLE (Contd.)

(1)	(2)	(3)
10.	The Maintenance of Internal Security Act, 1973 (Repealed in 1977)	(MISA)
11.	Conservation of Foreign Exchange and Prevention of Smuggling Activities Act, 1974	(COFEPOSA)
12.	The Jammu And Kashmir Public Safety Act, 1978	
13.	National Security Act, 1980	(NSA)
14.	The Assam Preventive Detention Act, 1980	
15.	The Maharashtra Prevention of Communal, Anti-Social and Other Dangerous Activities Act, 1980	
16.	The Maharashtra Prevention of Dangerous Activities of Slum Lords, Bootleggers and Drug Offenders Act, 1981	
17.	The Bihar Control of Crimes Act, 1981	(BCOCA)
18.	Tamil Nadu Prevention of Dangerous Activities Of Bootleggers, Drug Offenders, Goondas, Immoral Traffic Offenders And Slum-Grabbers Act, 1982	
19.	The Anti-Hijacking Act, 1982	
20.	The Suppression of Unlawful Acts Against Safety of Civil Aviation Act, 1982	
21.	The Punjab Disturbed Areas Act, 1983	
22.	The Chandigarh Disturbed Area Act, 1983	
23.	The Armed Forces (Punjab and Chandigarh) Special Powers Act, 1983	
24.	National Security Act (Amended), 1984	(NSA)
25.	The Terrorist Affected Areas (Special Courts) Act, 1984	
26.	The National Security (Second Amendment) Ordinance, 1984	(NSA)
27.	The Gujarat Prevention of Anti-Social Activities Act, 1985	
28.	The Karnataka Prevention of Dangerous Activities of Bootleggers, Drug Offenders, Gamblers, Goondas, Immoral Traffic Offenders and Slum-Grabbers Act, 1985	

29. The Uttar Pradesh Gangsters and Anti-Social Activities (Prevention) Act, 1986
30. The Andhra Pradesh Prevention of Dangerous Activities of Bootleggers, Dacoits, Drug Offenders, Goondas, Immoral Traffic Offenders and Land Grabbers Act, 1986
31. The National Security Guard Act, 1986
32. The Criminal Courts And Security Guard Courts Rules, 1987
33. National Security Act (Amended), 1987 (NSA)
34. The Terrorism and Disruptive Activities (Prevention) Act, 1987 (Repealed in 1995) (TADA)
35. The Jammu and Kashmir Prevention of Illicit Traffic In Narcotic Drugs And Psychotropic Substances Act, 1988
36. The Jammu And Kashmir Disturbed Areas Act, 1990
37. The Armed Forces (Jammu and Kashmir) Special Powers Act, 1990
38. The Madhya Pradesh Rajya Suraksha Adhiniyam, 1990
39. The Maharashtra Control of Organised Crime Act, 1999 (MCOCA)
40. The Madhya Pradesh Special Public Security Act 1999
41. The Karnataka Control of Organised Crime Act, 2000 (KCOCA)
42. The Andhra Pradesh Control of Organised Crime Act, 2001 (APCOCA)
43. The Prevention of Terrorist Act, 2002 (POTA) (Repealed in 2004)
44. Unlawful Activities (Prevention) Amendment Act, 2004 (UAPA)
45. The Chhattisgarh Special Public Security Act, 2005
46. The National Investigation Agency Bill, 2008
47. The Unlawful Activities (Prevention) Amendment Bill, 2008 (UAPA)

BRIEF OF SOME PRIME ANTI-TERRORISM LAWS

Unlawful Activities (Prevention) Act, 1967 (UAPA)

Issued - 1967
Amended - 1969, 2004, 2008

The National Integration Council appointed a Committee on National Integration and Regionalisation to look into, *inter alia*, the aspect of putting reasonable restrictions in the interests of the sovereignty and integrity of India. Pursuant to the acceptance of recommendations of the Committee, the *Constitution (Sixteenth Amendment) Act, 1963* was enacted to impose, by law, reasonable restrictions in the interests of the sovereignty and integrity of India. In order to implement the provisions of 1963 Act, the Unlawful Activities (Prevention) Bill was introduced in the Parliament.

Pursuant to the acceptance by Government of a unanimous recommendation of the Committee on National Integration and Regionalism appointed by the National Integration Council, the Constitution (Sixteenth Amendment) Act, 1963, was enacted empowering Parliament to impose, by law, reasonable restrictions in the interests of sovereignty and integrity of India, on the—

1. Freedom of Speech and Expression;
2. Right to Assemble peaceably and without arms; and
3. Right to Form Associations or Unions.

The object of this Bill was to make powers available for dealing with activities directed against the integrity and sovereignty of India. The Bill was passed by both the Houses of Parliament and received the assent of the President on 30th December 1967. The Amending Acts are as follows:

1. The Unlawful Activities (Prevention) Amendment Act, 1969;
2. The Criminal Law (Amendment) Act, 1972;
3. The Delegated Legislation Provisions (Amendment) Act, 1986;

4. The Unlawful Activities (Prevention) Amendment Act, 2004.

This Amendment, 2004 was enacted after POTA was withdrawn by the Parliament. However, in the Amendment Act, 2004, all provisions of POTA were incorporated.

The Unlawful Activities (Prevention) Act 1967 was amended by the Unlawful Activities (Prevention) Amendment Act 2004 and Unlawful Activities (Prevention) Amendment Act 2008, in order to incorporate the provisions of POTA, which was repealed by the Parliament in the wake of nation-wide protests against its draconian provisions. It may be recalled that not only 100 parliamentarians had signed a petition demanding repeal of POTA, but the National Human Rights Commission (NHRC) had also pointed out its misuse and certain sections violating of the Constitution.

The Maintenance of Internal Security Act, 1973 (MISA)

Issued - 1973
Repealed - 1977

The Maintenance of Internal Security Act was a controversial law passed by the Indian parliament in 1973 giving the administration to Prime Minister Indira Gandhi and Indian law enforcement agencies super powers of—indefinite "preventive" detention of individuals, super strength, search and seizure of property without warrants, flying, telephone and wiretapping, and x-ray vision—in the quelling of civil and political disorder in India, as well as countering foreign inspired sabotage, terrorism, subterfuge and threats to national security.

The legislation gained infamy for its disregard of legal and constitutional safeguards of civil rights, especially when "going all the way down" on the competition, and during the period of national emergency (1975-77) as thousands of innocent people were believed to have been arbitrarily arrested, tortured and in some cases, forcibly sterilized.

The legislation was also invoked to justify the arrest of Indira Gandhi's political opponents, including the leaders and activists of the opposition Janta Party.

The *39th Amendment to the Constitution* of India placed MISA in the 9th Schedule to the Constitution, thereby making it totally immune from any judicial review; even on the grounds that it contravened the Fundamental Rights which are guaranteed by the Constitution, or violated the Basic Structure.

The law was repealed in 1977 following the election of a Janata Party-led government; the *42nd Amendment Act of 1978* similarly removed MISA from the 9th Schedule.

Controversial successors to this legislation include the Terrorism and Disruptive Activities (Prevention) Act and the Prevention of Terrorism Act, criticized for authorizing excessive powers for the aim of fighting internal and cross-border terrorism and political violence, without safeguards for civil freedoms.

The Terrorism and Disruptive Activities (Prevention) Act, (Amended) 1987 (TADA)

Issued	-	1985
Amended	-	1987
Repealed	-	1995

The Terrorist and Disruptive Activities (Prevention) Act of 1987 [hereinafter TADA] was an antiterrorist legislation that was meant to apply throughout India. TADA allowed for the admission of confessions of detainees, in police custody, in legal proceedings against them. While the Criminal Procedure Code required identification to be made at a test identification parade, TADA allowed identification to be based on a witness having picked out the detainee's photograph. Section 2(1)(a)(ii) of TADA had defined Abetment as the passing on of *"any information likely to assist . . . terrorists."* The Supreme Court struck down this broad definition as it had criminalized an association with a terrorist even in situations where there was no criminal intent. Furthermore, TADA proscribed various *"disruptive activities"* which included not only acts that disrupt the sovereignty or territorial integrity of India, but also acts which *"question"* such sovereignty or territorial integrity, or *"support any claim . . . directly or indirectly... for the cession of and part of India, or secession of any part of India from the Union"*. Any of these advocacy crimes were punishable by up to life imprisonment. TADA also provided for the creation of "Designated Courts" which had the exclusive jurisdiction to try violations of its provisions. These Courts were closed to the public, and provided significantly diminished procedural protections for suspected terrorists. For example, where the potential punishment was not more than three years, the Court was authorized to conduct a *"summary trial"*, though it was free to recall witnesses or rehear a case where circumstances warranted. Finally, TADA created a presumption of guilt in situations where arms or explosives were found, in the possession of the accused, which were similar to those used in the terrorist act or in cases where the accused's fingerprints were found at the scene or vehicles used in the terrorist act, or where the accused rendered any financial assistance to a person accused of or reasonably suspected of a terrorist act. Of the 52,998 people detained under TADA at the end of 1992, a mere 434, or 0.81%, had been convicted. It is submitted that, the shadow of TADA continues to loom as, even though TADA is no longer in effect, as the State retains the power to charge suspected persons retroactively for crimes committed during its enactment.

The Prevention of Terrorist Act, 2002 (POTA)

Issued	-	2002
Repealed	-	2004

The events of 9/11 (11th of September) gave the Government of India the pretext it needed to launch yet another salvo in its own "strike against terror". Promulgated six years after the Terrorist and Disruptive Activities Act (TADA) lapsed in 1995, the Prevention of Terrorism Ordinance (POTO) is expected to come up for debate in Parliament during its winter session beginning on 19 November 2001. POTA is, according to the Government, "less draconian" than the defunct TADA. Other official explanations dwell on the "necessity" of new legislation to tackle "new" crimes. And for good measure, references are made to "similar" legislation in countries such as the United States of America and the United Kingdom. Closer scrutiny, however, reveals the lack of foundation for these arguments.

On the 13th of December 2001, five Pakistani Terrorists attacked the Indian Parliament, killing seven people and placing the country into a heightened State of alert. In response to the domestic pressures for the failure to crack down on terrorism, like its American counterpart, the Indian central government in March 2002, passed the Prevention of Terrorism Act, through a joint session of parliament, to enhance India's ability to crack down on possible terrorist threats. The criminalization of *"abetting"* a terrorist, which had been struck down in TADA by the Indian Supreme Court, was revived under POTA. It criminalizes the membership of an organization labeled *"terrorist"* by the Central Government, regardless of criminal intent or activity. The statute, however, was silent as to how the State must prove that a person indeed is part of such a terrorist organization. Section 20 of POTA presumes that an individual charged with being a member of a terrorist organization is a terrorist unless that person can show that he or she has not participated in terrorist activities and that the organization itself was not declared illegal by the State at the time when the person joined. Hence by placing this type of onus on the individual, the State inevitably inhibits those peaceful persons who might wish to join a non-mainstream association but fear that doing so could subject them to potential arrest, or at the very least to the hassle of having to prove their innocence. Furthermore, Section 57 of the Act gives governmental authorities immunity from prosecution under POTA, as long as the actions taken to combat terrorism are done in good faith. POTA had also retained the admissibility of confessions, a provision that many had pointed to as one of the sources of the high incidences of torture and brutality during TADA interrogations. Terrorist acts were placed outside the parameters of the criminal procedure code, which has been established to balance the rights of criminal defendants with the interests of the State. Moreover, POTA had established special Courts to handle cases of terrorism. These special Courts were vested with the discretion to hold trials in non-public places such as prisons and would have the power to withhold trial records from the public. Under section 49(2), of POTA the police may place a suspected terrorist in jail for up to ninety days without any Court proceedings. The abovementioned period may be extended by another three months if the prosecution submits a report to the Court explaining the State's need for additional time. When an individual is charged under POTA, section 49(7) permits the denial of bail to the accused for up to one year, as long as the prosecution's opposition to the bail request satisfies the Court.

Section 52(4) States that the accused is not entitled to have a lawyer *"present throughout the period of the police interrogation"*. Section 14 additionally States that "any individual" (not excluding defense lawyers) is obligated to provide to the State information of anyone who may be in violation of POTA. These limitations contravene the spirit of the United Nations Basic Principles on the Role of Lawyers [hereinafter BPRL] in two major ways. Firstly, Article 1 of the BPRL mandates that clients should have access to their lawyers during an entire police interrogation. Secondly, Article 22 of the BPRL emphasizes that the confidentiality between a lawyer and a client must be respected by the State; any effort to undermine this relationship are incompatible with international norms on the rights of the detained. On the 11th of July, 2002, in the State of Tamil Nadu, Vaiko, a leader of the opposition political party, was arrested and charged for the violation of section 21 of POTA which prohibits the promotion of any terrorist group explicitly banned by the statute. Viko had made remarks in support of the Liberation Tigers of Tamil Eelam, an organization deemed terrorist by the central government. According to the State government, on the 29th of June, 2002, Vaiko in a speech allegedly stated, *"I was, I am, and I will continue to be a supporter of the LTTE"*. Two weeks later, P. Nedumaran, another opposition leader in Tamil Nadu, was arrested under POTA for similar charges. In April 2003, Vaiko petitioned the Supreme Court to declare section 21 of POTA as unconstitutional. In December 2003, a two-judge bench of the Court refused to grant his release and upheld the validity of section 21, however it opined that the Special Courts could not find an individual guilty of violating this section for expressing only a *"moral support"* to a banned terrorist group.

A Special POTA Court in Delhi hearing the parliament attack case found Shaukat Hussain Guru, Geelani and

Mohammad Afzal guilty of violating section 3(2) of POTA read along with section 302 of the Indian Penal Code and sentenced them to death. The Court also ruled that Afsan Guru was guilty of concealing knowledge of the conspiracy and sentenced her to five years in prison and a fine of 10,000 rupees. The Delhi High Court sustained the verdicts against Shaukat Hussain Guru and Mohammad Afzal, although in January 2004, the Supreme Court issued a temporary stay of the execution orders until it could more fully review the matter. The convictions of Professor Geelani and Afsan Guru, however, were set aside by the Delhi High Court.

The Supreme Court reversed the Madras High Court's ruling that bail should be granted to journalist R.R. Gopal, who was arrested in April 2003, for possessing terrorist weapons and other materials prohibited by POTA. Gopal had contended that the State retaliated against him as he published stories critical of and embarrassing to members of the Tamil Nadu government. In overturning the Madras High Court's ruling, the Supreme Court deferred to POTA's provisions on bail: that when the prosecution opposes a bail request, a Court may grant bail only when there has been an abuse of discretion on the part of the government. It is reverently submitted that the Supreme Court's ruling, that a prima facie case had indeed existed, and that the Madras High Court should not have allowed its sympathy for the defendant's argument to cloud what was an obviously an easy call to deny bail is erroneous.

In Uttar Pradesh, twenty-five Dalits were arrested under POTA between April and July 2002. Tribals in the area claim that POTA has been used to characterize their struggle for worker's rights as membership in the banned, extreme leftist Maoist-Leninist groups known collectively as Naxalites. In one district, "nine out of twelve people arrested were bonded laborers who refused to return to work because of the physical abuse of their employer." POTA has been used in a similar way in the State of Jharkhand. On the 19th of February 2003, almost 200 people were arrested under POTA, including "a twelve-year-old boy and an eighty-one-year-old man."

After the Gujarat communal riots, the Gujarat police arrested hundreds of Muslims and charged them with violating POTA, not a single Hindu has been charged under POTA.

Article 14 of the Constitution of India reads, "the State shall not deny to any person equality before the law or the equal protection of the laws." Furthermore, Article 15 reiterates this tenet more specifically by prohibiting the State from discriminating against any citizen on the basis of "religion, race, caste, sex, place of birth or any of them. Although much of the litigation involving these two Articles has predominantly dealt with promoting affirmative action-type policies on behalf of lower castes and women, the preeminent Indian constitutional law scholar, S.P. Sathe, has noted that the Indian Supreme Court has explicitly held that the right to equal protection extends to all State policies.

The Ministry of Home Affairs (MHA) has justified POTA by claiming "an upsurge of terrorist activities, intensification of cross border terrorism, and insurgent groups in different parts of the country."

Most of the provisions contained in POTA can be found in statutes such as the *National Security Act, 1980; the Armed Forces Special Powers Act, 1958; the Disturbed Areas Act, 1990; the Unlawful Activities (Prevention) Act, 1967; the Prevention of Seditious Meetings Act, 1911; the Anti-Hijacking Act, 1982 No. 65 of 1982; the Suppression of Unlawful Acts against Safety of Civil Aviation Act, 1982, No. 66 of 1982; the Disturbed Areas Special Courts Act 1976; the Foreign Exchange Management Act, 1999; the Prevention of Black-marketing and Maintenance of Supplies of Essential Commodities Act, 1980; the Prevention of Illicit Traffic in Narcotic Drugs and Psychotropic Substances Act, 1988; the Indian Telegraph Act, 1885 or the Information Technology Act, 2000.*

The USA Patriot Act of 2001, enacted in the aftermath of the 11 September attacks, grants certain additional powers to the federal government and the Attorney General and establishes a new criminal prohibition against harboring terrorists.

What POTA seeks to do is hold the accused for a prolonged period of detention for upto 180 days without charging him, and effectively subverts the cardinal principle of the criminal justice system—the presumption of innocence—by putting the burden of proof on the accused, withholding of the identity of witnesses, making confessions made to the police officer admissible as evidence, and giving the public prosecutor the power to deny bail. Moreover, little discretion is given to judges regarding the severity of sentences. While the Terrorist and Disruptive Activities (Prevention) Act was reviewed every two years, POTA is not subject to review for a period of five years. POTA is also more likely to be used for preventive detention of all peaceful dissenters than for tackling terrorism.

Under Article 355 of the Indian Constitution, the Central Government has a duty to protect States from internal disturbances. Furthermore, the bedrock on which the edifice of any criminal justice system rests lies in the protection of the rights of the innocent and thereby punishing the guilty. There currently is a view that the Indian Criminal Justice System, which was devised more than a century back, has presently become ineffective as in a plethora of cases a large number of guilty go unpunished. Moreover, this system takes years to bring the guilty to justice and has thus ceased to deter perpetrators of heinous crimes.

Half a million cases in the High Courts have been on hold for 10 years or more, and almost 1 million in the lower Courts. Current trends indicate that terrorism is not a temporary phenomenon, but one that will continue and perhaps increase in the future. As a result, the effect of counterterrorism policies on civil liberties will be a substantial concern in coming years. The dramatics of the December 13th attacks on the Parliament building, combined with the September 11th atrocities in the United States, gave rise to the need of increasing the power of security forces despite the long history of past abuses. The United Kingdom's adoption of the Prevention of Terrorism Act and the United States' PATRIOT Act strengthened the notion that other countries had acknowledged the need to move beyond traditional domestic criminal procedure in order to properly battle terrorism. Thus, the Indian Government had enacted the Prevention of Terrorism Act [hereinafter POTA] which served as an anti terrorist legislation. It must be noted that on paper POTA did incorporate certain safeguards by which the Police were expressly barred from using coercion in order to obtain a Statement from an individual. Moreover, the State could punish any police official found abusing his authority with a fine and up to two years of imprisonment.

POTA also assured defendants a statutory right to appeal in a criminal conviction to a High Court of the concerned State both on facts and on law. Supporters of POTA have contended that sections 52(4) and 52(14) are in line with Article 22 of the Indian Constitution, which exempts the State from providing legal counsel to a person being held for *"preventive detention"* and implicitly places some limitations on the confidential relationship between a lawyer and client. With respect to the latter point, the Supreme Court of India has noted that lawyers do not have an absolute, *"sacrosanct right"* to keep privileged all communications from clients particularly those involving POTA-related crimes.

The Need

It is normally said that terrorism is a low intensity war. But the loss, which our country has suffered in the last two decades due to the rise of terrorist activities, has been on a very large scale. This country has fought four high intensity wars and in those wars we have lost more than 6000 people. We have already lost more then 70000 civilians. In addition, we have lost more than 9000 security personnel. Almost six lakh people in this country have become homeless as a result of terrorism. Outside the expenditure on our armed forces, merely for maintaining the entire set up to fight insurgency, to fight cross-border terrorism, the economic cost itself has been Rs. 45000 crore. The budgetary increase itself in the last 15 years, because of terrorism or anti-insurgency activities, has been 26 times. We have no record of the explosives that have been used in various parts of the country. We have a record of crime. But the explosives that have been confiscated by our security agencies weigh 48000 kilos. If our security forces had not been vigilant enough to confiscate these explosives, they would probably have been enough to take care of every inch of Indian soil.

It is not only Kashmir; Punjab too has suffered. Also Mumbai, Delhi and other regions of the country like the North East. Development has suffered, the economy has suffered. You have now a brand of Maoist terrorism; People's War Group and other groups. A large part of Andhra Pradesh, Orissa, Madhya Pradesh, Chattisgarh and Jharkhand right up to the Nepal border is affected. We had insurgency and terrorism in Tamil

Nadu. We lost two of our former prime ministers to this kind of terrorism.

In terms of our sovereignty, unity and integrity and our feeling of nationalism, terrorism strikes at each one of them. This is the enormity of the problem that we are addressing. But it is also said that our criminal law systems have broken down; it seems to be a sad fact to accept. *Are we aware of the conviction rate under the so-called ordinary laws—At times we try and conceal the figures and say that in India the conviction rate is 40%. But that 40% is actually a camouflage because every time there is a challan and somebody pays Rs 100 as fine, it is recorded as a conviction. Every time somebody feels guilty and pays a fine under company law, we take it as a conviction and then claim that the conviction rate is 40%. In heinous crimes like murder, the conviction rate under the so-called normal processes has come down to 6.5%.* There are several reasons for this. One is that when we deal with hardened criminals, some of our old notions of criminal law have to change. It is a sad reality that crime in India has become a low risk business. *It is a high profit business with a 93% probability that you can commit a hard crime and get away with it.*

So it becomes very necessary in a country like India that if a law regarding terrorism is enacted it should be made so stringent that the culprit be bought to book and does not go scot-free just because of the loopholes and lacunas in the ordinary law because when our neighboring nation Pakistan which is the cause of perpetrating terrorism in India and can have such stringent laws why cannot we have such laws.

The Birth of NIA by NIA Act, 2008

Why NIA ?

- Piloting the new laws, Home Minister Chidambaram said such legislations have been brought forward as the "country has been the victim of large-scale terrorism sponsored from across the border". There have been innumerable incidents of terrorist attacks, not only in the militancy and insurgency-affected areas and areas affected by left wing extremism but also in the form of terrorist attacks and bomb blasts in various parts of the hinterland and major cities. Also, the Prime Minister had promised the setting up of NIA soon after Mumbai attacks on November 26, 2008. Another reason for setting up NIA is complex inter-State and international linkages in smuggling of drugs and arms, pushing in and circulation of fake Indian currency and infiltration from across the borders. Keeping all these in view, it has for long been felt that there is need for setting up an Agency at the Central level for investigation of offences related to terrorism and certain other acts, which have national ramification.

PROVISIONS AT A GLANCE

The NIA Act is an Act to constitute an investigation agency at the national level to investigate and prosecute offences affecting the sovereignty, security and integrity of India, security of State, friendly relations with foreign States and offences under Acts enacted to implement international treaties, agreements, conventions and resolutions of the United Nations, its agencies and other international organisations. The superintendence of the agency has been vested in the Central Government.

On receipt of information, the officer-in-charge of the police station will forward the report to the state Government, which will further it to the Central Government. This will initiate the investigation procedure if the reported offence is a scheduled offence. Use of explosives, firearms, lethal weapons, and poisonous chemicals, biological or radiological weapons with the intention of aiding, abetting or committing terror act is a serious offence according to the Act. The punishment is jail term of up to ten years. Fund collection drive in India or abroad for terrorist activity will invite a five year jail term.

Stringent punishment will be awarded for those organising camps for training in terrorism, and for those recruiting persons for commission of a terrorist act. Special courts will try terror-related cases.

NIA has been endowed with powers to probe terrorism and other crimes having national ramifications across the country. Officers of the agency will enjoy all powers, duties, privileges and liabilities which the local police officers have in connection with cases related to terror. Elaborating on the provisions, though law and order being the state subject, officers of the NIA above the rank of sub inspector will have special powers to pursue and investigate any offence related to terror across the country.

Other Highlights of the NIA Act, 2008

The Act for constitution of the National Investigation Agency (NIA) to be applicable to whole of India, citizens of India outside India and persons on ships and aircraft registered in India—*Section 1.*

Officers of the NIA to have all powers, privileges and liabilities which the police officers have in connection with investigation of any offence.—*Section 3.*

The police officer in charge of a police station on receipt of the report of the offence shall forward it to the state government which in turn will send it to the Centre. If the Centre feels the offence is terror related, it shall direct the NIA for investigation.—*Section 6.*

Provision for transfer of investigation and trial of offences to state government with Centre's prior approval.—*Section 7.* NIA may investigate other offences connected with terror-related offences.—*Section 8.* A state government shall extend all assistance to NIA for investigation of terror-related offences.—*Section 9.*

Provisions of the Act with regard to investigation shall not affect powers of the state government to investigate and prosecute any terror crime or other offences.—*Section 10.* The Centre shall constitute special courts for trial of terror-related offences.—*Section 11.* Special Courts may sit at any place for any of its proceedings.—*Section 12.*

For speedy and fair trial, the Supreme Court may transfer any case pending with the special court to another special court in the same state or any other state, and the High Court may transfer such cases to any other special court within the state.—*Section 13.*

Offences punishable with imprisonment for less than three years may be tried summarily. Special court to have all powers of the court of sessions under CrPC for trial of any offence under the Act.—*Section 16.*

Proceedings to be held 'in camera' if special court deems it necessary.—*Section 17.*

Trial to be held on day-to-day basis on all working days and to have precedence over the trial of other offences.—*Section 19.* State governments empowered to constitute one or more special courts.—*Section 22.* No appeal shall be entertained after the expiry of 90 days.—*Section 21.*

2

National Security Laws and Human Rights

TERRORISM AND HUMAN RIGHTS

Terrorism is the phenomenon which produces terrorists and therefore, combating terrorism has a wider connotation which includes identification and eradication of the causes which give rise to, and promote the phenomenon of terrorism. That is the lasting remedy or cure of terrorism. Terrorism has no precise definition. Terrorism results in gross violation of human rights and must, no doubt, be dealt with a heavy hand. However, the methods to counter terrorism must not violate the human rights of innocents or else the innocents would be exposed to double jeopardy and suffer twin violation of their human rights. Prof. Noam Chomsky of MIT in one of his recent public lectures speaking on 'The New War Against Terror' describing terrorism referred to the Reagan administration which called it, plague spread by "depraved opponents of civilization," and said that, "terrorism is not the weapon of the weak, it is the weapon of those who are against 'us', whoever 'us' happens to be." He described it as 'primarily a weapon of the strong, overwhelming, in fact'.

So understood, it has wide ramification and amounts to 'intolerance' of any opposition of the strong. The source of strength may be any kind of power, even the power of the state. In that sense any weapon to combat terrorism which is not tempered with 'tolerance' and 'justice' may, itself, amount to an act of terrorism and be not within the ambit of 'rule of law'. Terrorism is a dastardly crime. In the case of crime, the rule of law requires finding the perpetrators and bringing them to justice under the law. In doing so, innocent people are not exposed to any danger or violation of human rights. If a criminal hides somewhere, the law does not contemplate assault on people all around to isolate and apprehend the criminal. The requirement of the rule of law in combating terrorism is similar.

Human rights are rights which inhere in every human being—man, woman or child from birth and which they are entitled to enjoy in every society. These rights recognize the essential worth of a human being and acknowledge the basic equality and dignity inherent in all human beings irrespective of race, colour, sex, religion or economic levels of living. These have existed in some form in all cultures and have been enjoyed by the people everywhere with varying degrees of emphasis. While this is a historical fact, it is also a part of our experience that powerful forces within the human race, at both the national and the international levels, have been conspiring to condemn millions of men, women and children in all regions of the world to a state of misery, deprivation and continuing exploitation, thereby violating their Human Rights. Over the years human rights have expanded not only vertically by ensuring their protection and promotion, but also horizontally by making human rights as the basis for good governance. These rights are non-negotiable and non-derogable and no compromise with their violation can be permitted by any civilized society.

The cult of terrorism strikes at the very root of human rights of innocent people. Terrorism, in all its forms, is the greatest violator of human rights. The aim of the terrorists is to destabilize the civil society and damage its socio-economic fabric. Right to life is the most basic of all rights. One of the rights incorporated in the Universal Declaration and in all other covenants, therefore, is the right to life. For only this right ensures the enjoyment of all other rights. The right to life is of crucial significance for every person, every group of people, every class and every nation and as a matter of fact, for all humanity. This very right to life of the innocent people is the target of terrorism. In democratic societies fundamental human rights and freedoms are more than paper or just pious aspirations. They form part of the law and, therefore, their protection becomes the obligations of those who are entrusted with the task of their protection.

There has been a growing consciousness amongst citizens all over the world against violation of human rights. Strong national and international movements against violation of human rights have emerged. Traditional thinking has been that it is the State that violates human rights but the violation of human rights by the terrorist is a reality, which poses a serious problem. It causes unlimited miseries to the hapless innocent and ordinary people whose death, injury; agony is aimed at the destruction of human integrity. Terrorism and human rights are natural enemies with no possibility of their co-existence. No person who supports human rights can support or condone terrorism, which results in a grave violation of human rights. Every violation of human rights wherever it occurs is a threat to the welfare of the entire human family.

Terrorism has to be distinguished from ordinary crime, which has been a part of human behaviour since the advent of human society. Black's Law Dictionary defines 'crime' as an act done in violation of those duties which an individual owes to the community and for the breach of which the law has provided that the offender shall make satisfaction to the public. This definition would have little application to organized violence like terrorism, as it is most vicious, irrational and senseless kind of violence, which aims at achieving personal, religious or political ends through acts of terror and travels beyond the effect of crime. Terrorists do not respect the law and norms of social life. They kill by-standers and inert people with an easy conscience to send shivers down the spine of the entire population. The main aim of such acts is not to kill or harm a particular person or persons but to create a sense of terror and fear among the people generally and senselessly violate human rights of innocent citizens.

Terrorism is a clear and present danger to world today; it strikes a fatal blow to human rights of innocent citizens. The ruthless, barbaric, inhuman killing of innocent people is carried out by the terrorists with a view not only to challenge the authority of the Government, but also to put the security and sovereignty of the country in jeopardy and bring trauma and perpetual grief to the families who suffer from such killings. Their grief and trauma cannot be adequately expressed but only sensed. It is, to say in one word, *terrible*.

While an acceptable definition of terrorism, despite huge debate over the years, still eludes the international community, the Supreme Court of India, as far back as in 1994, drew a distinction between a 'merely criminal act' and a 'terrorist act'. In its Judgment in *Hitendra Vishnu Thakur* v. *State of Maharashtra*,[1] the Supreme Court of India said:

> ". . . . It may be possible to describe it (Terrorism) as use of violence when its most important result is not merely the physical and mental damage of the victim but the prolonged psychological effect it produces or has the potential of producing on the society as a whole. There may be death, injury, or even deprivation of individual liberty in the process but the extent and reach of the intended terrorist activity travels beyond the effect of any ordinary crime capable of being punished under the ordinary penal law of the land and its main objective is to overawe the Government or disturb harmony of the society or "terrorise" people and the society and not only those directly assaulted, with a view to disturb even tempo, peace and tranquility of the society and create a sense of fear and insecurity. A 'terrorist' activity does not merely arise by causing disturbance of law and order or of public order. The fall out of the intended activity must be such that it travels beyond the capacity of the ordinary law enforcement agencies to tackle it under the ordinary penal

1. (1994) 4 SCC 602.

> law. Experience has shown us that 'terrorism' is generally an attempt to acquire helplessness in the minds of the people at large or any section thereof and is a totally abnormal phenomenon. What distinguishes 'terrorism' from other forms of violence, therefore, appears to be the deliberate and systematic use of coercive intimidation..."

Terrorists take recourse to different forms of violence to achieve their objectives—to subvert the system—by acts of terror and violence. They resort to "deliberate and systematic" use of coercive intimidation. More often than not, a hardened criminal today takes advantage of the situation and by wearing the cloak of terrorism, aims to achieve for himself some acceptability and respectability in the society because a terrorist is often projected and respected as a hero by his group and misguided youth. In many countries, ever-growing fundamentalism in its various forms and manifestations aimed at imposition of a religious or ideological will on the society is, today, another form of terrorism posing a serious threat to peace, order and harmony. While all faithfuls believe in harmony and brotherhood in religion, it is the misguided fanatics who do not value human life and in the name of religion resort to all types of attacks on human rights. These include forcible imposition of self-righteous social or moral code and undermining of freedom of expression and belief. Fundamentalism is sometimes used to exploit innocent citizens in the name of religion to secure *"political"* advantage over the rivals, unmindful of the harm their actions may cause to the nation by such exploitation. They contribute to a climate of religious bigotry, which leads to discrimination, harassment and attacks on all those who do not follow their dictates which may be right or wrong, on believers of other faiths. In doing so, they violate human rights of fellow citizens without any justification whatsoever. Terrorism grows and thrives on *'hatred policy'*—be that of rival political groups or fundamentalists or enemy agents. Indifference of the society to such acts encourages terrorists—loud and positive condemnation of their activities by the society, on the other hand is bound to discourage them. Today, we are exposed to a continuous impact of frightening possibilities against which individuals confine themselves by withdrawing in the psychological bunkers. Everyone must wake to meet the challenge of terrorism. A violent group whatever its politics, has no right to kill, and no claim to such a right must ever be allowed.

Global awakening about human rights and the threat that terrorism has posed to human rights of the people all over the world is necessary. There is no conflict between respect for human rights and combating terrorism. International humanitarian law is a part of human rights law applicable even in armed conflict. There is a growing convergence between the two since the object of both is the same and that is to respect human dignity and abjure needless violence. It is, therefore, necessary that respect for human rights must be accepted as an essential element of any strategy to counter terrorism. The fundamental concepts of laws of war are based on maintaining balance between military necessity and humanity, which include proportionality of the force used. Military necessity does not admit of cruelty or wounding in fight except or of torture to extract confessions. Geneva Conventions are for humane treatment even of the POWs. How a party to a conflict is to behave in relation to people at its mercy is governed by humanitarian laws. If humane considerations prevail even in armed conflict with an enemy, the treatment of persons to be dealt with in low intensity conflict cannot be harsher because they are often not even enemies of the nation. No doubt "the war on terrorism" has to be relentlessly fought but that should be done without going over-board and in effect declaring war on the civil liberties of the people. In addressing the Security Council on 18th January 2002, the Secretary-General stated:

> "While we certainly need vigilance to prevent acts of terrorism, and firmness in condemning and punishing them, it will be self-defeating if we sacrifice other key priorities—such as human rights—in the process"

It has to be remembered that the fundamental rationale of anti-terrorism measures has to be to protect human rights and democracy. Counter terrorism measures should, therefore, not undermine democratic values, violate human rights and subvert the Rule of Law. Consequently, the battle against terrorism should be carried out in keeping with international human rights obligations and the basic tenets of the Rule of Law. The protection and promotion of human rights under the Rule of Law is essential in countering terrorism. Let me emphasise that in countering terrorism, the approach should be humane, rational and secular. It must be consistent with democratic principles. Any kind of partisan and sectarian approach would be counter-productive. We need to strike a balance between the liberty of an individual and the requirements of security of state and sovereignty and integrity of the nation while keeping an open mind to fight terrorism. A limited approach may help eliminate some present terrorists but not the causes or the phenomenon of terrorism, which produces terrorists; and that too at the cost of violation of human rights of many innocents. A proper balance between the need and the remedy requires respect for the principles of necessity and proportionality. We must avoid a descent into anarchy—in which the only rule is 'might is right'– combating terrorism should not be used as an excuse to suspend all the rules of international law and domestic civil liberties by waging 'an undeclared war'. If human rights are violated in the process of combating terrorism, it will be self defeating. It is imperative that the essential safeguards of due process and fair trial should not be jettisoned.

Experience shows that one distressing feature of anti-terrorist operation is that the rubric of counter-terrorism can be misused to justify acts in support of political agendas, such as the consolidation of political power, elimination of political opponents, inhibition of legitimate dissent. Labeling adversaries as terrorists is a notorious technique to de-legitimize political opponents. It is during anxious times that care has to be taken that state does not take recourse to bend the Rule of Law to accommodate popular sentiment for harsh measures against suspected criminals. Response of the State even to all uncivilized acts must be civilized. It is now firmly believed that terrorism thrives and trades on the graver mistakes and misjudgments of security forces, bureaucrats, community and political leaders. It is, therefore, necessary that errors of over-reaction and repression are avoided so that population is not alienated and driven into terrorist folds.

It must, therefore, stand as a caution that in times of distress, the shield of necessity and national security must not be used to protect governmental actions from close scrutiny and accountability where the same affect enjoyment of human rights. In times of international hostility and antagonisms our institutions, legislative, executive and judicial, must be prepared to exercise their authority to protect all citizens from petty fears and prejudices that are so easily aroused. Terrorism is a challenge which has to be met with innovative ideas and approach. There can be no doubt that the State has not only the right, but also the duty, to protect itself and its people against terrorist acts and to bring to justice those who perpetrate such acts but the manner in which a State acts to exercise this right and to perform this duty must be in accordance with the Rule of Law. Proper observance of human rights is not a hindrance to the promotion of peace and security. Rather, it is an essential element in any worthwhile strategy to preserve peace and security and to defeat terrorism. The purpose of anti-terrorism measures must, therefore, be to protect Democracy, Rule of Law and Human Rights, which are fundamental values of our society and the core values of the Constitution. The Supreme Court of India has, in *DK Basu* v. *State of West Bengal,*[2] cautioned:

> "State terrorism is no answer to combat terrorism. State terrorism would only provide legitimacy to terrorism: that would be bad for the State, the community and above all for the rule of law. The State must, therefore, ensure that the various agencies deployed by it for combating terrorism act within the bounds of law and not become law unto themselves".

Rule of law is a basic feature of the Constitution of India and a part of its basic structure which is indestructible. The Supreme Court in *Indira Gandhi* v.. *Raj Narain*[3] observed that "the major problem of human society is to combine that degree of liberty without which law is tyranny with that degree of law without which liberty become license." The perennial dilemma

2. JT 1997(1) SC 1.
3. AIR 1965 SC 2299.

is to discover a measure of right balance appropriate to ever shifting tangle of human affairs. The device adopted by peoples devoted to liberal democracy to overcome the dilemma is the 'Rule of Law'. Article 21 in the Constitution of India has been judicially interpreted to mean right to life with dignity and not mere animal existence. Human dignity is the quintessence of human rights. Thus, Article 21 alone is comprehensive enough to encompass all human rights. Article 21 has also been construed to be applicable even to non-citizens along with Article 14 which guarantees right to equality, inclusive of the rule of non-arbitrariness.

The core values of our constitutional philosophy indicated in the Preamble to the Constitution are: dignity of the individual and unity and integrity of the nation. The two, obviously can co-exist, and are not incompatible. Otherwise, framers of the Constitution would not club them together in the Preamble as the core values. The message is clear. Every attempt must be made to balance the two in all state actions including legislation, its interpretation and implementation.

That is the demand of the rule of law in a true democracy. Combating terrorism under the rule of law must, therefore, mean compliance of the constitutional mandate. It is significant that Article 21 is non-derogable. After the emergency, an amendment of Article 359 of the Constitution provides that Article 20 (protection against testimonial compulsion) and Article 21 (right to life) cannot be suspended even during an emergency. War against terrorism cannot be more stringent. Methods for combating terrorism must conform to these constitutional requirements.

I may also make a passing reference to the provisions contained in the ICCPR and the Convention Against Torture which can be safely read into the constitutional guarantees in India by virtue of the decision in Vishaka[4] *which requires reading into the domestic law all provisions in international instruments not inconsistent with the domestic law which have the effect of enlarging the fundamental rights guaranteed under the Constitution. It is this wide canvass of rule of law which must determine the kind of laws and nature of other*

4. AIR 1997 SCC 3011.

strategies to combat terrorism in India. Enforcement and implementation of the same must be similarly regulated.

No Conflict between Human Rights and Combating Terrorism:

> Terrorism regardless of motivation has to be condemned and countered but this has to be done taking "all necessary measures in accordance with the relevant provisions of international law and international standards of human rights to prevent, combat and eliminate terrorism, whenever and by whomever committed". This has to be achieved within the framework of rule of law. The Vienna Declaration and programme of action adopted on 25 June, 1993 categorically asserted:
>
> "The acts, methods and practices of terrorism in all its forms and manifestations, as well as linkage in some countries to drug trafficking, are activities aimed at the destruction of human rights, fundamental freedoms and democracy, threatening territorial integrity, security of States and legitimately constituted governments. The international community should take the necessary steps to enhance cooperation to prevent and combat terrorism."

The responsibility for the security of our land, and the fight against terrorism, are patriotic duties and the integrity of the state must be preserved and the terrorism—the sworn enemy of civil society—which respects neither life, nor law nor any human rights, must be suppressed. Yet we must fight this just war using means that are righteous, that are in conformity with our Constitution, our law, and our treaty obligations. This is no easy task. But then it is never easy to live by ideals and it is the ideals that distinguish civilized people from barbarians.

It must be remembered that there is a clear and emphatic relationship between national security and the security and integrity of the individuals who comprise the state. Between them, there is a symbiosis and no antagonism. The nation has no meaning without its people. John Stuart Mill emphasized that the worth of a nation is the worth of the individuals constituting the nation. This is the emphasis laid in the Constitution of India which holds out the promise to secure both simultaneously.

Often doubt is raised about the possible conflict between respect for human rights and combating terrorism. There is really no such conflict. International humanitarian law is a part of human rights law applicable even in armed conflict. There is a growing convergence between the two since the object of both is the same and that is to respect human dignity and abjure needless violence. The fundamental concepts of laws of war are based on the balance between military necessity and humanity which includes proportionality of the force used. Military necessity does not admit of cruelty or wounding except in fight nor of torture to extract confessions. Geneva Conventions are for humane treatment even of the POWs. How a party to a conflict is to behave in relation to people at its mercy is governed by humanitarian laws. If humane considerations prevail even in armed conflict with an enemy, the treatment of persons dealt with in low intensity conflict cannot be harsher because they are often not even enemies of the nation. The whole regimen of Hague laws and Geneva laws covers the field and there is growing convergence between them.

No person who supports human rights can support terrorism which is a grave violation of human rights. There is no conflict between respect for human rights and combating terrorism. Ms. Mary Robinson, the UN High Commissioner for Human Rights, recently in India to receive the Indira Gandhi Prize for Peace, Disarmament and Development, emphasized this fact when she stressed that 'government action must be guided by human rights principles, which strike a balance between the enjoyment of freedoms and the legitimate concerns for national security.'

Various suspicion and voices have been raised by people NGO's under the pretext of constitution, constitutional provisions, and equality before law and civil rights. All these organizations must keep in mind that provisions are there in the constitution where reasonable restrictions can be enforced even upon the liberty of people and in view of the increasing terrorist activities in the nation more particularly in view of the 9/11 attacks on the World Trade Center which killed more than 3000 people and 13 December attack on the Indian Parliament and large number of terrorist activities not only in J&K, N.E., A.P., and other areas of our country need for promulgation of POTA type legislation becomes the need of the hour.

However there are numerous safeguards to prevent the abuse of above legislation by unscrupulous investigating officers, which are being ignored by various organization professing the repeal of such law. The attention of those who are against this legislation is invited to object and reason for which POTA was enacted. The repeal of Pota is just party politics to gain for their party's vote bank. *If you do not give to your security forces and investigative forces the legal power, human rights violations will be much worse.* Therefore, if you want, out of concern for human rights, the powers not to be misused, you cannot sustain a situation where you do not give powers to the police but put pressure on it to deliver. You will have a situation of anarchy.

Therefore, let us all understand the problem we are now dealing with. And this problem requires various kinds of provisions. Legitimate power has to be given because this is an extraordinary situation. *Extraordinary situations require extraordinary remedies.* Please do not advise us to use velvet gloves. Terrorism has several consequences that have to be faced in the context of a growing threat to the country. References have repeatedly been made to laws in other countries. It is very dangerous to quote selectively. Let us not selectively take our lessons from America. With all due respects to those great countries, when 3,000 people sadly died in the World Trade Centre, the US president said that a war had been launched on America. When 61,000 people and 8,000 security persons have died here, we are advised to show restraint. We are advised that this is the remedy; that we should deal with it under the normal procedure. Learning from this experience, I would urge the people who are opposing this law to once again reconsider their stand because posterity eventually will decide that this country, for its integrity, sovereignty and unity certainly needs this law. Quite clearly, there is a crying need to fight the menace of terrorism untidily. Partisanship of any sort in dealing with the ISI-sponsored terror attacks in India should be abandoned forthwith. Today terrorism has reached the heart of India in New Delhi's Parliament House.

To the extent it detracts from presenting a united front against terrorists, the governments myopic stand on POTO and MCOCA in Delhi represents a greater threat to national unity than even the threat of the ISI-sponsored terror. So it becomes very necessary in a country like India that if a law regarding terrorism is enacted it should be made so stringent that the culprit be bought to book and does not go scot-free just because of the loopholes and lacunae's in the ordinary law because when our neighboring nation Pakistan which is the cause of perpetrating terrorism in India can have such stringent laws then why cannot we have such laws. Indian law as it stands today has come around in strange circumstances as the earlier legislation was found capable of being misuse.

Now, it is obvious that for curbing terrorism and such like activities only Anti-Terrorism Laws like POTA can play important role and that's why almost all the provisions of POTA have been recalled by the later anti-terrorism laws, which can be better understood by the Table 1 given on the next page.

Who would have thought that India would need to tutor Australia on protecting individual human rights? Yet here we have the case of the Government of India summoning the Ambassador of Australia to remind his government of the need for due process in the treatment of an Indian doctor detained in Brisbane.

The case highlights the importance of a proper balance between civil liberties, individual human rights, and the responsibility of the state to protect inhabitants from terrorists. Before 9/11, western governments and human rights champions were prone to moral ambivalence between perpetrators of terrorism and efforts of legitimate governments to maintain national security and assure public safety. After 9/11, western governments began to view other countries' parallel wars against terrorism through the prism of a fellow-government facing agonising policy choices in the real world, rather than single-issue groups whose vision is not anchored in any responsibility for policy decisions. Many governments used to be at the receiving end of moral and political judgment about robust responses to violent threats posed to their authority and order from armed dissidents. They now get a more sympathetic

TABLE 1

Existence of Controversial Provisions of POTA

	During POTA		*After POTA*		
Sl. No.	*Controversial Provisions*	*POTA, 2002*	*UAPA, 2004*	*UAPA, 2008*	*NIA, 2008*
(1)	*(2)*	*(3)*	*(4)*	*(5)*	*(6)*
1.	Pre-trial Imprisonment	180 Days	Dropped	180 Days	Continued
2.	Police Custody	30 Days	Dropped	30 Days	Continued
3.	Onus to Prove Innocence	On Accused	On Prosecution	On Accused	Continued
4.	Prima-facie Offence	Presumed committed	Dropped	Presumed committed	Continued
5.	Confession before Police Officer	Admissible	Dropped	Dropped	Dropped
6.	Admissibility of Evidence Collected Through Interception of Communication	Admissible	Admissible	Continued	Continued
7.	Legal Presumption as to Possesion of Unauthorised Arms, etc.	Guilty of Terrorist Act	Guilty of Terrorist Act	Continued	Continued
8.	Compulsory Denial of Bail	Present	Dropped	Present	Continued
9.	Special Provisions	Obtaining samples of any accused person S/27	Dropped	Dropped	Dropped
		Punishment for malicious action for Police officer S/58	Dropped	Dropped	Dropped
10.	Protection of action taken in Good-Faith	Present	Present	Continued	Continued
11.	Obligation to furnish information	Present	Dropped	Present	Continued

hearing and mature understanding forged in the crucible of shared suffering.

This does not give any government a licence to trample rights won at great cost over many centuries: rights of people against governments. A human right, owed to every person simply as a human being, is inherently universal. Held only by human beings, but equally by all, it does not flow from any office, rank or relationship. The language of human rights embodies the intuition that the human species is one and every individual is entitled to equal moral consideration. It is vividly captured in the Second World War joke that they came after the workers; I was not a worker, so I did not object. They came after the homosexuals; I wasn't one, so I did not object. They came after the Jews; I wasn't one, so I did not object. Then they came after me: there was no one left to object. Success in defeating terrorism can come only if we remain true to values that terrorists reject. It is possible to resort to the lesser evil of curtailing liberties and using violence in order to defeat the greater evil of terrorism, but only if we do not succumb to the greater evil of destroying the very values for which democracies stand.

The way to do this is to require of governments that they justify all restrictive measures publicly, submit them to judicial review, and circumscribe them with sunset clauses to guard against the temporary becoming permanent. The safeguards are especially important because the history of the great democracies themselves suggests that most people privilege the security of the majority over the harm done to minorities deprived of their rights in the name of national security.

After 9/11, some western democracies recalibrated the existing balance between national security and civil liberties in their laws and practices. American priorities shifted to subordinate human rights to victory in the 'war' against terrorism. A counter-terrorism expert testified that "after 9/11 the gloves came off," while another official remarked that "if you don't violate someone's human rights, you aren't doing your job." There developed also the distasteful practice of "rendition to torture," sending prisoners to their home countries precisely because the latter were known to practise torture as a routine part of their interrogation.

Many other democracies joined the United States in shifting the balance of laws and administrative practices towards state security. In Australia, the post-9/11 hysteria was harvested by the government to introduce tough detention laws against illegal immigrants in defence of a policy of Fortress Australia that led to the detention of dozens of Australian citizens, one of whom was deported to her country of birth and another, a mentally ill woman, spent ten months in detention.

Thus terrorism has an impact on human rights in three ways. First, it is itself an extreme denial of the most basic human right, namely to life, and it creates an environment in which people cannot live in freedom from fear and enjoy their other rights. Secondly, the threat of terrorism can be used by governments to enact laws that strip away many civil liberties and political freedoms. One simple yet popular technique is to reverse the burden of proof: those accused of terrorist activities, sympathies or even guilt by association on the basis of accusations by anonymous people are to be presumed to be guilty until they can prove their innocence of unspecified charges. Thirdly, without necessarily amending laws or enacting new ones, governments can use the need to fight terrorism as an alibi to stifle dissent and criticism and imprison or threaten domestic opponents.

This is where the case of Dr. Mohamed Haneef is so very disturbing. On the evidence presented to the Brisbane court, he made the mistake of giving his prepaid SIM card to a second cousin in the United Kingdom because the card would not be of any use to him in Australia for whose sunny shores he was departing. The card was found in a car used by a terrorist a year later.

Hardly surprising that the magistrate granted bail. This is where the case gets curioser and curioser, as Alice remarked in her wonderland. Having spent 12 days in custody before being questioned, then granted bail pending trial, Dr. Haneef had his multi-year work visa cancelled on 'character' grounds. No country will strip its Immigration Minister of the power to cancel a visitor's visa. But the purpose is to prevent someone from entering or, if he is already in the country, to terminate his presence and deport him. In Dr. Haneef's case the primary motivation would appear to be to keep him in Australia under detention—and require him to pay for the privilege at the end of it all, even if he should be acquitted.To top it all, the government has made it clear that Dr. Haneef will be deported even if he is ultimately found innocent. A case perhaps of guilty even if proven innocent?

It is hard not to infer that this is a case of a serious misuse of power and political interference in the process of criminal justice.The dream of a world ruled by law is a shared vision. We must not privilege security and order to such an extent as to destroy our most cherished values of liberty and justice in the search for an unattainable absolute security. As Benjamin Franklin, one of the fathers of American independence, said, those who would sacrifice essential liberty to temporary safety deserve neither liberty nor safety.

The robustness and resilience of the civilised world's commitment to human rights norms and values will be judged in the final analysis not by the breaches in the aftermath of 9/11, but by the reversal and attenuation of the breaches through judicial and political processes as well as the pressure of domestic and international civil society. This is where the response of the Australian community to the prima facie abuse of executive power by the Australian Government is so reassuring: the legal fraternity, civil liberties groups, other sectors of society, and even the State Premier have either roundly condemned the extra-judicial detention of Dr. Haneef or demanded a public explanation from the government. The one disappointment has been the federal opposition Labor Party, which frightened of being wedged on an issue of national security, has once again resorted to "me tooism."If and when Dr. Haneef is tried in a court of law, the trial will be about him: his beliefs, actions, and links to terrorism. The manner, forum, and rules of procedure of the trial are not about him, but about the quality and credibility of the Australian justice system. Specifically, does the Australian government believe in, respect, and abide by the rule of law or disregard it as a mere inconvenience when judicially tested? The question of indifference or active concern about Dr. Haneef's fate in a foreign land is about Indian values and beliefs. A failure by the government to demand justice for him would be an abdication of its responsibility to protect citizens.Tough on terrorists.

Tougher on the causes of terrorism. But toughest of all on safeguarding the virtues of tolerance, human rights, civil liberties, and due process.

(A) INTERNATIONAL ASPECTS

The Security Council and CTC have not been sufficiently attentive to these inevitable human rights concerns, in either the initial drafting of the resolution or subsequent efforts to monitor and facilitate states' compliance.

At best, the CTC has failed to make consistency with human rights norms a sufficient priority, essentially disclaiming responsibility to be attentive to human rights standards when monitoring and facilitating states' efforts to implement Resolution 1373's antiterrorism requirements. At worst, the CTC may in some instances be enabling human rights violations by "push[ing] governments to show results without at the same time explicitly raising relevant and empirically well-founded human rights concerns."

Perhaps in part because Resolution 1373 does not affirmatively refer to any international human rights, humanitarian, or refugee law obligations to be heeded when implementing its antiterrorism requirements, the CTC initially took the position that its mandate did not encompass any human rights concerns at all. Soon after the CTC was established, its first chair, Jeremy Green stock, explicitly disclaimed any obligation to ensure that states implemented Resolution 1373 in a manner consistent with human rights norms. While pledging to "remain aware of the interaction with human rights concerns," Greenstock stated that "monitoring performance against other international conventions, including human rights law, is outside the scope of the CTC's mandate," and that instead, "it is . . . open to other organizations to study States' reports and take up their content in other forums." Greenstock reiterated the same message on other occasions, stating that the CTC would make its operations sufficiently transparent to permit NGOs and others to identify and bring concerns to the "established human rights machinery," but that the CTC had no responsibility to ensure that states respect human rights when implementing the resolution.[5]

Terrorism is highly correlated with the presence of human rights abuses, weaknesses in the rule of law, and major political grievances.[6] When governments violate human rights in their efforts to combat terrorism, they effectively "cede to terroriststhe moral high ground" and "provoke tension, hatred and mistrust of government among precisely those parts of the population where terrorists are most likely to find recruits."[7] In this context, respect for human rights is not merely an independent moral or legal obligation, to be compartmentalized and relegated to institutions dedicated exclusively to "human rights" as a freestanding set of concerns. Rather, respect for human rights is itself a strategic imperative, an integral element of any "comprehensive strategy" to combat terrorism.[8]

Resolution 1373 is, in essence, a call to implement a regime of law. If Resolution 1373 is properly implemented, the rule of law will be strengthened. In turn, human rights, which depend on the rule of law for their consistent vindication, will be strengthened. Despite the centrality of human rights to any successful campaign against terrorism, the CTC has not incorporated human rights norms into its operations to any significant degree. In its general guidance to states preparing their compliance reports, the CTC does not request any information concerning states' efforts to heed human rights obligations when implementing their antiterrorism initiatives.[9]

5. United Nations, Human Rights Committee Briefed on Work of Counter-Terrorism Committee, Press Release No. HR/CT/630, Mar. 27, 2003, available athttp://www.un.org/News/Press/docs/2003/hrct630.doc.htm [hereinafter U.N. Press Release, Mar. 27,2003] (discussing briefing by Curtis Ward)
6. Human Rights Watch, Hear No Evil, See No Evil: The U.N. Security Council's Approachto Human Rights Violations in the Global Counter-terrorism Effort 3 (2004), http://www.hrw.org/backgrounder/un/2004/un0804/index.htm [hereinafter HRW, Hear No Evil]; Int'lbar Ass'n, International Terrorism: Legal Challenges and Responses 30-31 (2003).
7. U.N. SCOR, 57th Sess., 4453rd mtg. at 5, U.N. Doc. S/PV.4453 (statement of Jeremy Greenstock); see also Rosand, at 340.
8. Human rights by incorporating attention tohuman rights "into decision-making and discussion throughout the work" of United Nations.
9. High Level Panel Report, 147-48; see Secretary-General, In Larger Freedom, 144 (discussing importance of mainstreaming").

Security Council went even further, suggesting that attention to human rights concerns arising from states' implementation of 4# U.N. SCOR, 57th Sess., 4561th mtg. at 21, U.N. Doc. S/PV.4561 (statement of Jeremy Greenstock). One official close to the Resolution 1373 was not only outside the CTC's mandate, but also unnecessary, since the CTC's efforts would invariably advance human rights norms based on the following syllogism: Rostow. This logic is flawed, however, for if "proper implementation" is notdefined to incorporate human rights concerns, then human rights may be undermined, rather thanstrengthened, by the CTC's efforts to promote compliance with the resolution's provisions mandatingantiterrorism measures.

Nor has the CTC appeared to identify and consider human rights concerns upon reviewing states' initial and subsequent reports. As one organization concluded based on its review of those reports in 2004, the CTC has typically failed to question or otherwise respond to states' descriptions of antiterrorism laws or other actions that quite apparently implicate human rights concerns, either on their face or as applied in states with known human rights problems, or to scrutinize assertions by states that are "demonstrably inaccurate."[10] In some instances, these human rights concerns have been foreseeable and apparent. More recently, the Security Council has clarified, in Resolutions 1456, 1566, and 1624, that attention to human rights must indeed play a central role in the antiterrorism initiatives required by Resolution 1373.524 To its credit, the CTC has made a sustained effort since its creation to engage in dialogue with OHCHR and other international institutions charged with ensuring compliance with human rights obligations. Successive

10. S.C. Res. 1456, supra note 488, 5 (Jan. 20, 2003) ("calling upon" states to ensure that their anti-terrorism measures "comply with all their obligations under international law," and to "adopt suchmeasures in accordance with . . . international human rights, refugee, and humanitarian law); S.C. Res.1566, pmbl (Oct. 8, 2004) ("[r]eminding" states to comply with international humanrights, refugee, and humanitarian law obligations); S.C. Res. 1624, U.N. Doc. S/RES/1624, para. 4 (Sep. 14, 2005) ("stress[ing] that" states' antiterrorism measures should comply with international human rights,refugee, and humanitarian law obligations).

High Commissioners for Human Rights and others with expertise in human rights issues have met with the CTC to convey their perspectives on how the CTC should increase its attentiveness to human rights issues.[11] In addition, the U.N. Human Rights Committee has been briefed by the CTC's legal expert and has been afforded an opportunity to convey its perspectives directly to the CTC.[12] Since its earliest days the CTC also has made efforts to ensure that its work is sufficiently transparent to permit outside institutions both to monitor and critique the compliance reports submitted by member states as well as to evaluate the work processes of the CTC itself.[13]

The CTC also has taken additional measures to incorporate the human rights mandate of Resolution 1456 into its work more directly than it had previously. Letters sent by the CTC to states since May 2003 have incorporated the language in Resolution 1456 reminding states that they must ensure that their antiterrorism measures comply with international human rights, refugee, and humanitarian law.

(B) NATIONAL ASPECTS

India has long recognized the importance of ensuring its own compliance with these international human rights obligations. While international treaties do not automatically become part of domestic law upon ratification,[14] the Constitution provides, as a Directive Principle of State Policy, that the government "shall endeavour to foster respect for international law and treaty obligations in the dealings of organized people with one another", and also authorizes the central government to enact legislation implementing its international law obligatio.

The Supreme Court of India has frequently emphasized that constitutional and statutory provisions should be

11. HRW, Hear no Evil, at 6-7.
12. U.N. Press Release, Mar. 27, 2003.
13. Rosand, at 335.
14. E.g., State of Madras *v.* G.G. Menon, A.I.R. 1954 S.C. 517.

interpreted in light of India's international law obligations [15] and has looked for guidance when interpreting the Constitution's fundamental rights provisions to the UDHR, which was adopted while the Constitution was being drafted.[16] India also is bound by customary international law norms, to the extent it has not persistently objected to those norms, and is absolutely bound by norms that have attained the status of jus cogen.[17] In 1993, India established the National Human Rights Commission, an independent government commission whose mandate is to protect and promote international human rights norms.[18] The NHRC is empowered to receive and investigate individual complaints of human rights violations, initiate such investigations on its own, monitor and make non-binding recommendations to the government on domestic implementation of international human rights norms, and promote public awareness of human rights standards.[19] To conduct these activities, the NHRC has the powers of a civil court, including the ability to compel appearance of witnesses, examine witnesses under oath, compel discovery and production of documents, and order production of records from

15. See, e.g., People's Union for Civil Liberties v. Union of India, A.I.R. 1997 S.C. 568; KesavanandaBharati *v.* State of Kerala, A.I.R. 1973 S.C. 1461; Jolly George Verghese *v.* Bank of Cochin, A.I.R. 1980S.C. 470, 473; JAIN, at 1394-95; Justice A.S. Anand, The Domestic Application ofInternational Human Rights Norms (1998), http://www.humanrightsinitiative.org/jc/papers/jc_2004/supplementary_papers/anand.pdf.
16. Durga Das Basu, Human Rights in Constitutional Law 27 & n.48 (Bhagabati Prosad Banerjee and Ashish Kumar Massey eds., 2d ed. 2003) (citing Maneka Gandhi *v.* Union of India, A.I.R. 1978 S.C.597).
17. Malanczuk, at 43, 46-48, 57-58.
18. Protection of Human Rights Act, 1993, No. 10 of 1994 [hereinafter PHRA]; see Vijayashri Sripati, India's National Human Rights Commission: A Shackled Commission?, 18 B.U. INT'L L.J. 1 (2000). The PHRA was enacted amidst a broader effort by the U.N. Commission on Human Rights and the General Assembly during the early 1990s to encourage the establishment of national human rights institutions to promote and protect human rights norms domestically. See G.A. Res. 134, U.N. GAOR, 48th Sess., U.N.Doc. A/RES/48/134 (Dec. 20, 1993).
19. PHRA, §§ 12-14. The NHRC issues annual reports and more specific reports regarding government abuses, and sponsors studies and other research programs.

courts and government agencies[20] recommend compensation to the victim or prosecution of those responsible.

(C) TERRORISM AND HUMAN RIGHTS

Does India Need Counter Another Counter-Terrorism Regime?

The threat of terrorism has in recent years been propelled to the forefront of the global agenda. Events such as those of 11 September 2001, the Bali bombings, the London underground bombing, the Madrid bombing and closer home, the attack on the Indian Parliament have entrenched the perception that terrorism is a global threat that is the concern of all nations to counter. The discourse surrounding the issue at the international stage is omnipresent and agonistic. The terms 'terrorism', 'terrorist', or 'terrorist organisation' have come to be used as generic terms for some vague notion of a wicked and criminal enemy, and for this reason, have been easily applied to describe a vast diversity of violence throughout the world. Although al-Qaeda and Osama bin Laden are largely the epitome of 'terrorism' within the US-led campaign entitled 'the war on terror', the term has certainly not been confined to applying to international networks of religious zealots who plan and perpetrate indiscriminate killing of civilians, but has applied liberally to all forms of non-State actors who resort to violence, regardless of whether that violence is directed against civilians or States. Despite decades of efforts, no uniform definition of terrorism currently exists in the international community. This is reflective of the high political stakes associated with the term. Nevertheless, in response to the events of 11 September 2001, the United Nations Security Council issued Resolution 1373, which placed an obligation on all member states to implement counter-terrorism laws with respect to financing, supporting,

20. *Id*. §§ 13-16. The chair of the NHRC must be a former Supreme Court chief justice, one member must be a current or former Supreme Court judge, one member must be a current or former High Court chief justice, and two members must "hav[e] knowledge of, or practical experience in, matters relating tohuman rights." Id. § 3(2).

planning, or perpetrating terrorist acts or harbouring terrorists.[21] Without an internationally accepted understanding of terrorism, States were thus obliged to implement counter-terrorism laws in the name of international peace and security based on their own understanding of terrorism.[22] Counter-terrorism regimes have generally bestowed a plethora of extraordinary powers on law enforcement agencies, being reflective of the perception that terrorism is a unique crime in the threat it poses not merely to individuals, but to the security of states and democratic culture. Such powers have included preventive detention, broad and invasive investigatory powers, and special rules of criminal procedure—many of which themselves offend basic principles of procedural justice and democratic rights.

As a consequence, combating terrorism has given rise to concerns regarding its own adverse affects on human rights and democratic polity. India's experience with political violence and terrorism long pre-dates the current era of terrorism's preponderance on the world stage. Indeed, India has possessed extraordinary security laws throughout its independent life, and before that, under British colonial rule. In fact, many of the lessons learnt in Ireland were sought to be applied in the 1920s and 1930s in India and in Palestine in the 1940s by the British colonial administrators. A brief characterisation of the scope of terrorism in India reveals that it is highly complex and varied. There is an insurgency as in Kashmir which has claimed between 40-67 thousand lives between 1989 to 2007,[23] is only one aspect of many that comprise India's understanding of the terrorist threat. Some examples of other causes for violence and terrorism can be found in the religious identity and political power struggles characterising Sikh militancy in the 1980s, the economic and political agendas that have given rise to separatist movements such as the United Liberation Front of Assam

21. Security Council Resolution 1373, 28 September 2001. (http://www.unodc.org/images/resolution%201373.pdf on 15 September 2007).
22. See for instance, T. Stephens, '*International Criminal Law and the Response to International Terrorism*', UNSW Law Journal, Vol. 27(2), pp. 457-461.
23. Project Ploughshares, Armed Conflicts Report January 2007, India Kashmir (http://www.ploughshares.ca/libraries/ACRText/ACR-IndiaKashmir.html#Deaths on 8 August 2008).

(ULFA) in Assam, the poverty and social oppression coupled with extreme left-wing political ideology that has come to be known as 'Naxalism' throughout many parts of the country, and ethnic armed opposition groups seeking independence from India such as in Manipur and Nagaland The multitude of forms and causes for violence are reflective of the huge diversity that exists in the heterogeneous nation which has more than 1600 language groups, six major religions, and entrenched social divisions.[24]

What is popularly known as terrorism in India is thus often a reflection of the deep discontent of sections of the Indian population, and not merely the universal and 'foreign' threat of international jihadist networks. The Indian Supreme Court has even recognised the popular advantage of being labelled 'terrorist 'It is a common feature that hardened criminals today take advantage of the situation and by wearing the cloak of terrorism, aim to achieve acceptability and respectability in the society; because in different parts of the country affected by militancy, a terrorist is projected as a hero by a group and often unfortunately even by many misguided youth.[25]

In 2004 the government published a statement that described terrorism and extremist violence as 'not merely a law-and-order problem, but a far deeper socio-economic issue' [26]

India's attempts to solve its problems with armed opposition and terrorism through draconian regimes have proved largely ineffective in preventing terrorist attacks. Furthermore, the toll inflicted on human rights has counteracted the very purposes of the laws: improper use of extensive executive powers has been used against political opponents, damaging India's democratic character; and the targeting of minority communities often associated with terrorism has caused their further alienation from mainstream society—

24. T. Mkandawire, Foreword to Jayal 2006, N.G. Jayal, Representing India, Ethnic Diversity and the Governance of Public Institutions (Palgrave MacMillan 2006), p. xv.
25. Madan Singh *v.* State of Bihar [2004] INSC 215.
26. Prime Minister's Office, *National Common Minimum Programme of the Government of India*, May 2004, p. 10 (http://pmindia.nic.in/cmp.pdf on 12 Aug. 2008).

increasing both the grievances endured and the likelihood that more will seek to find political voice through violence. The repeal of POTA in 2004, as with its predecessor TADA in 1995, was due primarily to such considerations. Presently, the question exists of whether India requires another extra-ordinary regime to counter terrorism. Such a regime would come on top of a host of existing laws for this purpose that provide for broad criminal offences for terrorism, under the UAPA as amended in 2004 and the power of preventive detention under laws such as the National Security Act (NSA).

It is contended that India's problems with terrorism and armed opposition may be better countered by a strategy different to its traditional recourse to extra-ordinary executive powers, namely, a strategy that seeks to reconcile the imperatives of state security and human rights—particularly, the human rights of marginalised sections of Indian society that are the most targeted by draconian laws, most beleaguered by mainstream political narratives, and in turn, most likely to resort to forms of armed opposition and terrorism.

It is unhelpful to draw comparisons with the experiences of other, notably Western, countries either with regard to the nature of the terrorism threats they face, or with respect to the ways in which those threats are countered. For one, Western countries themselves suffer from a serious crisis of legitimacy. Accounts of torture, prolonged periods of detention without trial, and intrusions into privacy through surveillance of communications systems point to the increasing erosion of rights in those countries.

It is, however, useful to consider that the justice systems in some of these countries have firmly struck down many of the extraordinary measures and policies formulated in the aftermath of terror strikes in the United States and in Europe. For example, the European Court of Human Rights recently reaffirmed the prohibition of torture was absolute. In June 2008, the United States Supreme Court ruled that foreign terrorism suspects held at the Guantánamo Bay naval base had the right to challenge their detentions in US courts.

The need to strike a balance between individual rights and national security is legitimate. For India, the solution clearly lies in the strengthening of the investigative machinery and the reform of institutions concerned with law enforcement. It is a cause for worry when investigations into major terror attacks founder due to lack of evidence. It is further disquieting to observe that a large number of those rounded up in the aftermath of terror attacks are found to have been detained on flimsy grounds, with all the attendant consequences—long periods of detention, the risk of torture, the stigma of having been detained, and the inevitable rise of hostility towards the State and its agencies.

Instead of bestowing greater powers on executive agencies already lacking in accountability, and thus increasing the potential for abuse and social harm, the plethora of extraordinary powers already in existence might be better replaced with reforms of the ordinary criminal justice system and police institutions. Only where justice is accessible to all, and state institutions are viewed to work impartially in the interests of all, can the State increase its legitimacy in the eyes of the broader population and consequently reduce the threat that the aggrieved will resort to violence against the State.

(D) STATES OF EMERGENCY : INDIA IN FOCUS (CORE E-HUMAN RIGHTS FEATURE)

As the United Nations' Commission on Human Rights is poised to convene next week for its 58th session, among many other human rights issues, it will be looking into the question of "states of emergency" all over the world. A state of emergency is a temporary situation declared within the territorial boundaries of a State during which certain fundamental liberties of its citizens are kept in suspension. According to established international law, such a state can only be declared by lawful means and some core human rights such as the right to life and the arbitrary deprivation of life, the right not to be tortured, the prohibition of forced labor, can never be derogated or set aside, even in a state of emergency.

States of emergency are a continuing focus of the UN's human rights monitoring activities under both its Charter as well as its Treaty-based bodies, in particular the Human Rights Committee. The General Assembly, the highest representative body under the United Nations Charter, has an independent expert reporting to the Secretary General annually on states of emergency. On the other hand, the Human Rights Commission (HRC), which was set up to monitor the implementation of one of the most important core treaties of the International Bill of Rights—the International Covenant on Civil and Political Rights (ICCPR)—also has a special focus on this extremely important aspect of civil and political. This worldwide concern arises from the close relationship between such emergency situations and democratic functioning of States.

This year, a human rights organization in special consultative status with the UN has submitted a written statement to the 58th Commission on Human Rights that strongly indicts the Government of India. The statement titled as "Undeclared state of emergency in India" that the South Asia Human Rights Documentation Centre has submitted describes a number of existing legislation, which it claims violates established principles that form the basis of a democratic State.

SAHRDC's statement is particularly pertinent to the continuous declaration of the entire State of Manipur, for the past 22 years, as a "disturbed area" thereby justifying the blanket suspension of inviolable fundamental liberties of over two million of India's population assured by the Constitution as well as by international treaty. Though the Supreme Court, in its highly controversial 1997 verdict, upheld the constitutional legality of this continued de facto state of emergency in Jammu and Kashmir, Nagaland, Manipur, Assam and parts of Tripura, wide legal and public opinion persist that the Government of India is blatantly and continuously acting in direct contravention to its legal obligations under the International Bill of Rights to which it is a State Party.

SAHRDC says: "India is awash in legislation that restricts fundamental liberties. Laws purporting to safeguard national security and public order have been employed to counter ambiguously defined threats. Applied over large swathes of the country—from the state of Jammu & Kashmir in the north to several states in the northeast as well as Andhra Pradesh in the south—these Acts contain provisions that are incompatible with the principles that form the basis of a democratic State.

"Preventive detention, extraordinary powers to the police and security forces to arrest, detain, and even shoot suspects—are measurers that normally follow the proclamation of a state of emergency, which, in turn, is justifiable only in the face of threats to the life of a nation. The extensive nature of these laws has ensured that virtually the entire country remains in a state of undeclared emergency.

"Some of the major legislative measures are summarized below: "The Disturbed Areas Act is in effect in the states of Assam, Nagaland, Manipur, parts of Tripura, Jammu & Kashmir, Andhra Pradesh, and in two districts of the state of Arunachal Pradesh. It gives police extraordinary powers of arrest and detention.

"The National Security Act (NSA) of 1980 provides for detention of a person "with a view to preventing him from acting in any manner prejudicial to" various State objectives including national security and public order. The maximum period of detention is 12 months. The Act limits the powers of the court to review detention orders. And while it requires the Government to refer all cases to an Advisory Board consisting of High Court judges within three weeks of the detention, it does not permit legal counsel to appear before the Board on behalf of the detenu. The proceedings of the Advisory Board are moreover closed to the public and its report to the Government in confidential. Finally, it gives legal immunity to any government officer acting in good faith in pursuance of the Act. At the end of 1997, according to Government records, approximately 500 persons were in detention under the NSA.

"The Jammu & Kashmir Public Safety Act (PSA) of 1978 applies similar procedures to the state of Jammu and Kashmir, allowing detention without trial for two years. According to Government records, updated as far as August 1997, nearly 1,600 persons were being held in five detention centers in Jammu and Kashmir as compared to 2,070 in 1995. Of these, 1,298 persons were held under the PSA.

"The Armed Forces Special Powers Act of 1958 remains in effect in Jammu and Kashmir, Nagaland, Manipur, Assam and parts of Tripura. It gives the Central Government the power to declare any State or Union Territory a disturbed area, allows security forces to fire at any person if it is considered "necessary

for maintenance of law and order." They can also arrest any person "against whom reasonable suspicion exists" with no obligation to inform the detainee of the grounds for arrest. Finally, security personnel are given immunity from prosecution for any acts committed by them in relation to the Act. The Prevention of Terrorism Ordinance (POTO) of 2001 is the latest in the series of measurers that often cause more harm than the threat they are meant to tackle. POTO provides for the holding of an accused person for a prolonged period of detention for up to 180 days without charges, and effectively subverts the cardinal principle of the criminal justice system - the presumption of innocence - by putting the burden of proof on the accused, withholding of the identity of witnesses, making confessions made to the police officer admissible as evidence, and giving the public prosecutor the power to veto bail.

Certain rights must be fully respected at all times and under all circumstances. These include the right not to be arbitrarily deprived of life, the right to freedom from torture, the right to a fair trial and the right to protection against discrimination. The Acts listed above lack the safeguards needed to ensure the protection of these basic rights.

"India is a party to the International Convention on Civil and Political Rights (ICCPR) and is therefore obliged to abide by its provisions. Furthermore, any derogation from its provisions is only permissible under three conditions. Firstly, it is only "in times of public emergency which threatens the life of the nation and the existence of which is officially proclaimed" that states may derogate from their obligations under the ICCPR. Also, such derogation must be "strictly required by the exigencies of the situation" and cannot be inconsistent with other international law obligations. The AFSPA, for example, was enacted without such an official proclamation of emergency and goes beyond the requirements of the situation. No official proclamation was made with regard to the application of the NSA or POTO either.

"Secondly, there can be no derogation from articles 6, 7, 8 (paragraphs 1 and 2), 11, 15, 16 and 18. The AFSPA violates three of these—Article 6 guaranteeing the right to life and prohibiting the arbitrary deprivation of life, Article 7 prohibiting torture and Article 8 prohibiting forced labor.

"Certain elements contained in this Acts violate other key provisions of the ICCPR. Article 4 of POTO violates Article 14(2) of the ICCPR which states that any person "charged with a criminal offence to be presumed innocent until proven guilty."POTO allows detention for a minimum of one year, and it is for the accused to prove his or her innocence, which is made more difficult by the courts' powers to convict a person using only the testimony of the arresting police officers.

"The NSA also derogates from rights guaranteed under the ICCPR, in particular Article 9 which provides that anyone who is arrested must be informed of the reasons for the arrest and the charges against him. Under Section 8(2) of the NSA, the authorities may not disclose the grounds on which the person has been detained. This is also in direct contravention of article 14(3) of the Covenant.

"Thirdly, under article 40 of the ICCPR, any state which derogates from the Covenant must inform the other States parties immediately, through the Secretary-General. It must also give reasons for the derogation and the date on which the derogations are terminated. India has not met this obligation with regard to any of the above legislation.

"In its Concluding Observations after having considered India's Third Periodic Report in July 1997, the UN Human Rights Committee expressed its concern 'at the continuing reliance on special powers under legislation such as the Armed Forces Special Powers Act, the Public Safety Act and the National Security Act in areas declared to be disturbed and at serious human rights violations, in particular with respect to Article 6, 7, 9 and 14 of the Covenant, committed by security and armed forces acting under these laws as well as by paramilitary and insurgent groups.' The Committee also expressed regret that by applying legislation such as the AFSPA, the State party was 'in effect using emergency powers without resorting to Article 4, paragraph 3, of the Covenant.' It recommended the close monitoring of the application of 'these emergency powers' to ensure strict compliance with the provisions of the Covenant.

"The September 11 attack in New York prompted many countries to adopt anti-terrorism policies and legislation. In this context, the High Commissioner for Human Rights, Ms Mary

Robinson, has pointed to the need to ensure that States conform to the standards set out in the ICCPR dealing with emergency measures. Such measures, the High Commissioner added, may be justified in principle in international law, provided they are demonstrated to be necessary and there are effective safeguards. However, she stressed, they may also require notice of derogation under the Covenant.

"The need to strike a balance between personal freedoms and national security will and must remain the major concern of States while framing policies and legislation. A good yardstick by which to measure State action is the set of standards laid down in the ICCPR. India, along with other countries, must be reminded of its obligation to conform to these standards. It must also submit its actions to scrutiny. That, as the High Commissioner pointed out, is the sign of a healthy democracy."

3

Indian National Security Laws and State Communities

New anti-terror legislation, drafted in response to the series of attacks in Bombay (Mumbai) on 26 November, was approved by the Rajya Sabha (the upper house of the bicameral legislature) on 18 December, having been approved by the Lok Sabha (the lower house) the previous day. The Unlawful Activities (Prevention) Act provided new powers for the security services, most controversially the ability to hold suspects for six months without charge. It also made provision for the establishment of a National Investigating Agency responsible for gathering and processing intelligence and investigating terrorism.

The new anti-terror law was written in response to attacks in Bombay on 26-29 November. These attacks were carried out by 10 gunmen who attacked predominantly tourist and Jewish targets. The attackers killed an estimated 183 people and injured many more before all but one of them was killed. One gunman was captured and interrogated by the Indian authorities. The attacks took place over four days, partly due to the slow response of the Indian security forces.

The attackers apparently arrived in Bombay by sea on the evening of 26 November. They immediately dispersed around the city to attack a train station, the Taj Mahal and Oberoi Trident hotels, a hospital, a cafe, and the Nariman House Jewish centre. People were killed indiscriminately at all the locations, then hostages were taken at the hotels and the Jewish centre. The Indian security forces surrounded the hotels and the Jewish centre and eventually commandos stormed all three buildings. Several hostages were freed from the hotels but all the hostages in the Jewish centre were killed.

Mumbai has suffered several attacks in the last 10 years, including the train bombing of 2003, other bombings later in 2003 and the 2006 commuter train bombings. The police response to these attacks was widely criticised as insufficient. There was little success in bringing the perpetrators to justice and Pakistan was blamed to a greater or lesser extent in each case.

The Unlawful Activities (Prevention) Act was passed by the bicameral legislature with the support of both main parties, but was criticised by some smaller parties and by human rights and minority rights groups. Amnesty International said that, while they recognised the duty of the Indian government to provide security, anti-terror laws should not infringe human rights. The Communist Party of India also released a statement affirming its opposition to the legislation on human rights grounds. An earlier anti-terrorism Act was repealed by the current government because minorities, especially Muslims, felt it was used to unfairly target them.

Questions remained over the level of involvement by Pakistani militant groups and the Pakistani government in the attack. The Indian government insisted that the militant captured during the attack was Pakistani and stated that the militants were coordinated by the Pakistani authorities. The Joint Police Commissioner of Crime for Mumbai, Rakesh Maria, stated that the attackers were trained in Pakistani Kashmir by former officers of the Pakistani army. However, the government of Pakistan maintained that it had not received any tangible evidence that the attacker was one of its citizens and categorically denied being behind the attacks.

The US government put pressure on Pakistan to co-operate fully with India in investigating the attacks and bringing the perpetrators to justice. After meetings with the Indian foreign minister on 3 December, US secretary of state Condoleezza Rice said: "This is the time for everybody to co-operate and do so transparently."

The US government reportedly sought to avoid a military buildup on Pakistan's Indian border that could divert Pakistani resources away from dealing with the militants on its Afghan border.

India was first united in the 3rd century BC by the Maurya Empire and Buddhism was spread within India by the Maurya emperor Ashoka. After the fall of the Maurya Empire, India was ruled by patchworks of states and Hindu empires until the arrival of Islam. In the 13th century a number of Muslim sultanates were established but proved short-lived. In 1526 the Mughal Empire again united the country; the Mughals reigned until colonial times despite being a Muslim empire ruling a predominantly Hindu population.

The British set-up their first Indian trading post in 1619 and the British East India Company grew increasingly influential over the following century. In 1764 the East India Company conquered Bengal and set-up an administration, which expanded to encompass most of the sub-continent by 1857. After the Indian Mutiny the British Crown took direct control of India and dissolved the remains of the Mughal Empire. The Indian independence movement grew from this time, through World Wars I and II until the withdrawal of the UK in 1947. Most notable among the independence leaders was Mahatma Gandhi who advocated non-violent resistance to UK rule.

At independence India underwent "Partition" into predominantly Muslim Pakistan and predominantly Hindu India. Sectarian rioting at the time of Partition led to around 500,000 deaths and contributed to mass migrations of minority communities. After Partition the princely state of Jammu and Kashmir joined India, having been invaded by Pakistani forces. India sent its army to Kashmir and fought the first Indo-

Pakistani war within the state. No clear victor emerged and a ceasefire established the Line of Control (LOC) which has remained the de facto international border.

India and Pakistan fought three further wars after 1947. In 1965 the two countries fought a five-week war over Kashmir, which was also inconclusive. The two countries fought a brief war at the time of Bangladeshi independence in 1971, when India invaded East Pakistan in support of Bengali rebels. The East Pakistani forces surrendered, leading to the independence of Bangladesh. The most recent war took place in 1999 and was fought entirely in Kashmir. Neither side made any territorial gains.

India has suffered many outbreaks of sectarian strife since independence. In 1984 a Sikh militant independence movement was crushed in the storming of the Golden Temple, Sikhism's most holy shrine. This led to widespread anger among Sikhs and the assassination of Indira Gandhi by Sikh members of her bodyguard.

Hindu-Muslim tension was inflamed by the destruction in December 1992 of the Ayodhya mosque by Hindu extremists. Subsequent rioting led to the deaths of more than 1,200 people.

The Hindu-Muslim violence continued with massacres and attacks including the assault on the Indian Parliament (2001), the riots in Gujarat (2002) and bombs in Bombay (2003, and 2006) and Delhi (2005).

A. NEPAL

Introduction

Self-preservation is the mainspring of a national security strategy. National security is a highest, public good; the benefits of its outreach include all the citizens. In the absence of national security neither democracy, nor development not even peace can be organized. The UN defines security as freedom from want and freedom from fear. This means secure citizens are those whose basic needs, civic freedoms and identity are guaranteed and they are not intimidated by any force, internal and external. National security essentially means the state of the health of the nation within which citizens enjoy life, liberty, property and participation in the productive life of society.

Political stability, economic well-being and equitable distribution of resources are its essential preconditions. If any society has a high incidence of death, violence, crime, killing, kidnapping and extortion, whatever the causes, the citizens living there will never feel safe and sound. Ordinary citizens measure the standard of national security through the ability of national leaders "to rise above narrow and special economic interests of parts of the nation", and "focus their attention on the more inclusive interests of the whole" (Wolfers, 1968:148). The peacefulness of environment of a nation is based on the sound civil defense, amodicum of trust among citizens themselves and with the national institutions of governance. The sources of threat can be extra-systemic (inter-state tension, cross-border terrorism, unwanted immigration, climate change, fuel and financial crises, refugees etc.) or intra-systemic (civil war, poverty trap, inequality and exclusion of citizens from ecological, social, economic and political resources). One source of threat reinforces the other systemically and is linked with macro and micro issues. The comparative and competitive strengths of any nation in material possessions, such as hydropower, ecological diversity, tourism, manpower and productive potential and the proper utilization of these resources can contribute to its viability. This means the *government cannot construct a national security without understanding the systemic crises* at five dimensions: protection of national "community values vs. the destructiveness of warfare; the behavior of economy vs. the structure of the polity; the location of ecological system vs. political boundaries; pluralistic cultural identities vs. loyalty to a given state; and human rights vs. state sovereignty norms" (Brown, 1992:117). The optimal resolution of these systemic crises is crucial to the state-society harmony within the nation-state and safe adaptation in the international system.

How can civil and defense security agencies of Nepal collaborate to safeguard national and public interest and ensure the well-being, dignity and freedom of all Nepalese citizens? How can they exercise professionalism, impersonality and neutrality to beef up national integrity system when each change in government involves massive reshuffle of security and administrative personnel? How does security as a highest collective good is equally distributed in society so that citizens are free to pursue their productive life? What are the legitimate ways to achieve the synergy of hard capital of state institutions and soft social capital of civic institutions (political parties, civil society, media and other socialization agencies) for the coherence of state-society ties in achieving governance goals1 and implementation of peace accord through constitutional process? In the introductory note, this paper defines national security, the second section narrates the nation's geopolitics, the third section explains the changing patterns of security and stability in Nepal, the fourth section focuses on modernization of public security agencies and the fifth section suggests measures for democratic control of security mechanism.

Governance goals are :

> National security, law and order, voice, civic participation, service delivery and non-violent resolution of multi-polar and multi-layered conflicts.

Geopolitics of Nepal

Nepal occupies a central part of Asia geopolitics between two advanced technological super states—China in the north and India in the east, south and west each with over one billion population, leading infrastructure, software technology industries, high growth markets and highest engagement of multilateral institutions. This potentially makes it a transit corridor for increased Sino-Indian competition for trade and commerce. Its location in the geopolitical underbelly of China, Tibet and India's heartland states of Uttar Pradesh, Bihar and West Bengal constitutes its strategic geography vital to their security, stability, progress and peace. An increasingly open and democratic Nepal in the future is more likely to be swayed by the ongoing geo-strategic competition between them and the great powers for their influence. As globalization will unglue its historically evolved centripetal forces and denationalize them on the basis of self-chosen linkages, the nation will become a site of internal conflicts of elites nourished by geo-strategic contest of external drivers of conflict in search of internal allies. Existence of over two-dozen insurgent groups in Tarai, Nepal's southern flat land, and simmering crisis in Tibet involve the high stake of neighbors as they pose an external security dilemma. Similarly, internal security dilemma has kept a powerful brake on the pacification of Nepali politics through the enforcement of peace accord. In this context, understanding the nation's geopolitics is crucial to maintain a balanced foreign and security policy of the country. As Nepal's ecological, social, economic and technological spheres transcend the domain of the statehood confined to its territorial sovereignty, an imperative exists to see security beyond national defense planning as development and defense needs are competitive and interdependent. Human security needs today are defined by the universal ideologies of human rights, democracy, social justice and peace. They have made Nepal's survival and vital interests interdependent with the neighbors and global powers. In this context, international cooperation is essential to abolish the Hobbesian state of nature existing at various levels of security—*individual, sub-national, state, regional and international system and foster norm-based sociability and collective action*. A well-functioning polity features "an essential *congruence* between the effective authority possessed by society's governing institutions and the behavior that must be constrained in order to maintain or further society's values" (Brown, 1992:115).

Changing Patterns of Security and Stability in Nepal

Nepal's political institutions now rest on the commitment to popular sovereignty, parliamentary supremacy and political openness. But, the political process of Nepal revolves around powerful personalities rather than institutions. The familial and dynastic succession of leadership has bred a patrimonial culture. Poor political institutionalization 2 has blurred the boundaries between various institutions of society. From the unification days until recently there is a continuity of the state institutions, such as monarchy, Nepal Army, police, bureaucracy, tradition and law and discontinuity and fragmentation of civic institutions.

Lack of a balance between the state and society created authoritarian culture in the nation. But, the security agencies of the nation have expressed absolute loyalty to those in power under all regimes monarchy, Ranarchy, oligarchy, liberals and even communist-led regime and helped to maintain the unity and security of the nation through state-orientation notion of security politics. Their preference for loyalty, discipline, patriotism and hierarchy has earned their image abroad in peace keeping missions.

After the unification of Nepal in 1769 AD Nepal's security was based on a policy of active defense. The advent of Rana regime in 1846 modified this policy as it maintained special security relationship with British India and isolation from the rest of the world. But, the concept 2 According to Robert A. Scalapino political institutionalization is the "process whereby a political structure is made operational in accordance with stipulated rules and procedures, enabling more regularized, hence predictable, patterns of political behavior, minimum trauma in power transfer, and a foundation for the effective development of policies as well as the application of justice" (1986: 59) of national autonomy and cultural self-expression of diverse groups were not completely clocked. Nepal's traditional political system fused executive, legislative and judiciary function into a single, centralized structure as it performed overlapping functions although there was a semblance of judiciary. Police controlled and pacified the population internally, the army provided external protection and the culture provided sources of nationalism and world view. Legitimacy was based on tradition and there were minimal functions of the state—security, stability, revenue collection and conflict resolution.

The innovation of modern constitutional state in 1950 expanded participatory resources as society demonstrated its capacity for collective action and legitimacy stemmed from election, performance and international recognition. The democratic experiments of 1950s subsequently expanded the size and scope of the state due to the need to perform many welfare functions. The state adopted the policy of diversification in international relations. During the 1960-90 period, the reason of state held the primacy over civic rights and the state and the states persons acted as guardian of diverse society. Public education, communication, health and economy mediated the state-society relations and helped the regime to maintain a policy of equidistance in regional and global geopolitics. Following the success of movement for democracy the post-

1990 regimes of all hues, however, de-linked the state from society through privatization, denationalization, deregulation and globalization and abdicated policy-making responsibility in favor of market forces. The withdrawal of state from society created security and authority vacuum and the onset of People's War. Vicious poverty trap for the many and resource monopoly for a few thus triggered the cycles of violence and counter violence, violation of human rights, declaration of the state of emergency by democratic governments and emigration of youth abroad to avert livelihood crisis and the fear of being drafted into civil war. These measures eroded the efficacy of democratic institutions—civil society, political parties and parliament and resurrected the role of security agencies in conflict resolution. If conflicts are managed through coercion, then the institutions of coercion become more powerful and they in turn hold bigger say in the way future conflicts are resolved (Weiner, 1986:311).

After the success of mass movement of April 2006 against King Gynendra's active rule the political classes removed the traditional base of Nepali identity built on monarchy, Hindu state and unitary polity and declared Nepal a federal democratic republic. The Nepal Army has been brought under civilian control. But, Nepali state is being treated by the international community as soft, fragile and weak because of its inability hold legitimate monopoly on power, control competitive violence, perform "core state functions" and successfully handle important post-conflict issues, needs and problems confronting the Nepalese society. Nepal is weak because it lacks financial resources to undertake a self-sufficient state-building processes financed by its own tax revenues and reshape conflict moderating structures and policies. It is the least institutionalized with respect to its presence in huge rural society. As a result, the tasks of stabilization of national unity and orderly participation of citizens in constitution-making, state building and the peace process in a satisfactory way remain tantalizing. The Nepalese urban civil society and NGOs are organized in segmentary style and opposed to legitimate state power and sovereignty. Most of the political parties are faction ridden, organized through the stabilization of client networks and are less interested in the transformation of peoples into citizens. The most difficult problem remains that of political and constitutional instability caused by a move of constitutional actors from consensus to competitive politics, free-riding tendency of some actors who are enjoying more power than their actual social representativeness, distributional struggle of social movement actors for power, resource and identity and extra-constitutional activities of armed non-state actors thus spoiling peace and security.

The Constituent Assembly (CA) election has broadened the social, gender and intergenerational bases of political power. But, there is a lack of educational, economic, technological, institutional and leadership preconditions of modernity to sustain these bloated political classes and structural reforms as tax contributes only 12 percent to GDP. In the future, continuous gap between traditional politics of patronage and right-based socioeconomic revolution spawned by rising expectation of participation of citizens in decision-making will continue to make the government and political system unsteady. Incapacity of ruling political classes to cope with multiple challenges has posed the problem of governability. The unstructured, fluctuating, unsystematic, anomic and multidimensional participation of Nepalese citizens subsuming the absolutization of mini-identities of gender, class, caste, ethnicity, region and religion rather than meta-identity of citizen has made conflict an open-ended exercise. These multiple identifications of citizens have weakened their loyalty to the state, eroded any respect to rule of law and opened a new security problem. The deadlock created by the opposite conception of adjustment of armed forces, meager trust between civil and military and conflicting vision of democratic republic versus peoples' republic have provided various armed groups to free-ride causing security and authority deficit and shrinkage of development space. The adoption of extra-constitutional mode of conflict resolution and political change every time has established the utility of a political culture of militancy of youth wing in every party and offensive understanding of politics thus compelling the Home Minister Bam Dev Gautam to admit *his inability to improve security situation in the country*. Political parties and civil society can only release the potential for national integration if the state and political system are stabilized, leadership develops institutional capacity for conflict resolution and rules of the game are accepted by all actors—actual, potential and left out. To this end, it should proceed within institutional frameworks that are capable of countering the danger of territorial, political and ethno-religious conflicts over "distributional issues" (Wimmer and Schetter, 2002:3) and enabling a mutually acceptable framework for democratic peace.

Modernization of Public Security Mechanism

Modernization of security sector involves the professionalization of security agencies, rationalization and democratization of their authority, differentiation of their institutions and responsibilities and inclusion of left out groups of society through common process of laws. Sensitivity to humanitarian laws is a crucial aspect of democratization. The disagreement between the Maoist's concept of security sector reform (SSR) and non-Maoist notion of demilitarization, demobilization and reintegration (DDR) of combatants in the nation's productive life must be resolved with viable, long-term and rational strategies of right-sizing, professionalization and relative autonomy of security agencies so that they serve general public and national interest. The DDR is linked with the peace process and abolition of all sorts of non-state violence from politics while SSR is linked to locally-owned broader development, training and capacity building and democratization of public security agencies. Both aim to abolish the culture of impunity and the state of nature. Creation of an interface between civic groups and security like the community police (Shrestha, 2004:438-461), can refurbish the image of security agencies thus offering relief, rehabilitation and peace dividend at the local level. The concept of democratic oversight was never practiced in Nepal due to a lack of political will, financial constraints, inter-institutional coordination and communication and absence of expertise to do so. But, this is important to remove the trade off between security's over preoccupation with nationalism than democracy and political parties' excess preoccupation with democracy than nationalism and establish a correlations between the two as both democracy and nationalism make these institutions accountable to sovereign citizens. There is also a need to strength cross-bonding social capital at inter-institutional level so as to overcome the problems of collective action in the maintenance of security and rule of law. Samuel P. Huntington has developed four central concepts as measurement and durability of the state focusing on the degree to which the political system is *"adaptable, complex, autonomous and coherent"* (1968:13). These measures are important for the institutionalization of political parties and security agencies in Nepal. Crisis management and structural transformation require the capacity of state to redress the root causes of conflict and create structures that fulfill basic human needs and security. The key to the future of national security is civil-security collective action in areas of public and national interests including the development of stable democratic political culture responsive to public needs as well as preservation of its changing environment caused by continuous political turmoil (Webersik and Thapa, 2008:1).

Democratic Control of Security Agencies

This is the central aspect of creating a legitimate public order where different actors accept the rules of social conduct and undertake mutual accountability. Key strategies are:

- *The reason of state establishes that its legitimate monopoly on power is prerequisite to defend the citizens from external threat and performance governance functions.* Without a strong, unified and disciplined security structure the democratic state cannot protect its citizens from external encroachment and internal conflict and pursue national development policies.
- *Modern democracy requires the primacy of civilian control* (elected parliament and government) *over security components especially on matters of security expenditure, the disposition of structure, control over internal promotions, the kind of military technology to be acquired, purchase of equipments, military tasks, doctrine and security strategy.* In Nepal it is essential to separate clear responsibilities between the Nepal Army, APF, Police and Intelligence Agencies to determine each

other's jurisdictions and establish unified security governance.

- *Institutionalization of civil-security relations is important for coherence and synergy of the tasks and prevent the rise of militarism occurring at societal (armed groups, militant youth wings and radicalism in political party) levels.* Institutionalization helps to gain legitimacy to both sides—political parties and the security agencies, establish relationship with political structures and leadership and cope with the societal challenges jointly.
- *Professionalism of security agencies on public affairs and parliament and government on security matters are crucial to build mutual confidence.* For this, establishment of special committee in the parliament and political parties on security affairs and regular dialogues on civil security relations are important to build trust and confidence between the two. It also helps monitoring the compliance of democratic values and civilian oversight. It is difficult to develop professionalism of security agencies if high level of personalized authoritarianism in the government and political parties coexists with impersonal political and legal institutions of the state and state mechanism are often utilized to expand the party leaders' political constituencies than serving the ordinary citizens.
- *A project of civic education (enlightenment) is essential* to provide exposure and constructive engagement of all the stakeholders on the principles and practice of national security, democracy, human rights, constitutionalism and rights and responsibilities of citizens so that they develop cultivated capacity to take effective roles in the political system and learn the art of compromise for good governance.

Conclusion

A sound civil-security relation is central to enhance national security in Nepal and contribute to achieve three national tasks—building modern state, inclusive democracy based on a new social contract and sustainable peace rooted on the realization of human security. But, this requires the political leadership to remove the five defects of democracy, such as skewed access of public to power, denial of opponent groups' claim to power, erosion of the legitimate state monopoly on power, narrow power base restricting pluralistic politics in opinion and democratic will formation and the mode of rule violating basic democratic values (Meyer, 2004:34-35). Rectification of the defects of democracy and democratization of security agencies must be accompanied with a formulation of national security doctrine, institutionalization of dialogue and regular identification of sources of threat by various stakeholders of society; and strengthening of National Security Council through interdisciplinary team of experts coordinated by Defense and Home Ministeries who can also inform about early warning of fault line Conflicts and suggest measures for early response. Mutual appreciation of each other's roles and responsibilities between civil and security forces is crucial for the construction of a post conflict Nepal and build a shared, peaceful future.

B. SRI LANKA

In Sri Lanka anti-terrorist legislation is of comparatively recent vintage, having been introduced not, as is commonly supposed, in response to escalating violence originating in the demand by Tamil guerrilla groups, most notably the Liberation Tigers of Tamil Eelam, for a separate Tamil homeland in northern Sri Lanka, but rather in an attempt to prevent the Tamil population from voicing its demands through democratic channels for an end to social and economic discrimination. Although it was not until 1983, when the Tigers under their leader Prabhakaran carried out a daring attack on an army convoy in Jaffna, that the situation was perceived to call for extraordinary legislation, emergency legislation conferring wide powers upon the government had been in effect since 1979. That year, the Sri Lanka Parliament adopted the Prevention of Terrorism (Temporary Provisions) Act, as though to suggest that this act was comparable with the like-named legislation in the United Kingdom. In point of fact, as various observers have noted, the Sri Lankan law in 1979 was so fearsomely draconian that in some respects, for instance with respect to the power of the state to impose restriction orders on suspects, it bore comparison with legislation then in force in South Africa.

Where the British Prevention of Terrorism (PTA) Act allows preventive detention for only one week, the Sri Lankan PTA allows detention without the levying of charges for eighteen months; similarly, where the British PTA confers special powers only to combat "acts of terrorism", defined as "the use of violence for political ends", the Sri Lankan PTA confers powers of search, arrest, and seizure without warrant in connection with "any unlawful activity". The Sri Lankan Prevention of Terrorism Act does, in effect, confer *carte blanche* upon the forces of 'law and order', and indeed some of its provisions, such as the infliction of 20 years imprisonment for defacement of public notices, are nothing short of being fascist. It is not surprising that the Act also guarantees officers of the state immunity from prosecution for any action taken under the Act. Wide as are the powers that the Sri Lankan government has on account of the Prevention of Terrorism Act, this is not the only legislation of its kind in force. The Emergency (Miscellaneous Provisions and Powers) Regulations made under the Public Security Ordinance, the origins of which go back to the days of colonialism, empower the executive to arrest and detain suspects without charge, proscribe political parties, and ban publications. Regulation 15A, which dates to 3 June 1983, is susceptible to even greater abuse. This Regulation entitles police officers or other authorized persons to take possession of a dead body and determine the manner in which it is to be disposed. This Regulation was brought into force after the Jaffna Magistrate returned a verdict of homicide at the inquest into the death of K.T. Navaratnarajah, who died in army custody from numerous external and internal injuries inflicted by blows and weapons. By preventing an inquest from taking place, Regulation 15A can only encourage functionaries of the state in the belief that indiscriminate and retributory exercise of their power will remain unpunished. Sri Lankan legislation shows with greater clarity than anti-terrorist legislation in Northern Ireland and Britain how democratic norms are easily subverted on the plea that the state must be equipped to meet any emergency, especially one that appears to pose grave threats to national security. Although the Sri Lankan Prevention of Terrorism Act (1979) was promulgated while an emergency was officially in effect, and the emergency was lifted on December 27 of that year, the legislation was not removed, merely because Section 29 of the Act provided for the retention of the Act for "three years"; moreover, a subsequent amendment to the Act has given it an indefinite life.

C. BANGLADESH

The Second Amendment of the Constitution gave the scope to allow national security legislation to be passed into law under its emergency provision; and under this emergency provision, the Special Powers Act of 1974 was enacted. It was passed especially to suppress and detain the opposition political activists who were challenging the then-regime. Most of these political activists were from the left-wing movements, and about 20,000 of them were killed by the government's action because they wanted to establish a revolutionary system after the liberation war of Bangladesh in 1971, and this goal was opposed by the regime at the time. In addition, thousands of these political activists were arrested from 1974 until the early '90s. After the 1990s, the Special Powers Act was not applied as much as it was during the '70s and '80s, but it still exists. Now we have been informed by official sources that 143 people are presently being detained. Another aspect of this Special Powers Act was the detention of the ethnic minority people of the Chittagong Hill Tracts, or CHT, which happened mostly during the autocratic regime of Gen. Muhammad Ershad in the 1980s. Hundreds of Chittagong Hill Tracts people were detained in those days, and they didn't know how to look for redress. These laws came into being to protect a political regime instead of the people, and that is why there is a difference between national security and people's security. The people became insecure, and the regime wanted to feel secure. This is the rationale behind how the Special Powers Act of 1974 came to be enacted. There are legal aid organisations that provide legal aid to file habeas corpus applications before the High Court Division of the

Supreme Court or to challenge these matters under the criminal jurisdiction of the Supreme Court. These organisations are doing good work in respect to getting these detainees out. There are public-spirited lawyers in different bars who will also take up these cases. At one time, four of us organised a team to handle the cases of the detainees of the Chittagong Hill Tracts, and about 300 people were released because of the filing of these habeas corpus cases. In the days of the early '90s, the National Committee for the Protection of Fundamental Rights in the Chittagong Hill Tracts was also quite instrumental in campaigning for the release of the detainees of the CHT. Even human rights organisations, like Odhikar, which normally would not provide legal aid because there are other organisations doing so, took up the case of the detention of 15 young children who were between the ages of 12 and 14 who were detained because they were allegedly conspiring to attack the former prime minister in early 2001. there is a strong movement from civil society, particularly from the human rights organisations, professional organisations and the media, to repeal this law, the Special Powers Act, and even the present prime minister as part of her election campaign promises said during the 2001 election that she would repeal this law. People are waiting to see whether, in fact, she'll keep her commitment to repeal this law before her term ends in 2006. Bangladesh's judiciary is independent as such. The question is whether the lower judiciary is controlled by the Supreme Court or is controlled by the administration. That is why there is a big move to bring about change. There is a demand from the public that the separation of the judiciary should take place. Separation means complete separation from executive control and bringing the lower judiciary under the control of the Supreme Court since the Supreme Court is the custodian of the Constitution. The Supreme Court has given a timetable for this separation to be completed, and the last date for this separation is April 2004.

There were earlier attempts though to curb the independence of the judiciary. On 25 January 1975, through the Fourth Amendment of the Constitution, the judiciary was put under the executive, and Bangladesh came under a single-party system. On 15 August 1975, there was a bloody power change, and Bangladesh has seen several power changes subsequently and more bloodshed. However, the revival of the supremacy of the judiciary by the Fifth Amendment in 1979 was not to many a complete revival because the position of the chief justice and the appointment of judges was not completely revived as it was before the enactment of the Fourth Amendment to the original 1972 Constitution of Bangladesh. That is why the bar associations, retired judges and civil society are constantly campaigning and advocating for a complete code regarding the appointment of judges and to secure its independence in whatever form is possible.

Another problem that we have faced during the marital law regimes is that our retired chief justices were not hesitant to become the president of the military regimes or were not hesitant to support the undemocratic regimes. Human rights groups still feel that the judges of the Supreme Court have not fulfilled the commitments they made in their oath to protect the Constitution, for they continued their service whenever there has been a military regime and did not resign from their positions even though they could not honour the commitments they made in their oath to the Constitution.

D. PAKISTAN

In Pakistan : In 2002, ordinance was issued for the inclusion of military officers in the panel of judges to try terrorist offences. This not only undermines the independence of the judiciary but makes the anti-terror law in the country even more draconian Described as necessary that appropriate administrative and judicial measures be adopted to fight a spate of terrorist activities and commission of heinous offences in Pakistan these anti-terrorism laws opened the door to grave violations of human rights including the right to life, the prohibition of torture, the right to liberty and security and the right to fair trial. Inter alia, they provide for the creation of anti terrorist courts and give wide powers of arrest and interrogation to the police and army. Amnesty International has criticized the legislation in its report.

Legalizing the Impermissible: the new anti-terrorism law. It is important to note that the existing legal and judicial system is already equipped to deal with offences referred to in the act.

The problem then seems to be a lack of implementation, not a lack of laws. However, in an attempt to hide this inefficiency, Pakistan adopted the anti-terrorist acts which provide speedy trial without necessary guarantees for the accused, unfair trials and license to kill etc.

The right to shoot to kill 1997 Anti-Terrorism Act Under Section 5(2)(1): an officer of the police, armed forces and civil armed forces may: (i) after giving prior warning use such force as may be deemed necessary or appropriate, bearing in mind all the facts and circumstances of the situation, against any person who is committing, or in all probability is likely to commit a terrorist act or a scheduled offence, and it shall be lawful for any such officer, or any superior officer, to fire, or order the firing upon any person or persons against whom he is authorized to use force in terms hereof The enactment of broad provisions empowering summary executions is not the way a modern civilized state ought to act. Rather the government should set strict limits to the circumstances in which firearms could be used to prevent arbitrary killing by the security forces. The broad powers given to the police and consequently, to the military and civil armed forces contravene major international standards of human rights. Indemnity for acts done in good faith: Section 39 of the act says: No suit, prosecution or other legal proceedings shall lie against any person in respect of anything which is in good faith done or intended to be done under this act.? This is tantamount to providing impunity to the security forces for abuses, including extra judicial killings. To explicitly place any acts of police or other law enforcement personnel, including possibly random resort to lethal force, outside scrutiny and accountability may give law enforcement personnel the impression that they may commit such acts with impunity if only they can claim to have done them in good faith. It breaches a basic requirement of the rule of law, namely its equal and exception less application to everyone. Confessions to police made admissible in court: The provision in the act in section 26 which says: The special court may, for admission of the confession in evidence, require the police officer to produce a video tape together with the devices used for recording the confession.

Article 14(2) of the Constitution of Pakistan prohibits the use of torture, though only in the limited context of extraction of confessions: No person shall be subjected to torture for the purpose of extracting evidence. However, Pakistani law enforcement officials, to extract confessions from the accused, routinely use torture. Lending greater legal weight to confessions and putting pressure on police to speedily resolve crime may indirectly contribute to the continued and perhaps increased use of torture.

The right to be tried in a public place without prejudice to the defendant Section 15 of the 1997 Anti-Terrorism Act states. The government may direct that for the trial of a particular case, the court shall sit at such place including the place of occurrence as it may specify. This is intended to expose the defendant to public expressions of outrage, anger or even violence for his deeds, to humiliate him and to deter others by the specter of public exposure; it does not appear to serve the purpose of helping the judiciary establish the truth and do justice in a detached circumspect manner and in calm circumstances. The right to be presumed innocent: The act lays down that only special courts may grant bail to people tried for offences under the act but they may not release a defendant on bail if there are reasonable grounds for believing that he has been guilty of the offence with which he has been charged and unless the prosecution has been given an opportunity to? Show cause why he should not be released. This gives the prosecution the right to veto to deny bail.

The right to appeal: Section 31 of the act reads: A judgment or order passed, or sentence awarded, by a special court, subject to the result of an appeal under this act shall be final and shall not be called in question by any court. The possibility of the defendant to appeal to a court in the regular judicial system, either to the provincial high court or the Supreme Court of Pakistan is therefore excluded. People convicted and sentenced by the special courts are clearly disadvantaged in so far as their legal remedies are restricted: they have only one possibility of appeal, whereas people convicted by regular courts may also appeal to the Supreme Court. This provision violates the principle of equality before law laid down in the Constitution of

Pakistan. It is one of the fundamental principles of international human rights law. Moreover, the right to appeal is restricted in so far as it is subject to severe time limitations. The defendant may not in seven days be able to present an adequate appeal while the prosecution has 15 days for the appeal.

Moreover, the right to appeal of those facing the death penalty also appears to be seriously infringed under the act. Death penalty: Under Section 7(1) of the 1999 Amended Anti-terrorism Act, for terrorist acts resulting in death, courts have to mandatory impose the death penalty. This does not give any discretion to the judiciary. Section 22 of the 1997 Anti Terrorism Act, The government may specify the manner, mode and place of execution of any sentence passed under this act, having regard to the deterrent effect which such execution is likely to have?. Section 22 opens the possibility for public executions of the death penalty.

E. U.S.A.

Since its passage following the September 11, 2001 attacks, the Patriot Act has played a key part and often the leading role in a number of successful operations to protect innocent Americans from the deadly plans of terrorists dedicated to destroying America and our way of life. While the results have been important, in passing The Patriot Act, Congress provided for only modest, incremental changes in the law. Congress simply took existing legal principles and retrofitted them to preserve the lives and liberty of the American people from the challenges posed by a global terrorist network. Congress passed the USA PATRIOT Act in response to the terrorists attacks of September 11, 2001. The Act gives federal officials greater authority to track and intercept communications, both for law enforcement and foreign intelligence gathering purposes. It vests the Secretary of the Treasury with regulatory powers to combat corruption of U.S. financial institutions for foreign money laundering purposes. It seeks to further close our borders to foreign terrorists and to detain and remove those within our borders. It creates new crimes, new penalties, and new procedural efficiencies for use against domestic and international terrorists. Although it is not without safeguards, critics contend some of its provisions go too far. Although it grants many of the enhancements sought by the Department of Justice, others are concerned that it does not go far enough.

Criminal Investigations

Tracking and Gathering Communications-Federal communications privacy law features a three tiered system, erected for the dual purpose of protecting the confidentiality of private telephone, face-to-face, and computer communications while enabling authorities to identify and intercept criminal communications. The Crime Control and Safe Streets Act of 1968s give authorities a narrowly defined process for electronic surveillance to be used as a last resort in serious criminal cases. When approved by senior Justice Department officials, law enforcement officers may seek a court order authorizing them to secretly capture conversations concerning any of a statutory list of offenses.

Foreign Intelligence Investigations

The Act eases some of the restrictions on foreign intelligence gathering within the United States, and affords the U.S. intelligence community greater access to information unearthed during a criminal investigation, but it also establishes and expands safeguards against official abuse. More specifically, it: permits roving surveillance (court orders omitting the identification of the particular instrument, facilities, or place where the surveillance is to occur when the court finds the target is likely to thwart identification with particularity).

Alien Terrorists and Victims

The Act contains a number of provisions designed to prevent alien terrorists from entering the United States, particularly from Canada; to enable authorities to detain and deport alien terrorists and those who support them; and to provide humanitarian immigration relief for foreign victims of the attacks on September 11.

New Crimes

The Act creates new federal crimes for terrorist attacks on mass transportation facilities, for biological weapons offenses, for harboring terrorists, for affording terrorists material support, for misconduct associated with money laundering already mentioned, for conducting the affairs of an enterprise which affects interstate or foreign commerce through the patterned commission of terrorist offenses, and for fraudulent charitable solicitation. Although strictly speaking these are new federal crimes, they generally supplement existing law by filling gaps and increasing penalties.

New Penalties

The Act increases the penalties for acts of terrorism and for crimes, which terrorists might commit. More specifically it establishes an alternative maximum penalty for acts of terrorism, raises the penalties for conspiracy to commit certain terrorist offenses, envisions sentencing some terrorists to life-long parole, and increases the penalties for counterfeiting, cyber-crime, and charity fraud.

Other Procedural Adjustments

In other procedural adjustments designed to facilitate criminal investigations, the Act: increases the rewards for information in terrorism cases; authorizes? Sneak and peek? search warrants; permits nationwide and perhaps worldwide execution of warrants in terrorism cases; eases government access to confidential information; allows the Attorney General to collect DNA samples from prisoners convicted of any federal crime of violence or terrorism; lengthens the statute of limitations applicable to crimes of terrorism; clarifies the application of federal criminal law on American installations and in residences of U.S. government personnel overseas; and adjust federal victims? compensation and assistance programs.

F. AUSTRALIA

In the 2 years since the tragic events in America of September 11 2001, we have seen the war on terrorism become "one of the defining conflicts of the early 21st century" internationally and 'counter-terrorism' become the spearhead for a resurgence and expansion in security practice nationally. In this post-September 11 security environment, many western nations have enacted dramatic and unprecedented domestic counter-terrorism measures to deal with the threat of international terrorism. And Australia has been no exception.

In 2002 the Australian parliament passed legislation which introduced crimes of 'terrorism' for the first time in federal law, we have debated and ultimately rejected a proposal to allow the Attorney-General the power to proscribe or ban, on his own determination, terrorist organisations, and have instead introduced an attenuated form allowing for the proscription of organisations listed by the United Nations as 'terrorist organisations'. Finally, of most recent and continuing controversy, in June this year the Australian parliament passed amendments to the Asia Act which would allow Asia, under warrant, to detain for up to 7 days and interrogate for up to 24 hours within that 7 day period, Australians not suspected of any involvement in a criminal offence but who may have information relating to terrorism.

Nevertheless, Australia remains the only liberal-democratic nation to have proposed the detention and interrogation of non-suspects in this way. You can see why the Joint Parliamentary Committee which examined the Bill, described it in its original form as 'one of the most controversial pieces of legislation considered by the Parliament in recent times' and one '[which] would undermine key legal rights and erode the civil liberties that make Australia a leading democracy'.

There is no doubt that these counter-terrorism measures represent the greatest contemporary challenge to relations between the arms of government (the judiciary, the parliament and the Executive) and to long established civil and political rights since the liberal Prime Minister Robert Menzies' several failed attempts, through three spheres of governance, to pass the Communist Party Dissolution Bill. First through legislation, in the face of a successful High Court challenge and then through referendum in 1951. In the debate which surrounded the Communist Party Dissolution Act's provisions, then and since, what was highlighted was not so much the potential for an Executive abuse of a power to outlaw political organisations in this way, but that such a power was *itself* an abuse through its disavowal of judicial review in this process, one which endangered the often fragile relations between the arms of government. Menzies view, expressed following the High Court's dissallowance of the Act, was that, "the judgment of the relationship between this law and national defence and security ... is to be that of this Parliament and of no outside body". Justice Williams perhaps had this in mind when he queried during argument, "Does this mean that Parliament could say that the existence of John Smith, an ordinary citizen, is a menace to the security of Australia and require that he be shot at dawn?".

These concerns to maintain judicial protections and the trial process are particularly clear in the historic judgments of the majority High Court justices in this case in 1951. It is a decision which asserted the finality of the axiom of judicial review which permeates our Constitution and which, in doing so, protects all of us from the arbitrary abuse of executive power. It was, as Professor George Winterton has described it, "truly an 'epochal' decision, probably the most important ever rendered by the Court". The central issues raised throughout that intriguing struggle over the Communist Party Dissolution Act, "about the limits of legislative and executive power and supremacy of the judiciary in deciding such question", also remain at the heart of the current debate over national security needs and democratic practice. And yet, despite the obvious political parallels between arguments for enhanced and exceptional security powers during the Cold war, and those of the current day, the widespread community concern over the passage of the proscription provisions in particular, has not been matched by a widespread public debate. What this silence represents is the inevitability, the necessity, of national security imperatives. That, in the aftermath of September 11, the interests of national security have been unassailable and arguments to the contrary are largely seen as off the scale and scarcely worth reporting. The current counter-terrorism response rests on a universalised notion of threat rather than any specific threat, in this way the justification for extreme measures is shifted away from the present and into the fear of an unknown future. In this intellectual fortress in which anything is possible and therefore we must guard against everything, arguments for an expanded security sector are no longer based in present day realities but in the threat of the unknown, and debate on these terms becomes difficult, if not impossible. The current security environment neither encourages such debate nor would willingly accept its conclusions. Nevertheless, there is now the means for such detailed debate and consideration to take place particularly in relation to the Asio Act. Thanks to substantial Senate amendment of the original Asio Bill, there is now a 3 year sunset clause which is preceded by a process of review of the Act's provisions and enforcement. Several key features of the debate that we have not had, remain and ought now to be addressed: what has the Australian experience of terrorism been; what is the level of terrorist threat in Australia; what are Australia's existing powers and structures to counter terrorism and are they adequate to meet this level of threat? These questions mirror the legal concerns for the introduction of exceptional measures, or for the derogation from established criminal justice procedures, that such measures be proportional, appropriate and proximate. These requirements need to be considered politically as much as legally before we determine on a path which takes us into the uncharted terrain, for Australia, of introducing exceptional powers to deal with terrorism. In a sense we are witnessing what might be called a 'second wave' of counter-terrorism in Australia, one which further develops a network and structure of counter-terrorism first set in place in the mid-1970s and cemented following the Hilton Hotel bombing of 1978. Two distinct models of domestic counter-terrorism in liberal democratic states can be identified in this first wave of counter terrorism: a militarised strategy which draws clearly from counter-insurgency theory and practice and which treats terrorism as a war-like domestic insurgency; and secondly a counter-terrorism structure developed within the existing criminal justice system and which treats terrorism as essentially a peace-time, criminal, matter. In the earlier development of counter-terrorism, Australia drew heavily on the British model, despite clear differences in the nature and extent of political violence. The British model in turn has been essentially a militarised one, reflecting its focus on Northern Ireland, drawing clearly on five main aspects of counter-insurgency theory and practice: the use of exceptional legislative measures; the maintenance of vast intelligence collections; the development of pre-emptive controls on political activity; military involvement in civil disturbances and the development of a strategy of media management in times of crisis. The exception to the wholesale adaptation of this model in Australia's counter-terrorism strategy however had been, to date, in our continued use of the existing criminal law against terrorist offences. Unlike Britain, Australia's broadly counter-insurgency based approach has retained this important element of the 'criminal justice model' and, until the events of September 11 2001, had not adopted the particularly problematic use of around. It is view which the new Attorney-General Philip Ruddock reiterated just last week in his comment that; "the unavoidable fact is that any tightening of security arrangements does involve some diminution of rights". It is, in my view, a flawed equation. And it is the dichotomy suggested in this popular view, the argued trade-off between liberty and security, that lies at the heart of what has been described as the "startling surrender of fundamental democratic principles" in the heightened security environment of post-September 11. National security and individual liberties, far from being in competition with one another in a simplistic zero-sum game, are in fact mutually reinforcing; but will constitute the very means of sustaining it. In this view, democracy "is not limited by the rule of law but rather is defined by it". Taken overall the current revised security powers establish a new orthodoxy in Asio's activities, moving it clearly into the arena of 'security policing', merging its activities with those of domestic policing. It also marks the closure in Asio's gradual shift towards a universalised strategy of pre-emptive surveillance of an ever-present internal 'enemy', an end to the political struggle waged really since Asio was established in 1949 but particularly during the 1970s, to maintain a more focused, more democratic, a transparent and accountable notion of national security. Yet the need for such 'formidable powers' has been questioned by one of Australia's most experienced security officers. The former senior security adviser to the Defence and Attorney-General's departments, Allan Behm, has expressed grave concerns about such a dramatic expansion in Asio's already extensive powers and over the removal of fundamental rights such as independent legal advice during detention and the capacity to It can be seen also in the process of the proscription legislation. In a similar trajectory the government, never happy with the Parliament's removal of the minister's power to proscribe and its replacement with a United Nations listing process, has proposed an amendment to the Act as negotiated through the Parliament. The proposal, which is still before the Parliament, would simply remove the united Nations Security Council basis for listing terrorist organisations in Australia and replace it with the ministerial discretion originally proposed. It would overturn, in other words, the negotiated Parliamentary compromise over proscription and simply reinstate the original proposal for ministerial discretion. The Greens Senator Bob Brown strongly criticised this aspect of the mode of government, in the final hours of the parliamentary session late last year following the Senate's initial rejection of the Asio Bill: "When . . . the Prime Minister and the government won't brook amendments, then it is democracy itself that is being questioned by the PM".

References

Brown, Seyom, 1992. *International Relations in a Changing Global System: Toward a Theory of the World Polity*, Boulder:

Westview Press. Huntington, Samuel, P., 1968. *Political Order in Changing Societies*, Bombday: Vakils, Feffer and Simons.

Meyer, Thomas. 2004. *Military and Democracy*, Jakarta: FES.

Scalapino, Robert, 1986. "Legitimacy and Institutionalization in Asian Socialist Societies", eds. Robert A. Scalapino, Seizaburo Sato and Jusuf Wanandi, *Asian Political Institutionalization*, Berkeley: University of California.

Shrestha, Chuda Bahadur, 2004. *Nepal: Coping with Maoist Insurgency*, Kathmandu: Chetana Lokshum. Webersik, Christian and Manish Thapa. 2008. "Nepal: Climate Change and Security Factsheet", Tokyo: United Nations University.

Weiner, Myron, 1986. "Institution Building in South Asia", eds. Robert A. Scalapino, Seizaburo Sato and Jusuf Wanandi, *Asian Political Institutionalization*,

Berkeley: University of California.Wimmer, Andreas and Conrad Schetter, 2002. *State Formation First: Recommendations for Reconstruction and Peace Making in Afghanistan*, No. 45. Bonn: ZEF. Wolfers, Arnold, 1968. *Discord and Collaboration: Essays on International Politics*, Baltimore: The Johns Hopkins University Press.

Note: Presentation made at a seminar organized by Nepal Ex-Policemen Organization and Friedrich-Ebert-Stiftung, November 16, 2008, and Nepal Police Academy in Kathmandu on Nov. 20.

This paper draws on the author's recently published *Terror Laws: ASIO, Counter-terrorism and the threat to democracy* UNSW Press, Sydney, 2003

Michaelson, C. 'International Human Rights on Trial—The United Kingdom's and Australia's Legal Response to 9/11' *Sydney Law Review* 2003, Vol. 25, pp. 275-304; p. 276.

4

National Security Laws and Global Effect of National Security

A. NATIONAL SECURITY LAWS : INTERNATIONAL LEGAL ASPECTS

One issue that states around the world have all been struggling with is security: to define what constitutes national security, enact appropriate provisions, ensure applications and provide security. At the outset it is important to remember that the states have duties to protect their nationals and those living within their territories including protection of their national frontiers.

In this fast evolving world, nature and actors of threats to security change frequently and unexpectedly. In fact, non-state actors, organisations, loose networks and even unconnected individuals could pose grave national security threats than ever before in present days as opposed to conventional threats emanating from another state or states which premised international relations so far. States have responded very differently to traditional and to these new brands of national security threats and concerns largely by introducing new laws and measures, and even, on occasions, acting beyond laws. There are widespread legitimate concerns about impacts of floods of new laws both at international and national levels on individuals and societies. Questions abound whether, on the one hand, laws intended to provide safety, security and freedom in reality are restricting freedoms, or on the other hand, restrictive measures put in place deny space and freedom that in turn create further or aggravate resentments. Many believe that the world changed on 9/11 in 2001: bunch of young men blew themselves and the planes they were on, used those aircraft as weapons of mass destruction and killed numerous unsuspected civilians. These individuals and those associated with them committed a serious crime under international law, crimes against humanity. Since 9/11 and even before, nations around the world experienced their own versions of 9/11, UK's 7/7 and in case of Bangladesh, the 17th August 2005 when there were synchronized bombings all over Bangladesh, except in one district. Although some would argue that enough early warnings were there but nonetheless, no country ever experienced what Bangladesh did on that day, peace time bombings in all cities and towns in a widespread and systematic manner. Since 9/11 and even before, nations around the world experienced their own versions of 9/11, UK's 7/7 and in case of Bangladesh, the 17th August 2005 when there were synchronized bombings all over Bangladesh, except in one district. Although some would argue that enough early warnings were there but nonetheless, no country ever experienced what Bangladesh did on that day, peace time bombings in all cities and towns in a widespread and systematic manner. Since 9/11 and even before, nations around the world experienced their own versions of 9/11, UK's 7/7 and in case of Bangladesh, the 17th August 2005 when there were synchronized bombings all over Bangladesh, except in one district. Although some would argue that enough early warnings were there but nonetheless, no country ever experienced what Bangladesh did on that day, peace time bombings in all cities and towns in a widespread and systematic manner.

This Counter Terrorism Committee, which receives reports from the States and analyses compliance of Security Council Resolution 1373 issues guidelines and shares expertise on counter terrorism matters.The new versions of security laws adopted in different countries have surprisingly common features, such as, newer crimes, extra-territorial application of laws, civilians tried under military commissions, monitoring of correspondences, wiretappings, preventive detentions, prolonged and indefinite detention with or without judicial process, shifting burden of proof on the accused, withholding identity of witnesses, making confessions before police admissible, giving prosecutor power to deny bail, banning of organisations, allowing pre-emptory actions, authorising governments to declare emergency, to designate areas for special measures, arrests without warrants, detaining members of the families of the persons sought, withholding details of disappeared individuals, use of excessive force at the time of arrest, aggressive and invasive search, shoot to kill, indemnity of security personnel against legal process, barring suspects freed on bail to visit public places, sanction of tortures, contracting out tortures, aggressive interviews, house arrest, limitation on travel within and out of the country, imposing restrictions or otherwise banning media to report, vague imprecise and wide definition of crimes, harsher punishments, more death sentences, authorising or tolerating extra-judicial executions, restricting fair trails, denying judicial review, limiting access to judiciary, reduced accountability of security forces, summary trials, reduced or denying defence rights, limiting access to lawyers and families, silencing dissenting views, orders preventing entry to particular areas, banning of public gatherings, criminalisation of political and religious activities, sanction of custodial violence, monitoring money transfers and transactions, restricting access to information and knowledge, profiling individuals and communities, relaxing data protection laws etc, and if you like, this list could go on and on and on.

This illustrates how governments around the world have responded to ensure national security concerns to ongoing and new threats. It's true that we live in a much more dangerous world than anytime before, where, because of globalisation, technology and other factors, smaller groups and even individuals could cause havoc as people of Oklahama City experienced some years back, when, a disgruntled loner brought down a federal building with fertilisers and other implements and killed hundreds.However, the challenge is, how to approach these threats coming form all directions mixed with ideology, religion, nationalism, ethnicity, culture, economic and natural resources. One option is to adopt all or some of the measures listed above, which, in fact, numerous states have already done. Such restrictive and repressive approach got two problems, firstly, its impacts are often for shorter periods and threats not only persist, but in cases aggravate, which then requires even harsher measures. Take airline safety as an example, which, by the way, is still the safest mode of transport. In early seventies, few individuals evaded security, boarded planes with guns and grenades and hijacked airplanes. Of course, search and security was strengthened along with laws against hijacking. Then the 9/11 perpetrators hijacked the planes virtually without any significant weapons. Again, a host of stringent laws followed and along with procedures to secure against hijacking. Sophisticated scanners and secondary searches became routine practice, until revelation of alleged plots to use liquid explosives to blow off transatlantic flights from London. It seems, terrorists set the agenda and the governments react with restrictive measures and new laws! The second problem is, most of these security laws contravene international norms and laws that evolved out of ashes of First and Second World Wars which resulted in monumental destructions thankfully the world has not witnessed since. It appears that states to address such threats have literally tossed off universally accepted norms, practices and mechanisms.

The Universal Declaration of Human Rights, the International Covenant on Civil and Political Rights, the European Convention for the Protection of Human Rights and Fundamental Freedoms, the American Convention on Human Rights, the African Charter of Human and People's Rights, the Arab Charter of Human Rights fairly balances national security concerns and fundamental freedoms, which these restrictive laws are intended to protect.The International Covenant on Civil and Political Rights provides derogating mechanism in case public emergency. Article 4 states, "In time of public emergency which threatens the life of the nation and the existence of which is officially proclaimed, the States parties to the present Covenant may take measures derogating from their obligations under the present Covenant to the extent strictly required by the exigencies of the situation, provided that such measures are not inconsistent with their other obligations under international law and do not involve discrimination solely on the ground of race, colour, sex, language, religion or social origin".

In other words, derogating measures must be of an exceptional and temporary nature. Moreover, ICCPR requires that some rights cannot be derogated from under any circumstances whatsoever such as, right to life (article 6), prohibition of torture or cruel, inhuman or degrading punishment (article 7), the principle of legality in the field of criminal law (article 15), the recognition of everyone as a person (article 16), freedom of thought, conscience and religion (article 18) etc.

Torture, for example, is absolutely prohibited under Article 2(2) of the Convention against Torture and Other Cruel, Inhuman or Degrading Treatment or Punishment, which no creative interpretation of law could justify. The provision is very clear, "No exceptional circumstances whatsoever, whether a state of war or threat of war, internal political instability or any other public emergency, may be invoked as a justification of torture". Article 3 of the Convention also provides an absolute prohibition on expelling, returning or extraditing a person to another State where there is risk of torture.The Convention on the Rights of the Child also applies in case of emergencies and in that, all rights of the child, meaning persons under 18 years of age, must be protected even during emergency periods.

Internal Security Forces

In addition to looking at the security laws, it is important that security forces, which often apply these laws, be examined. To address security concerns, governments create new security forces, remodel or give extra powers to existing forces. Equally, most allegations of violations are labeled against members of forces.

The United Nations Code of Conduct for Law Enforcement Officials adopted by the General Assembly was intended to have universal applicability. It certainly is an important guideline with which to measure the internal security forces, but there seems to be an absence of clearly defined international standards for accountability and operations of the internal security forces, such as, an International Convention on the Internal Security Forces. The States obviously are duty bound to create institutions to promote and protect human rights, which is what internal security forces are supposed to do, but such laws and institutions don't have minimum set standards to reach. Human rights and other norms have set parameters, but it is important that a common universally acceptable standard is set for all, as other instruments have done. Such a Convention could elaborate on nature of internal security forces, its legal basis, provisions relating to control of such forces, a code of conduct, recruitment and training, other operational aspects, consequences of violations of rights, monitoring and accountability by the government as well as by media and other stakeholders, etc. Both activists and experts present could take it up and discuss and endeavor to work for such an instrument.

In fine, both laws and security forces are there to protect rights and that should be operative part of any legal measures, and examined accordingly. The measuring rod of a law should be, whether it protect rights or not.

B. NATIONAL SECURITY AND THE INTERNATIONAL CONTEXT

The debate on national security is also framed within an international context and that context is one where the United States and the Western powers have exercised varying degrees of control over the globe. In the case of India, the links that the United States has had with Pakistan have shaped her foreign policy. Pakistani support for militancy in the Kashmir valley and its funding of training camps as well as financial and other support has shaped the debate. It is not an academic matter but rather seen as affecting the integrity and stability of the country.

This confrontation is seen by many as one between a secular India, where all religions are equal and a theocratic Pakistan. This is the unfinished agenda of partition. The Hindu right frames it to counterpoise a tolerant Hindu civilisation against an aggressive and intolerant Islam.In the international context the role of news media, non-governmental organisations such as Amnesty International (established 1961) or Helsinki Watch (1975) and other more humanitarian organisations have created a space for civil action across state boundaries. These powerful pacific weapons (in the words of Hardt and Negri) use the language of human rights to prepare the ground for Western domination. The argument that nations are operating in different conditions and should be allowed to operate on their own principles goes back to the state's indivisible claims of sovereignty. The landmark European Convention on Human Rights, a charter to enforce security arrangements in post war Europe that established the European Court of Human Rights in Strasbourg in 1953 marked the beginning of what has developed into a global human rights movement. It allowed dissidents in East Europe, such as Jiri Hajek, Czech Foreign Minister under Dubcek, on the basis of the human rights clauses in the Helsinki Act (1975) to argue that it was illegal for governments to dismiss or jail people for their political beliefs. Hajek went on to found Charter 77, the major Czech human rights group. Important as these groups have been they have constraints and limitations: largely elite organisations with no mass following, supported by foundations (Ford, MacArthur) and working often worked closely with the U.S government. What has become important in the last decades is that it is no longer just the strong repressive states that have become the target of intervention but so-called rogue or collapsing states where increasingly large scale intervention is carried out to "save" entire populations. The attack on Afghanistan to eliminate the Taliban have brought to the fore the argument that to protect national security a state can attack another state. There are historical examples of such arguments but these questions need to be addressed in a global context. The dilemma of supporting military intervention to save a population or the alliances generated by the 'war on terror" that have removed the activities of repressive regimes (Russia, China, Pakistan) from the international agenda indicate the questions that are being generated'The realisation of individual and community rights has been supported by global networks that often work to support small, marginal groups in their struggle against the state. The nation-state, particularly in regional alliances still has an effective role as a bulwark against global powers. This has resulted in the formation of a national arena for debating rights but this arena overlaps the global arena so that there are points of commonality. The demands of a global standard, not just in the specifications of machinery or in statistics but also in the way business is conducted is also being fought for in areas such as work conditions and political life. If capital can have the right to invest anywhere in the world then workers can also be entitled to demand a global wage standard. What is national security or constitutional rights in this context. The absolute value of national security can then be debated from positions that lie outside narrow national self interest as defined by those in power B.

Elements of National Security

National security is an undertaking lower in complexity only to the International security. It directly or indirectly encompass much of the national public administration. At its basic, national security can be divided into internal natiosecurity and external national security.

National security is concerned with ensuring state legal codes are not transgressed, and prevention of attacks on public infrastructures and their personnel by implementing civil defense and emergency preparedness measures (including anti-terrorism legislation), and ensuring the resilience and redundancy of critical infrastructure. This also includes using counterintelligence services or secret services to protect the nation from internal threats sponsored from the outside. The executive authority for internal national security is the expression of political power, preferably through democratic process of selecting national leaders. Internal national security is also the management of national finances free from economic problems that can lead to large scale public dissatisfaction with the government, and public disorder through protests. External national security is generally the scope more often associated with national security in democratic states. It encompasses national border security as a means of immigration control, national environment security where the environmental threat originates from sources external to national territory, territorial waters and airspace, and assurance of international trade safety through the state borders. Further removed from the national borders are the external security concerns derived from measures taken by other states or non-state groups to directly or indirectly, through use of economic instruments, interrupt, damage or attack economic systems that would adversely influence national quality of life, resulting in an Economic warfare. If an economic conflict can not be resolved through diplomacy to rally allies and isolate threats, it generally escalates into a larger and more acute military conflict that necessitates maintaining effective national armed forces. It is usual that armed conflicts threaten territorial integrity of states, and require development of a military doctrine as part of the national defence policy that guides armed forces posture, and the concepts, methods and technologies that are to be use in securing the preventing loss of this integrity. External national security generally requires using intelligence services to detect and defeat or avoid threats and espionage, and to protect classified information.

History of National Security

The first known use of the term "national security" was in the Clark Memorandum of 1928.The concept of security of a nation goes back to the dawn of nation-states themselves. Armies for domestic peacekeeping and maintaining national sovereignty have existed since the dawn of recorded history.

Civil and national police forces have also existed for millennia. Intelligence agencies and secret services of governments date back to antiquity such as the Roman Empire's *frumentarii* and *agens in rebus*. While the general concepts of keeping a nation secure are not new, the specific modern English term "national security" itself came into common parlance in the 20th Century. Methodologies to achieve and maintain the highest possible desired state of national security have been consistently developed over the modern period to this day.

National Security of the United States

Over the history of the United States, policies such as the Monroe Doctrine, the domestic establishment of the United States Secret Service in the wake of the American Civil War, and the so called "big stick" corollary to the Monroe Doctrine by President Theodore Roosevelt all show a maturation of policies and systems of establishing and ensuring diplomatic, military, and economic security. Each nation has its own history of establishing national security mechanisms.

The modern concept of national security was introduced in the United States after World War II and became an official guiding principle of foreign policy in the United States when the *National Security Act of 1947* was signed on July 26, 1947 by U.S. President Harry, S. Truman.[1]

The majority of the provisions of the Act took effect on 18 September 1947, the day after the Senate confirmed James V. Forrestal as the first Secretary of Defense. Together with its 1949 amendment, this act: created the National Military Establishment (NME) which became known as the Department of Defense when the act was amended in 1949, created a separate Department of the Air Force from the existing United States Army Air Forces, subordinated the military branches to the new cabinet level position of the Secretary of Defense, and established the National Security Council (NSC), a central place of coordination for National Security policy in the Executive Branch, as well as the Central Intelligence Agency, the United States' first peacetime intelligence agency. During the Cold War's bipolar system, states often relied heavily on the two superpowers and other aligned nations to assist their national security. This principal is referred to as collective security, a term which came into vogue after the Armistice of World War I. Since the breakup of the Soviet Union and the end of the Cold War, and with the rise of terrorism, national security has had to shift its focus dramatically. Security Sector Reform (SSR) and Security Sector Management (SSM) is needed in many nations for different reasons. Some are nations emerging from

1. "History of the National Security Council, 1947-97". White House. August 1997. http://www.whitehouse.gov/nsc/history.html. Retrieved on 8 February 2007.

repressive regimes or recovering from civil wars. Others are developing nations with weak governments where national security sectors never existed or were never strong before. The United States saw its own security sector overhaul with the establishment of the Department of Homeland Security in the wake of the 9/11 terrorist attacks.

C. CRITICISM OF NATIONAL SECURITY

Rights and Freedoms

The measures adopted to maintain national security in the face of threats to society has led to ongoing discussion, particularly in liberal democracies, on the scale and role of authority in matters of civil and human rights. Tension sometimes exists between the preservation of the state (by maintaining self-determination and sovereignty) and the rights and freedoms of individuals. Although national security measures are imposed to protect society as a whole, such measures will necessarily tend to restrict the rights and freedoms of individuals. The concern is that where the exercise of national security laws and powers is not subject to good governance, the rule of law, and strict checks and balances, there is a risk that "national security" may simply serve as a pretext for suppressing unfavorable political and social views. Taken to its logical conclusion, this view contends that measures which may ostensibly serve a national security purpose (such as mass surveillance, and censorship of mass media), could ultimately lead to a police state. In the United States, the controversial USA Patriot Act and other government action has brought some of these issues to the forefront, raising two main questions: To what extent, for the sake of national security, should individual rights and freedoms be restricted *and* can the restriction of civil rights for the sake of national security be justified?

Human Security

Others believe that the national security approach has outlived its usefulness to the international community since many of the sources of global insecurity today (such as terrorism or global warming) are immune to unilateral state military responses. In response to this growing sense of dissatisfaction, growing numbers of scholars, NGOs, and policy makers have argued for the adoption of a new people-centered model for security—Human Security.[2] Human Security argues that global security is best enhanced when state leaders focus on reducing human vulnerabilities as the best pathway to enhancing state security.[3]

D. NATIONAL SECURITY AND CYBER SECURITY

India does not have technical resources and expertise as well as legal framework to tackle terrorism and cyber terrorism. Indian citizens must come together in this hard time and provide their valuable suggestions and inputs to the government.

National Security and cyber security in India is passing through a bad phase. The recent terrorist attacks have unambiguously proved the deficiencies and weaknesses of Indian defence mechanisms. India failed to cope up with both traditional terrorism as well as contemporary technology driven cyber terrorism. The technology has further complicated the situation because we have a weak cyber law in India in the form of Information Technology Act, 2000 (IT Act, 2000). A weak cyber law accompanied with absence of legal framework for terrorism is coming heavily upon India. Is it that difficult for the government of India to appreciate this bitter truth and act accordingly?

India does not have technical resources and expertise as well as legal framework to tackle terrorism and cyber terrorism. The citizens of India must come together in this hard time and provide their valuable suggestions and inputs to the government of India. One such novel and timely action has already been undertaken. Letters regarding "Constitutionality" of the proposed Information Technology (Amendment) Bill,

2. "Centre for Security Sector Management at Cranfield University". http://www.ssronline.org/. Retrieved on 8 February 2007.
3. For a clearer idea of these supporters, see the Human Security Network website, http://www.humansecuritynetwork.org/menu-e.php.

2006 and National Security Policy of India have been sent by Praveen Dalal, Managing Partner of Perry4Law, to the Prime Minister of India (Dr Manmohan Singh), President of India, Parliament Members (Lok Sabha and Rajya Sabha), Government of India (GOI), Department of Information Technology (DIT), Department of Science and Technology (DST), CERT-IN, etc. The same has been done before the Parliament's winter session started so that the suggestions and recommendations contained in them may be incorporated in the National Policies of India. We must also share our responsibility and provide our thoughts, inputs, suggestions, etc for the larger interest of India. If we do not raise a voice now, we may again face another attack of similar, perhaps graver, nature.[4]

According to Praveen Dalal, the Leading Techno-Legal Specialist of India, "The Indian security infrastructure and workforces are not in good shape and require rejuvenation. We need a techno-legal security workforce and not personnel who do not have even the basic facilities and technological means and knowledge. The terrorist attacks have really shattered the deep pervasive false sense of security present in the Indian government mentality.

We have to think and act against such internal and external threats by going beyond a "political debate". We can fool ourselves by bragging about India's capabilities and victories against terrorism and cyber terrorism and keep on facing future attacks and bear the traumatic casualties. Alternatively, we must accept our weaknesses against such attacks and take constructive steps to anticipate, prevent and counter such future terrorist and cyber terrorism activities".

We request the stakeholders and citizens of India to share their suggestions either with the government of India directly or through Perry4Law by sending an e-mail at perry4law (at) yahoo (dot) com. A consolidated reply would be provided to the Parliament of India and government of India so that necessary action may be taken at the top level. Further, the consolidated reply would also be posted at the first and exclusive working

4. See *Human Security Now*, http://www.humansecurity-chs.org/finalreport/index.html

group on Cyber Law that has been formed to act as a bridge between the government and citizens of India. We hope to get your full support in this regard.

E. CONFLICTING DEMANDS IN A DEMOCRACY

In all democracies all over the world there is a widespread acceptance of the need for special laws to strengthen the hands of law enforcers to fight terrorism. Already special laws which are much more severe than the Indian ones of the past are in force in the UK, USA, Canada and many countries of the European Union. Even jurists have conceded this requirement in number of cases in many countries including India. For instance former Chief Justice J.S. Verma, later the Chairperson of the National Human Rights Commission (NHRC) while inaugurating the first Law Commission seminar on the POTA bill in December 1999 advocated the necessity for a special law to fight the terrorist activities in unequivocal terms, keeping in mind the extraordinary situation prevailing in the country. [However, Justice J.S. Verma as Chairman of National Human Rights Commission had disputed the necessity of such ordinance after the NDA government promulgated POTO ordinance on October 24, 2001]. Another former chief justice of India M.N. Venkatachaliah, when specifically asked whether POTA should be scrapped, said that what was necessary was regulation and not the scrapping of POTA. However, in India while we have several laws in force in different parts of the country to deal with violence, militancy etc there is no central law specifically to deal with terrorism in the absence of POTA. Why there is tardiness in the democratic political process in evolving comprehensive legislations to ensure the rights of the citizen for security from acts of terrorism while ensuring the just rights to the accused in a due process of law? Some reasons for the lack of readiness among our politicians in strengthening the fight against terrorism through a better and comprehensive legislation are routed in the democratic political process itself. These are :

Majority Rule

Democracies, particularly those that follow the Westminster model and based on a single vote provide for rule by the majority even if it is by one vote. So minorities of different hues feeling threatened by the majority feel insecure and struggle to retain their exclusive identity of race, religion, caste, ethnicity, language etc. This is what has happened to Muslim minority (most of whom are immigrants from Asia) in Britain after 9/11. They had to bear the brunt of public wrath due to the close racial, ethnic, religious identity of the perpetrators of the 9/11 attacks. This feeling of insecurity had been dormant for sometime among sections of Muslims in India after the partition of the country based on religious lines. However, subsequently a number of factors including Pak sponsorship of terrorism in India, growth of Wahabism, reservations etc have further exacerbated the feeling of insecurity of large sections of Muslim population So any legislation brought to fight terrorism is examined not objectively by political parties in order not to lose Muslim vote banks which often tilt the results of elections. The political parties in the UK have also of late exhibited this 'vote bank' mindset.

Playing Opposition

Ruling party-opposition politics is fundamental to democratic exercise. So opposition always tends to find fault with ruling party's legislations whatever be their merits. Typical is the Congress opposition to terrorism laws brought in force by BJP at the Centre, while Congress ruled Maharashtra had no hesitation in using an equally 'draconian' Maharashtra Control of Organised Crimes Act 1999' enacted earlier by the Maharashtra Government ruled by Shiv Sena—BJP alliance. This mindset has also been noticed in the Tory mindset in the UK.

Misrule and Lack of Legal Redress

For all citizens concerned with police excesses and lack of quick and inexpensive legal remedies in democratic societies such restrictive laws spell disaster. Governments all over the world invariably ignore human rights violations by those wielding power. This is more so in India, where many state governments have ignored rule of law. As law and order is a state responsibility the affected citizen has limited options available to him. Thus there is genuine concern that draconian provisions of terrorism enactments will impinge upon democratic freedoms of the common man unless the accountability of legislators, political parties, executive and the state machinery improves. Though all political parties, including the left, pay only lip service to this concern; in practice human rights is not their political priority. Misuse of police machinery by criminalized politicians and the slow process of justice due to outdated judicial procedures and criminal justice say have compounded this problem further.

Conclusion

The globalisation of terrorism has added a new dimension to the multitude of internal security threats in India. The connivance of our neighbours in using terrorists for 'slow bleed' operations to serve their own ends in India has not disappeared. In this context it is time India took radical measures to carry out systemic improvements. Otherwise the ordinary citizen will continue to pay a price with his life, rights and security. It is the responsibility of the civil society to root for this cause. In this respect, some measures that come in my mind are: A comprehensive legislation specifically for handling terrorism giving greater powers to law enforcing agencies.

- Enforce police commission recommendations to improve the performance of police forces with better accountability.
- Strengthen judicial process by modernizing the criminal and civil procedural laws, weed out outdated provisions, appoint more judges, increase the use of information technology for processing of judicial documentation etc.
- Ensure rule of law by prosecuting police officers and other government officials including ministers for violation of laws of the land. The political parties should include this in the common minimum programme.

- Strengthen national security apparatus for integrated information management among intelligence and law enforcing agencies. This will enable more fool proof law enforcement.
- Introduce a witness security programme; this will reduce instances of perjury so common while prosecuting criminals in terrorism cases.

Strengthen NGOs involved in human rights holding public hearings with parliamentary committees.

5

National Security Laws and Constitution

INTRODUCTION

The question of constitutional rights, understood as the fundamental rights and liberties that citizens enjoy by their right as citizens, comes into conflict with the obligations of the state and inevitably the dominant language of this debate takes the right of the nations as inviolable; the collective over the individual. This language is used to justify special legislation or temporary ordinances that curtail, suspend or violate the very rights that are considered as fundamental and held to be unique characteristics of a democratic system. Democratic systems have used these special legislation to restrict and curtail the very freedoms they seek to protect and in doing so they evoke the same sense of crisis that we can find in repressive systems of government. Their means of ensuring acquiesce is grounded in the increasing specialised nature of the legislation and the rhetoric of threat and danger to our normal lives. The creation of the enemy through the media and the educational system is a vital component of the process of building an informed citizenry that will support state policies. State policies while crafted through a political process that owes as much to party interests as to the "national needs" are then projected as the collective wish.

Enactment of special legislation around the world after September 11 to counter threats to their security, legislation that gives wider powers and allows for a pro-active policy to perceived threat as well as the projection of terrorism and rogue states as the international enemy is just the latest example of this process.. As in the movie, crimes can now be tackled before they are committed. The statements coming form the United States, whether Bush or Colin Powell, reinforce the argument that a nation can take any measures to protect itself from a threat or perceived threat. It can do this both within its borders, by using special legislation as well as outside its border, where it can use methods ranging from an appeal to legal processes to air strikes and even war.

A counter current that flows against this discourse of the states is that of the people. Its history can be traced to earlier civil rights movements that sought to break the sanctity of the state and its machinery and force governments to justify and explain the rationale of its polices. Similarly outside the boundaries of the nation trans-national movements sought to check state sanctioned practices: for example, the anti-slavery movement, revolutionary movements that sought to establish a political order based on the will of the people, or national liberation struggles. All of them, however, confronted the dilemma of ends and means. The Gandhi an emphasis on non-violence was a clear stand on this issue but while its has been influential the problem has not been resolved.

The absolute inviolability of the nation state has also been eroded in a variety of ways. The movement of people, the explosion in the speed and rate of diffusion of ideas have given immediacy to events and allowed people from disparate corners of the globe to come together around a common cause. These bonds of affinity interact with national and regional ties in complex ways and influence the way national security is debated.

In the period of imperial expansion the ideological agenda sought to enforce global standards both in the material world as well as in other spheres of private and public life. Civilisation was measured by the approximation to a European ideal. In the post WWII world this legacy continues to play a role as does the emergence of alternative visions that often are regressive and authoritarian

The language of politics whether framed within the nation-state perspective or expressed in the language of civilisation allows for the denial of individual rights in the interest of the nation. These state-centric arguments carry the force of authority backed as they are by a wider dissemination and greater claims on legitimacy.

A. NATIONAL SECURITY LAWS, PUBLIC ORDER AND RULE OF LAW

India : The Legal Machinery to Maintain Security and "Public Order"—'Rule of Law'

"Public Order" is something more than ordinary maintenance of law and order. Public Order is synonymous with public peace,safety and tranquility."

This is the context within which each individual situation needs to be understood. Indian legal codes, in many cases, have continued colonial laws and have added their own variations to deal with new problems. The early legislation to control insurgency began under the Nehru government when it passed the Northeast (Armed Forces Special Powers Act (1958) to quell Naga militancy. This act, amended in 1972, allowed arbitrary arrest and search without warrant giving a free hand to the authorities for the exercise of arbitrary power. The declaration of Emergency by Indira Gandhi was a major milestone as was the legislation (TADA) to control militancy in Punjab and later the National Security Act (1980) However, there were a host of other legislation such as : The Unlawful Activities (Prevention) Act (1967), the Prevention of Seditious Meetings Act of 1911, the Religious Institutions (Prevention of Misuse) Ordinance, the Anti-Highjacking Act (1982), the Suppression Unlawful Acts against safety of Civil Aviation Act (1982) and Disturbed Areas Special Courts Act (1976), the Indian Telegraph Act and the Information Technology Act (2000) and the Prevention of Terrorism Ordinance reintroduced in March 2002 (an earlier version introduced October 2001 had met with opposition). These are just the national legislation, the states have their won specific legislation that mirror and build on these acts.

The National Security Act of 1980 (NSA) is to prevent individuals acting against the interests of the state (national security, public order, maintenance of essential supplies, industrial unrest etc. but these are nowhere defined) and provides for detention for up to a year without charge or trial. It is valid in all states except Jammu and Kashmir (there the Jammu and Kashmir Public Safety Act of 1978 is applicable). Between 1984-1988 there have been five amendments to increase the power to act without judicial supervision.

Equality before Law

The concept of equality does not mean absolute equality among human beings which is physically not possible to achieve. It is a concept implying absence of any special priv ilege by reason of birth, creed or the like in favour of any individual, and also the equal subject of all individuals and classes to the ordinary law of the land. As Dr. Jennings puts it : "Equality before the law means that among equals the law should be equal and should be equally administered, that like should be treated alike. The right to sue and be sued, to prosecute and be prosecuted for the same kind of action should be same for all citizens of full age and understanding without distinctions of race, religion, wealth, social status or political influence."[1]

Rule of Law

The guarantee of equality before the law is an aspect of what Dicey calls the rule of law in England.[2] It means that no man is above the law and that every person, whatever be his rank or conditions, is subject to the jurisdiction of ordinary courts. "With us", Dicey wrote "every official from the Prime Minister down to constable or a Collector of taxes is under the same responsibility for every act done without legal justification

1. Jennings— Law of the Constitution, p. 49 (3rd ed.).
2. Dicey — Law of the Constitution, p. 49 (3rd ed.)

as any other citizen." Rule of law requires that no person shall be subjected to harsh, uncivilised or discriminatory treatment even when the object is the securing of the paramount exigencies of law and order.[3]

Professor Dicey gave three meanings of the Rule of Law thus:

1. *Absence of Arbitrary Power or Supremacy of the law.* It means the absolute supremacy of law as opposed to the arbitrary power of the Government. In other words—a man may be punished for a breach of law, but he can be punished for nothing else."
2. *Equality before the law.* It means subjection of all classes to the ordinary law of the land administered by ordinary law courts. This means that no one is above law with the sole exception of the monarch who can do no wrong. Everyone in England, whether he is an official of the State or a private individual, is bound to obey the same law. Thus, public officials do not hold a privileged position in Great Britain. In Great Britain there is one system of law and one system of courts for all i.e., for public officials and private persons.
3. *The Constitution is the result of the ordinary law of the land.* It means that the source of the right of individuals is not the written constitution but the rules as defined and enforced by the courts.

The first and the second aspects apply to Indian system but the third aspect of the Dicey's rule of law does not apply to Indian system as the source of rights of individuals is the Constitution of India. The Constitution is the Supreme Law of the land and all laws passed by the legislature must be consistent with the provisions of the Constitution.

Equal Protection of the Laws

The guarantee of equal protection of law is similar to one embodied in the 14th Amendment to the American

3. *Rubinder Singh* v. *Union of India, AIR* 1983 SC 65.

Constitution.[4] This has been interpreted to mean subjection to equal law, applying to all in the same circumstances.[5] It only means that all persons similarly circumstance shall be treated alike both in the privileges conferred and liabilities imposed by the laws. Equal law should be applied to all in the same situation, and there should be no discrimination between one person and another. As regards the subject matter of the legislation their position is the same.[6] Thus, the rule is that the like should be treated alike and not that unlike shuold be treated alike.[7]

The rule of law imposes a duty upon the State to take special measure to prevent and punish brutality by police methodology.[8] The Rule of Law embodied in Article 14 is the *"basic feture"* of the Indian Constitution and hence it cannot be destroyed even by an amendment of the Constitution under Article 368 of the Constitution.[9]

The words *'any person'* in Article 14 of the Constitution denotes that the guarantee of the equal protection of laws is available to any person which includes any company or association or body of individuals. The protection of Article 14 extends to both citizens and non-citizens and to natural persons as well as legal persons. The equality before the law is guaranteed to all without regard to race, colour or nationality. Corporations being juristic persons are also entitled to the bebefit of Article 14.[10]

Exceptions to the Rule of Law

The above rule of equality is, however, not an absolute rule and there are number of exceptions to it : *First* 'equality before the law' does not mean the "powers of the private citizens are the same as the powers of the public officials." Thus, a police officer has the power to arrest while no private person has this power.

4. The 14th Amendment says : "Nor shall any State—deny to any person equal protection of laws".
5. *Ibid.*
6. *State of West Bengal* v. *Anwal Ali Sarkar,* AIR 1952 SC 75.
7. Dr. V.N. Shukla— Constitution of India, p. 27 (5th ed.)
8. *Raghubir Singh* v. *State of Haryana,* AIR 1980 SC 1087
9. *Indira Nehru Gandhi* v. *Raj Narain,* AIR 1975 SC 2299
10. *Chiranjit Lal* v. *Union of India,* AIR 1951 SC 41.

This is not the violation of the rule of law. But the rule of law does require that these powers should be clearly defined by law and that abuse of authority by public officers ust be punished by ordinary courts in the same manner as illegal acts committed by private persons. *Secondly*, the rule of law does not prevent certain classes of persons being subject to special rules. Thus, members of the armed forces are controlled by military laws. Similarly, medical practitioners are subjected to the regulations framed by the Medical Council of India a statutory body, are immune from the jurisdiction of ordinary courts. Article 361 of the Indian Constitution affords an immunity tothe President of India and the State Governors. Article 361 provides that the President or the Governor of State shall not be answerable to any Court for the exercise and performance of the powers and duties of the office or for any act done or purporting to be done by him in the exercise and performance of those powers and duties. No criminal proceeding shall be instituted or continued against the President or the Governor of a State in any Court during his term of office. No process for the arrest or imprisonment of the President or the Governor of State shall be issued from any Court during his term of office. *Thirdly*, today ministers and other executive bodies are given very wide discretionary powers by statute. A minister may be allowed by law 'to act as he thinks fit' or 'if he is satisfied'. Such power is sometimes abused. Today, a large number of legislation is passed in the form of delegated legislation, i.e., rules, orders or statutory instruments made by ministers and other bodies and not directly by Parliament. These rules did not exist in Dicey's time. *Fourthly*, certain members of society are governed by special rules in their professions, i.e., lawyers, doctors, nurses, members of armed forces and police. Such classes of people are treated differently from ordinary citizens.

Exclusion of Article 14 : The Constitution itself contains provisions which under certain circumstances, limit the effectiveness of Art 14.

1. The scope of right to equality under Article 14 has been considerably restricted by the 42nd Amendment Act, 1976. The new Article 31-C added by the Amendment Act provides that laws made by the State

for implementing the Directive Principles contained in clause (b) or clause (c) of Article 39 cannot be challenged on the ground that they are violative of Article 14. *Such laws will thus be an exception to Article 14 of the Constitution.* In *Sanjeev Coke Mfg. Co.* v. *Bharat Cooking Coal Ltd.,*[11] the Supreme Court has held that "where Article 31-C comes in, Article 14 goes out".

2. Art. 359 (1) provides that where a proclamation of emergency is in operation the President may, by order, declare that the right to move any court for the enforcement of such rights conferred by Part III (except Arts. 20 and 21) shall remain suspended. Thus, if the President of India issues an order, where a Proclaation of Emergency is in operation, enforcement of Art. 14 may be suspended for the period during which the Proclamation is in force.
3. Art. 36 lays down that the President and the Governors are exempted from any criminal proceeding during the tenure of their office.
4. Under International law, foreign sovereign and ambassadors enjoy full immunity from any judicial process. This is also available to enemy claims for acts of war.

"The Debate Over Special Powers"

There are a number of problems associated with these acts: are they necessary or are there existing provisions that serve the same purpose, are these acts being implemented arbitrarily, and so forth. For instance, a common complaint is that these measures are used more in areas where there is no insurgency. More importantly, as Ryan Goodman points out, the courts have developed little in the way of preconditions for the executive's subjective satisfaction so that judicial oversight is limited e.g. one judgement reads "The Court cannot substitute its own opinion for that of the detaining authority by applying an objective test to decide the necessity of detention for a specified purpose". (Ryan Goodman p. 21) As with other laws they are also open to abuse and transgression. Between 1980-90 over

11. (1983) 1 SCC 147.

two-thirds of the 16,000 detentions under this law were deemed invalid. (Ryan p. 22) Since 1990 the number of detentions has risen and, as one example out of many, to show the scale of the problem: out of 3,783 detained under NSA in Maharastra in 1993, 483 were released after scrutiny by the state, 1,332 by the advisory board, and 932 by the court. (Ryan p. 23). Again there is no correlation between levels of violence and detentions under the Act. Detainees are held because of political or ideological differences or suspected criminals, the former a gross violation of the fundamental rights and the later unnecessary.

The NSA is often used to deal with large strikes e.g. thus the leader of a campaign against the location of a steel plant was detained under the NSA in 1996. Again here such examples can be multiplied and instances from across the country can be cited. In its use against criminal acts, which while illegal can hardly be seen as a threat to national security points to the necessity to distinguish between public order and law and order. A Supreme Court judgement has suggested three concentric circles: the largest is law and order, the middle public order and the smallest security of state so that an act can affect law and order but not public order or security of state. A clear definition is not available and this is perhaps one area that needs to be worked on to limit arbitrary use of such legislation.

The question of national security has an emotive appeal and it is argued that the existing laws are inadequate, the judicial machinery too slow allowing known terrorists the freedom to operate with impunity. An influential police official K.P.S.Gill argues that today given the resources and technology that is available to terrorist organisations the arid formalism of the justice system cannot cope and what is needed is "real time legislative response". He suggests that weak laws far from being merely ineffective create situations where power is exercised arbitrarily so that they create dangers and that there can be no freedom and no rights unless there is security of life and property. In fact he argues that social activists who only look at the issue from the point of the culprits should understand that today we have a terrorised society. How can this society be freed from this terror is what has to be answered.

But the National Human Rights Commission of India (NHRC) rejects these arguments and says that the Criminal

Procedure Code (CrPc) and Indian Penal Code (IPC) are adequate. The provisions of POTA are similar to that available in the existing criminal codes. There is also a contradiction for while the government statistics show a reduction of incidents in Jammu and Kashmir, a decline in killings and an increase in militants killed they argue for the necessity of anti-terrorist legislation to counter the threat of increasing terrorism.

The conviction rates under these laws is remarkably low, for instance under TADA ever since the law came into force the rate has been 0.84%. For example, in 1994 of 67,000 detained since the beginning only 8,000 cases were even tried and just 725 were convicted. This means that 59,509 were detained needlessly (Chakma p. 30) The fear that these acts are being misused to target political opponents, minority groups is not misplaced as innumerable examples attest. Provisions in POTO make the law much more repressive and easily open to abuse. Its definitions of terrorism, terrorist activity, membership of a terrorist organisation, and other key terms are vague and unclear. The effectiveness of such legislation is a moot question. There have been cases where it is the political willingness to address the issues from both sides that has led to a solution such as with the Mizo Peace Accord but there are examples where political settlements have not worked. The debate on national security of course is not confined to the question of terrorism but includes other areas of life. The educational policies are a crucial element in building and sustaining a climate of crisis by inculcating a closed and one-sided view of history. Today, in India, government policy with regard to textbooks and the content of textbooks is of crucial importance and is being actively debated. Similarly the recent clampdown on internet cafes in Kashmir because militant groups were using them reflects the need to evolve mechanisms to address such issues. Control over information has been exercised by the state through censorship or through a monopoly over television and broadcast systems. Censorship has been exercised in limited ways and today with private broadcasters and satellite television, as well as the internet, many of these controls have been diluted. Yet, as the example of many countries does show, its possible to block sites on the net, even if these controls can be circumvented.

It should also be noted that the government spends massive amounts on national security, by one calculation 22% of its total expenditure. Aside fro the expenditure on the armed forces (22,500 crores) there is large outlay on paramilitary forces. The MHA plans to raise 209 battalions by 2004-05 or about 200,000 because of an increased threat perception. The cost of one battalion is around 26 crore and costs for maintaining it so that this would mean an extra expenditure of 2,000 crores per annum. The aim is to remove the army from internal security where as much as 50% of it is deployedtoday.

Conclusion

In conclusion I would like to note that, in the case of India, the expansion of the legal and policing machinery in the name of national security coupled with a policy to impute all problems as caused by cross border terrorism has given anti-democratic forces a very strong handle to selectively apply its special powers to curtail civil rights. In the case of Gujarat, the central government took an inordinately long time to wake up to the problem and did nothing to curb the state sponsored terrorism against the Muslim population and still continues its provocative policy of encouraging decisions within the state. The use of extraordinary powers, which give virtual immunity from prosecution, robs the citizens of their rights. This also diminishes the role of civil police and erodes the democratic functioning of the state. India prides itself on being a democratic society with an effective press, impartial judiciary and an active civil rights movement yet all these are put in jeopardy if the rights of people are eroded. Political problems need to be addressed politically and not blamed solely on outside intervention. Today it would seem that struggle in many societies is not to enact legislation to guarantee rights but to act to prevent legislation that would curtail civil liberties in the name of the guaranteed life and liberty.

B. PREVENTIVE DETENTION

Introduction

According to Article 21 no person can be deprived of his life a personal liberty except according to procedure established by law. This means that a person can be deprived of his life or personal liberty provided his deprivation was brought about in accordance with the procedure prescribed by law. Article 22 provides those procedural requirements which must be adopted and included in any procedure enacted by the Legislature. If these procedural requirements are not complied with, it would then be deprivation of personal liberty which is not in accordance with the procedure established by law. Thus Article 22 prescribes the minimum procedural requirements that must be included in any law enacted by the Legislature in accordance with which a person may be deprived of his life and personal liberty. Article 22 deals with two separate matters; (1) persons arrested under the ordinary law of crimes; (2) persons detained under the law of 'Preventive Detention'. The first two clauses of Article 22 deal with detention under the ordinary law of crimes and lay down the procedure which has to be followed whe a man is arrested and the remaining clauses (3), (4), (5), (6) deal with persons detained under a preventive detention law and lay down the procedure which is to be followed when a person is detained under that law.

Article 22 not a complete Code

At one time it was thought that Art. 22 was a complete Code in regard to laws providing for preventive detention and that the validity of an order of detention should be determined strictly according to the terms within the four corners of Article 22. It was held in *Gopalan's* case that a detenu cannot claim the freedoms guaranteed by Article 19(1)(d) if it was infringed by his detention and that the validity of the preventive detention law was not to be tested in the light of the reasonableness of the restrictions imposed thereby on the freedom of movement, nor on the ground that his right to personal liberty was infringed under Art. 21 otherwise than according to the procedure established by law. The view has now been shown to be wrong in *R.C. Cooper* v. *Union of India.*[12]

Although this case is concerned with Article 31(2) but in *Maneka Gandhi's* case the Court has applied it in relation to

12. AIR 1978 SC 597.

Article 21 also. According to this view a law relating to preventive detention must now satisfy not only the requirements of Art. 22 but also the requirtements of Art. 21 of the Constitution. In other words, the procedure prescribed under the preventive detention law myst be reasonable and just and fair under Articles 14, 19 and 21 of the Constitution.

Preventive Detention Laws

Clauses (4) to (7) of Article 22 provide the procedure which is to be followed if a person is arrested under the law of 'Preventive Detention'. There is no authoritative definition of the term 'Preventive Detention' in India law. The word 'preventive' is used in contra-distinction to the word 'punitive'. It is not a punitive but a preventive measure. While the object of the punitive detention is to punish a person for what he has already done, the object of preventive detention is not to punish a person for what he has already done, the object of preventive detention is not to punish a man for having done something but to intercept him before he does it and to prevent him for doing it. No offence is proved nor any charge is formulated. The sole justification of such detention is suspicion or reasonable probability of the detenu committing some act likely to cause harm to the society or endanger the security of the Government, and not criminal conviction which can only be warranted by legal evidence.[13]

Necessity of such Provision

Preventive Detention laws are repugnant to democratic Constitution and they are not found in any of the democratic countries of the world. No country in the world has made these laws integral part of the Constitution as has been done in India. There is no such law in U.S.A. It was resorted to in England only during war time. In England for the first time, during the First World War, certain regulations framed under the Defence of Realm Act provided for preventive detention at the satisfaction of Home Secretary as a war measure and they ceased to have effect at the conclusion of hostilities. The same thing happened

---

13. *Liversi v. Anderson* 1942 AC 206; *A.K. Gopalan v. State of Madras*, AIR 1950 SC 27 at p. 91 (Mukherjee. J.)

during the Second World War. These regulations were upheld by British Court.[14] Indian Constitution, however, recognises preventive detention in normal times also. In *A.K. Gopalan* v. *State of Madras*[15] Patanjali Shastri, J., explaining the necessity of this provision said: "The sinister looking feature, so strangely out of place in democratic Constitution, which invests personal liberty with the sacrosanctity of a fundamental right, and so incompatible with the promises of its preamble, is doubtless designed to prevent the abuse of freedom by anti-social and subversive elements which might imperil the national welfare of the infant republic."

The Preventive Detention Acts

The first Preventive Detention Act was enacted by the Parliament on 26th February, 1950. The object of the Act was to provide for detention with a view to preventing any person from acting in a manner prejudicial to the defence of India, the relation of India with foreign powers, the Security of India or a State or the maintenance of public order, the maintenance of supplies and services essential to the community. Section 3 empowered the Central and the State Governments and certain officers under them to make orders of detention if they were satisfied that it was necessary to detain a person with a view to prevent him from acting in any manner prejudicial to the things mentioned above.

The Act was purely a temporary measure and was to cease to have effect on 1st April, 1951. But its life was extended from time to time till it lapsed on December 31, 1969. But the Preventive Detention Law was revived in the form of Maintenance of Internal Security Act, 1971, (MISA), in less than two years time after the lapse of the first Preventive Detention Act, 1950. This Act continued to be in operation until the year 1977. That Act was repealed by the Janata Government in 1978 which came to power after the defeat of the Congress Ministry headed by Smt. Indira Gandhi. But in less than two years time after the repeal of the MISA the caretaker Government headed

14. *Liversidge* v. *Anderson*, (1942) AC 206, *Rex* v. *Holiday* (1917) AC 263 (Held, personal liberty can be sacrificed for the national success in war.)
15. AIR 1950 SC 27.

by Mr. Charan Singh again revived the Preventive Detention Law in the form of *Prevention of Blackmarketing and Maintenance of Supplies of Essential Commodities Act*. Its object is to prevent blackmarketing, hoarding of essential commodities. It requires the detaining authority to furnish grounds of detention within a period of 5 days from the date of detention, extendible to 10 days in exceptional cases. Within 3 weeks the Government is required to place grounds of detention along with detenu's representation before the Advisory Board. The Board must submit its report to the Government within 7 weeks from the date of detention. The maximum period for which a person could be detained after the confirmation by the Advisory Board has been restricted to 6 months from the date of detention. The aggrieved person has right to move the courts under Arts. 32 and 226 of the Constitution.

Again in, 1980 the President issued the *National Security Ordinance* providing for preventive detention of persons responsible for communal and caste riots and other activities prejudicial to the country's security. The Ordinance has become an Act now. It provides for detention upto a maximum period of 12 months but does not bar, the detenu from challenging his detention in a court of law on grounds, amongst others, of infringement of his fundamental rights. The detenu will be conveyed the grounds of the detention within 10 days of his detention. He shall have rights to represent to the Advisory Board against his detention. It also provides for detention of a person with a view to preventing him from acting in any manner prejudicial to the security of the State or the maintenance of public order or supplies and services essential to the life of the community.

The N.S.A. was amended by an Ordinance in 1984 in order to make it more effective. The amended Act 1984 separates each of the grounds for detention and allows further detention of a person whose earlier detention had either expired or had been removed. Such a provision already exists in the case COFEPOSA. Prior to this amendment, grounds on which the detention was based was held to be infirm the entire detention order was considered bad in law by the court. The new Section 5 which has been inserted in the Act provides that a detention order under Section 3 of the Act for which two or more grounds have been mentioned, would not be deemed to be invalid or inoperative merely because one, or some of the grounds are considered *vague, nonexistent, non-relevant, unconnected or invalid*. The amendment to Section 14 has been made to remove any bar on another detention order being issued under Section 3 against the same person. Section 14-A has been amended to substitute the words, 'two years' in place of "twelve months" *for Punjab and Chandigarh*. The amendment was necessitated by the extraordinary situations prevailing in the State of Punjab due to Akali agitation.

The amendment limits the scope of judicial review of preventive detention laws considerably. It thus nullifies the effect of numerous decisions of the courts in which the detention orders have been struck down on the ground that one of the several ground" of detention was found to be vague, non-existent or unconnected with the grounds of detention supplied to detenu.

The only difference between the earlier preventive laws and the present one is that the present laws give the detenu a right to go to the court and challenge the validity of his detention.

In *A.K. Roy* v. *Union of India*,[16] popularly known as the NSA case, the Supreme Court by 4 : 1 majority upheld the constitutional validity of the NSA and the Ordinance which preceded the Act. The Court held that Act was neither vague nor arbitrary in its provisions providing for detention of persons on certain grounds, as acting in a manner prejudicial to the 'defence of India,' 'security of India', 'security of the State', and to 'relations with foreign power'. While upholding the validity of the NSA and Ordinance preceding it, the Court issued a number of directions with a view to safeguarding the interests of detenues detained under the NSA. The Court directed: (1) that immediately after detention his kith and kin must be informed in writing about his detention and his place of detention; (2) the detenu must be detained in a place where he habitually resides unless exceptional circumstances require detention at some other place; (3) that detenu is entitled to his

16. AIR 1982 SC 710.

book and writing materials, his own food, visits from friends and relatives; (4) he must be kept separate from those convicted; (5) no treatment of a punitive character should be meted out to him and he should be treated according to the civilised norms of human dignity.

The majority, though disapproved the delay on behalf of the Government in not bringing into force the 44th amendment but held that it could do nothing. It said that the power to amend Constitution is different from that of bringing the concerned amendment into force. The 44th Amendment had itself left it to the Central Government to bring the amendment into force by a notification. Since it has not been brought into force it does not form the part of the Constitution and therefore the NSA is valid even though it does not provide for the setting up of the Advisory Board in accordance with the amendment. Gupta and Tulzapurkar, JJ., dissented from the majority on this point and issued a *mandamus* to the Union Government to bring the amendment into force. It is submitted that the minority view on this point is correct. The amendment must be brought into operation within a reasonable time by the Government. It would appear to be anomalous that Parliament can pass an amendment which cannot be brought into operation at all. Section 3 of the 44th amendment was intended to be a safeguard against misuse of the power of preventive detention by the Government and provided for the setting up of Advisory Bodies which would be a much more independent and impartial body. By not bringing into force the provisions of the 44th Amendment, the Central Government had not performed 'its' constitutional duty and the majority have abdicated its power to issue mandatory direction to the Government to bring the amendment into force.

Thus the petitioner was denied a very important right, that is, the right to have his representation considered by the Board as set up in accordance with the provisions of the 44th Amendment.

Terrorist and Disruptive Activities (Prevention) Act, 1987 (TADA)

TADA was primarily passed with a view to dealing with specific situations of terrorism in Punjab, Kashmir and even parts of the north-east. The Act vests sweeping powers in the Sate Governments which in effect means local politiciations and the Police—which is likely to be misused. There were widespread complaints of misuse of the provisions of the Act.

In *Kartar Singh* v. *State of Punjab*[17] the Supreme Court has considerably narrowed down the scope and ambit of the TADA and held that unless the crime alleged against an accused could be classified as a "terrorist act" in letter and spirit he should not be charged under the Act and should be tried under ordinary penal laws by the regular courts. The Court held that Section 3 of the Act operates when a person not only intends to overawe the government or create a terror in people etc. but also when he uses the arms and ammunition which results in death or likely to cause deaths and damages the property. In other words, the court held that *"a person becomes a terrorist or is guilty of terrorist activity when his intention, action and consequence all the three ingredients are found to exist together"*.

Thus an activity which is sought to be punished under Section 3(1) of TADA has to be such which cannot be classified as a mere law and order problem and cannot be tackled under the ordinary penal law.

The validity of the Act was challenged by more than 500 under-trials.

Another safeguard laid down by the court against the misuse of the Act was that of speedy trial of accused which is an essential part of the fundamental right to life and liberty under Art. 21 of the Constitution.

The Court also struck down Section 22 of the Act as violative of Art. 21 of the Constitution. Section 22 permitted identification of an accused on the basis of his photograph.

Referring to violation of human rights by the state law enforcing agencies the court said that these acts were in utter disregard and in all breaches of humanitarian law and universal human rights as well as in total negation of the constitutional guarantee and human decency.

The Court held that the Act did not provide a blanket power of unlimited detention without trial and a citizen should be entitled to bail in case the police fail to complete the

17. (1994) 3 SCC 569.

investigations within 6 months, extendable to maximum of one year with the permission of designated court.

Constitutional Safeguards against Preventive Detention Laws

Though the Constitution has recognised the necessity of laws as to Preventive Detention, it has also provided safeguards to mitigate their harshness by placing fetters on legislative power conferred on the Legislature. It is for this reason that Article 22 has been given a place in the Chapter on "guaranteed rights."[18] Clauses (4) to (7) guarantee the following safeguards to a person arrested under Preventive Detention Law :

(a) Review by Advisory Board.
(b) Communication of grounds of detention to detenue.
(c) Detenue's right of representation.

(a) Review by Advisory Board

Clause (4) of Art. 22 has been amended by the Constitution (44th Amendment) Act 1978. The effect of the Amendment is discussed below:

Prior to 44th Amendment Act, 1978

Clause (4) provided that no law providing for preventive detention shall authorise the detention of a person for a longer period than *'three months'* unless an Advisory Board constituted of person who are or have been qualified to be High Court Judge has reported before the expiration of the said period of three months that there is in its opinion sufficient cause for such detention. If in the opinion of Advisory Board the detention was not justified the Government was bound to revoke the detention order.[19] If the Advisory Board reported that the detention was justified then the detaining authority would determine the period of detention. However, the period of detention could not be indefinite. The detention cannot exceed in any case beyond the maximum period prescribed by any law made by Parliament for that class of detenu under sub-clause (b) of

18. *Pankaj Kumar* v. *State of Bengal,* AIR 1970 SC 97.
19. *Shibban Lal* v. *State of U.P.,* AIR 1954 SC 198.

clause (7). Any law providing for detention for a longer period of 3 months without obtaining the opinion of the Advisory Board must provide the class or classes of cases and also the circumstances under which a person may be detained for more than 3 months. It means that the Parliament must provide both (a) the classes or cases, and (b) the circumstances under which detention for a longer period of 3 months can be made.[20] Clause 7 of Article 22 contained an exception to clause (4). It empowered Parliament to enact a law and provide for a detention for more than three months without the opinion of the Advisory Board. Thus the opinion of the Advisory Board was not necessary in the cases (1) when period of detention does not exceed three months, and (2) when Parliament by law prescribed the maximum period for which a person may be detained under clause (4) (b) and clause (7) (a) (Now deleted). *The above amendment has not yet been brought into force.*

*After the 44th (Amendment) Act, 1978**

The 44th Amendment Act, 1978, has substituted a new clause for clause (4) which now reduces the maximum period for which a person may be detained without obtaining the opinion of the Advisory Board from '3 months' to '2 months'. The detention of a person for a longer period than two months can only be made after obtaining the opinion of the Advisory Board.

The Amendment has also changed the composition of the Advisory Board. The Advisory Board shall now be constituted in accordance with the recommendation of the Chief Justice of the appropriate High Court. It shall consist of a Chairman and not less than two other members. The Chairman of an Advisory Board shall be sitting Judge of the appropriate High Court and the other members shall be a sitting or retired Judges of any High Court. Thus an Advisory Board as envisaged under the Amendment Act of 1978 shall now be an independent and impartial body, *i.e.* free from executive control.

The Amendment has thus abolished the provision for preventive detention without reference to an Advisory Board as

---

20. *S.N. Sarkar* v. *Union of India,* AIR 1973 SC 1425.

* The Amendment Act has not been brought into force.

provided in unamended sub-clause (a) of clause (7) of Art. 22. The amendment therefore deletes sub-clause (a) of clause (7) of Article 22. Under Art. 22(7) (a) Parliament was empowered to make law for preventive detention without obtaining the opinion of an Advisory Board beyond the period of three months. After 44th Amendment a person can be detained beyond the period of two months only after obtaining the opinion of an Advisory Board. The deletion of clause (a) of Art. 22 (7) has thus removed the greatest blot on preventive detention in India.[21]

The amendment thus provides for two categories of preventive detention: (In) detention for a maximum period of two months under a law made by a legislature, and (2) detention for a period longer than two months provided the Advisory Board gives its opinion in favour of it. The Advisory Board will decide whether the detention is justified or not. It is a safeguard against executive highhandedness. If the Advisory Board reports that the detention is not justified, the detained person must be released. If it reports that the detention is justified the detaining authority will determine the period of detention.

The Advisory Board is bound to submit its report before the expiration of the said period of two months. Failure to do so would render the detention illegal. In absence of Advisory Board's clear opinion that there was sufficient cause for the continued detention of the detenu, it was held that their detention for more than one year was without legal sanction and hence illegal.[22]

In *Abdul Latif Abdul Wahab* v. *B.K. Jha*[23] petitioner was in jail awaiting trial on a charge of murder and was due for release on June 23, 1986. On that day, an order for preventive detention was made under the Gujarat prevention of Anti-Social Activities Act, 1985. On that date there was no Advisory Board in existence to which a reference could be made under Section II of the Act and whose report was required to be obtained within 3 months under Art. 22(4) of the Constitution. On August 7, 1986

21. H.M. Seervai, Constitutional Law of India, Vol. III, p. 12 ed. (1899)
22. *Sattar Habib* v. *K.S. Dilip Singhji*, 1986 SC 418.
23. (1987) 2 SCC 22.

when the order of detention dated June 23 was revoked a fresh order of detention was made. The Advisory Board was constituted on August 18, 1986 and a reference was made to it on Aug. 20. The Advisory Board made its report on Sept. 26, 1986 which was more than 3 months after the first detention order though within 3 months of the second order of detention. The Court held that the detention order was illegal being violative of Art. 22(4) which required that the report of the Advisory Board must be obtained within 3 months from the date of detention. This requirement cannot be evaded by making successive orders for detention before expiry of 3 months of the earlier order of detention. It is not sufficient to say that the procedural requirements of the Constitution have been complied with before the date of hearing of the case. The detention order was passed knowing fully well that there was no Advisory Board in existence to whom a reference could be made and report obtained as required by the Act and the Constitution. Such a casual and indifferent approach to citizen's rights has to be deprecated.

In *Nand Lal* v. *State of Punjab*,[24] the order of detention under Sections 11, 12.and 13 of the Prevention of Blackmarketing and Maintenance of Supplies of Essential Commodities Act, 1980, was challenged on the ground that the procedure adopted by the Advisory Board in allowing legal assistance to the State and denying such assistance to the detenu was both arbitrary and unreasonable and thus violative of Art. 21 read with Art. 14 of the Constitution. The detenu had made a request in writing for the assistance of lawyer during the hearing before the Advisory Board. The Court held that although under sub-section (4) of Section 11 of the Act a detenu had no right to legal assistance in the proceedings before the Advisory Board, but it did not preclude the Board to allow such assistance to the detenu when it allowed the State to be represented by an array of lawyers. Thus, the Board blindly applied the provisions of sub-section (4) of Section 11 of the Act to the case of the detenu that it could not allow legal assistance to the detaining authority and deny the same to the detenu. It is this arbitrariness in the procedure

24. AIR 1981 SC 2041; see also *Hemlata* v. *State of Maharashtra*, AIR 1982 SC 9.

adopted by the Board which had vitiated the order of detention in the instant case. The Supreme Court held that the principle of reasonableness is an essential element of equality and the procedure contemplated by Article 21 must satisfy the test of reasonableness in order to be in conformity with Article 14. Thus it is in the discretion of the Advisory Board to provide for legal assistance to detenu before it or not. But discretion should not. be exercised arbitrarily. But where no request for legal assistance is made by the detenu it was held that there was no denial of procedural fairness under Article 21.[25]

Parliament is empowered to prescribe the procedure to be followed by the Advisory Board in an inquiry under clause (4).

In a significant judgment in *Hitendra Vishnu Thakur* v. *State of Maharashtra,*[26] a case relating to TADA the Supreme Court has held that the designated court has no power to remand a TADA accused to custody if the police fails to complete investigation within six months to one year. Irrespective of the gravity of offence the accused has under Section 167 (2) of Cr.P.C. and Section 20(4)(b) of the TADA indefeasible right to be released on bail if the police fails to complete the investigation within 180 days or with the permission of the Court in one year. Art. 22(4) of the Constitution as well as the Cr. P.C. expects that an arrested person shall not be kept in custody for any unreasonable time and the investigation must be completed as far as possible within 24 hours. But realising that it may not be possible to complete the investigation in every case within 24 hours Parliament enacted the proviso to Section 167 (2) of the Cr.P.C. prescribing the outer limit. Section 167(2) was amended by amending Act 1993, substituting "180 days" for "one year" and providing for extension to one year when public prosecutor demands for specific reasons. The Court held that if the period of 180 days prescribed by clause (b) of Section 20(4) of T ADA has expired and the Court does not grant an extension on the report of the public prosecutor seeking extension of time to complete investigation the Court shall release the accused on bail.

25. *Smt. Kavita v. State of Maharashtra,* AIR 1981 SC 1641.
26. (1944) 4 SCC 602.

Accordingly, the Court held that the petitioner, Hitendra Vishnu Thakur, an MLA of Maharashtra Legislative Assembly, an accused under T ADA was entitled to be released on bail as the police had failed to complete the investigation within the prescribed period.

Section 167 read with Section 20 (4) of TADA is not a provision for "grant of bail" but deals with the maximum period during which an accused person may be kept in custody.

However, an accused person seeking bail under the provision of TADA has to make an application to the designated court for grant of bail on ground of "default" of the prosecution.

The court held that the Amendments of 1993 were of procedural naturel and therefore retrospective in nature and also apply to pending cases.

(b) Grounds of Detention must be Communicated to the Detenu

Article 22(5) gives two rights to the detenu : (a) the authority making the order of detention must "as soon as may be" communicate to the person detained the grounds of his arrest, that is, the grounds which led to be subjective satisfaction of the detaining authority, and (b) to give the detenu "the earliest opportunity" of making a representation against the order of detention, that is, to be furnished with sufficient particulars to enable him to make a representation.

The clause (5) imposes an obligation on the detaining authority to furnish to the detenu the grounds for detention "*as soon as possible*". The grounds of detention should be very clear and easily understandable by the detenu. The sufficiency of the particulars conveyed to a detenu is a justiciable issue, the test being whether they are sufficient to enable the detenu to make an effective representation. "Communicate" is a strong word. It requires that sufficient knowledge of the basic facts constituting the grounds should be imparted effectively and fully to the detenu in writing in a language which he understands, so as to enable him to make a purposeful and effective representation. If the grounds are only verbally explained to the detenu and nothing in writing is left with him in a language which he understands then that purpose is not served, and the constitutional mandate in Article 22(5) is infringed.[27] Thus where the detenu did not know sufficient English to understand the grounds communicated to him; it was held that there was no sufficient compliance with the requirements laid down in the Constitution.[28] Similarly in *Lallubhai Jogibhai Patel* v. *Union of India*,[29] the detenue did not know English but the grounds of detention were drawn in English and the detaining order stated that the Police Inspector while serving the grounds of detention fully explained the grounds in Gujarati to the detenu; but no translation of the grounds of detention into Gujarati was given to the detenu. It was held that there was no sufficient compliance of Article 22(5), and hence the order of detention was invalid. In *Kubic Darusz* v. *Union of India*,[30] the grounds of detention was served to the detenu in English and he acknowledged the receipt thereof putting his signature in English. After one month thereafter, he made a representation that he knew only Polish language and not English. It was held that there was no violation of Article 22(5) as the detenu had working knowledge of English but he was showing ignorance.

The grounds of detention must be in existence at the time of making the order. No part of such ground can be held back nor can new ground be added thereto.[31]

In *Shibban Lal* v. *State of U.P.*,[32] the petitioner was supplied with two grounds of his detention. But later on the detaining authority revoked one of the grounds communicated to him earlier. The detenu challenged the detention as illegal. The State contended that the remaining ground was sufficient to sustain the detention. The Court held the detention illegal and observed, "To say that the other ground, which still remains, is quite sufficient to sustain the order, would be to substitute on objective judicial test for the subjective decision of the executive

---

27. *Kubic Darusz* v. *Union of India*, (1990) 1 SCC 568 : *Harkrishan* v. *State of Maharashtra*, AIR 1962 SC 911; *Surjeet Singh* v. *Union of India*, AIR 1981 SC 1153.
28. *Ibid*.
29. (1981) 2 SCC 427, *Nainmal Pratapmal* v. *Union of India*, AIR 1980 SC 2129.
30. (1990) 1 SCC 568.
31. *State of Bombay* v. *Atma Ram* AIR 1954 SC 157.
32. AIR 1954 SC 179; see also *Kamalakar Prasad Chaturvedi* v. *State of M.P.* (1983) 4 SCC 442.

authority which is against the legislative policy underlying the statute. In such cases, we think, the position would be the same as if one of these grounds was irrelevant for purposes of the Act, or was wholly illusory and this would vitiate the detention order "as a whole".

In *Kishori Mohan* v. *State of W.B.*,[33] the petitioner was detained under Section 3 of the MIS A 1971, "with a view to prevent him acting in any manner prejudicial to the maintenance of the pubic order or security of the State". The grounds of detention supplied to the petitioner was as follows:- (1) that you along with your associates held a meeting at a place and decided to kill *jotedars* and richmen of the locality; (2) that you along with your associates attacked S.K. Ismail and tried to assault him by the tanga and dagger with intent to kill him; (3) that you and your associates addressed a meeting and impressed upon the gathering to use arson to establish common Raj in the country and for the same purpose urged killing policemen and collect guns and arms and ammunition from them, etc.

The Court held that the detention order stating that the detention was necessary to prevent the detenu from acting in a manner prejudicial to the "maintenance of public order or security of State" shows that either the magistrate was not certain whether the activities of the detenu endangered public order or security of the State or that he merely reproduced mechanically the language of Section 3 of the MIS A. When the language used did not make it clear whether his alleged activitics fell under one head or the other or both, it was not difficult to appreciate that a detenu might find it hard to make an adequate representation to the Government and the Advisory Board. The inclusion of an extraneous ground of detention vitiates the detention order since it is impossible to predicate whether without it the requisite satisfaction by the authority making the order could have been reached. The ground No. 2 was clearly extraneous to any of the heads and therefore the detention was invalid.

The grounds supplied to the detenu must not be *'vague'*, *'irrelevant'* or *'nonexistent'*. If the grounds are vague or irrelevant

33. AIR 1972 SC 1749.

to the object of the legislation the right of detenu under clause (5) is violated. A ground is said to be irrelevant when it has no connection with the satisfaction of the authority making the order of detention. The inclusion of an irrelevant or non-existent ground among other relevant grounds is an infringement of the rights of a detenu. The inclusion of even a single irrelevant or obscure grounds is an invasion of the detenu's constitutional right because it precludes the court from adjudicating upon the sufficiency of the grounds.[34] In *Ram Bahadur* v. *State of Bihar*,[35] it was held that where the order of detention was based on distinct and separate grounds and if any of the grounds was vague, or irrelevant the entire order would fail. In *Fogla & S.K. Jalil* v. *State of West Bengal*,[36] where one of the reasons for detention was not communicated to the detenu, it was held that the detenu had no opportunity to make an effective representation to the Government and therefore the detention was violative of Article 22(5) and must be set aside.

Amendment in N.S.A.

In view of the amendments in the N.S.A. the scope of judicial review of preventive detention laws has been considerably reduced. The 2nd amendment in N.S.A. provides that a detention order made under the Act for which two or more grounds had been mentioned would not be deemed to be invalid or inoperative merely because some of the grounds were considered vague, non-existent, not relevant unconnected or invalid. The grounds of detention is separable and a person can be detained again and again on the same ground. The amendment has nullified the effect of several decisions of the Court in which detention orders were struck down on one or the other grounds mentioned therein.

In *Shafique Ahmad* v. *District Magistrate, Meerut*,[37] it has been held that even where one of the grounds was found to be bad and unsustainable the detention under N.S.A. would not be vitiated if remaining grounds are valid.

---

34. *Mohd. Yusuf* v. *State of J. & K.*, AIR 1979 SC 1925.
35. AIR 1975 SC 223.
36. AIR 1975 SC 245.
37. AIR 1990 SC 220.

(c) Right of Representation

The other right given to the detenu is that he should be given the earliest opportunity of making a representation against detention order. It means that the detenu must be furnished with sufficient particular of ground of his dentition to enable him to make a representation which on being considered may give him relief.[38]

The '*grounds*' under Article 22(5) means all the "basic facts" and materials which have been taken into account by the detaining authority in making the order of detention and on which, therefore, the order of detention is based. Nothing less than all the basic facts and materials which influenced the detaining authority in making the order of detention must be communicated to the detenu. This is the plain requirement of the first safeguard in Article 22(5). The second safeguard in Article 22(5) requires that the detenu shall be afforded the earliest opportunity of making representation against the order of detention. No available delay: no shortfall in the materials communicated shall stand in the way of the detenu in making an earlier, yet comprehensive and effective representation in regard to all basic facts and materials which may have influenced the detaining authority in making the order of detention depriving him of his freedom. These are the legal safeguards enacted ~y the Constitution-makers against arbitrary or improper exercise of the vast power of preventive detention which may be rested in the Executive by a law of Preventive Detention.[39]

The reason why grounds are required to be communicated 'as soon as possible' is two-fold: Firstly, it acts as a check against arbitrary and capricious exercise of power. The detaining authority cannot whisk away a person and put him behind bars at its own sweet will. It must have grounds for doing so. Secondly, the detenu has to afforded an opportunity of making a representation against the order of detention. But if the grounds are not supplied to him it is not possible for him to

---

38. *Lawrence, D. Souzza* v. *Bombay State*. AIR 1956 SC 531, see also *Mohd. Yousuf* v. *State of J. & K.* AIR 1979 SC 1925.
39. *Hansmukh* v. *State of Gujarat, AIR 1981 SC 28; Khudiram Das* v. *State of W.B., AIR 1975 SC 550.*

make effective representation and in fact the right to make representation would become illusory.

The 'materials and documents' relied on in the order of detention must he supplied to the detenu along with 'grounds'. The supply of 'grounds' simpliciter would give him not a real but merely an illusory opportunity to make a representation and would thus make the procedure unjust and unreasonable which would be liable to be struck down.[40] Inordinate delay in considering the representation under Section 8 of N.S.A. by the detaining authority will make detention order invalid.[41]

Similarly, the non-supply of the copies of documents relied on by detaining authority will make the detention illegal.[42]

The word "and shall afford" in Article 22(5) cast a duty on detaining authority to inform the detenu while serving the order of detention that he has a right to make representation against the order of detention and also a right to be heard by the Advisory Board. This procedural safeguard must be observed strictly and the failure to comply with this requirement would vitiate the order of detention. But where a detenu who was an enlightened person and had been in active politics and was there fore, fully cognizant of his right to make representation under Article 22(5) and Section 8 of the N.S.A. and he, in fact, appeared before the Board and was personally heard by the Board, it was held that failure to comply with the above requirement would not have the effect of vitiating the order of detention.[43]

But merely because the detenu was not "simultaneously furnished with the grounds of detention along with the order of detention" it cannot be said that the detenu was thereby deprived of the right of being afforded the earliest opportunity of making a representation against the order of detention. Thus when the detenu did not allege that the detention was for non-existent grounds, nor did he attribute any mala fide on the part of the detaining authority the order of detention could not

40. *Kamla* v. *State of Maharashtra,* AIR 1981 SC 814.
41. *Rajkishor Prasad* v. *State of Bihar,* AIR 1983 SC 320.
42. *Yumnam Mangibabu Singh* v. *State of Manipur,* AIR 1983 SC 300. See also *Abdul Aziz* v. *Delhi Administration,* AIR 1981 SC 1389.
43. *Wasi Uddin Ahmad* v. *District Magistrate, Aligarh,* AIR 1981 SC 2166.

become invalid merely because the grounds were furnished two days later. The law is that he detaining authority must, communicate to the detenu the grounds of detention which is specified under Section 48 of the N.S.A. i.e., within 5 to 10 days, depending upon the circumstances of each case.[44]

Under Article 22(5) the Government is bound to consider the petitioner's representation as expeditiously as possible. Delay in deciding detenu's representation will make the detention illegal.[45] Delay in considering the representation of the detenu must be property explained otherwise it will make the detention illegal.

Similarly it has been held that refusal on the part of the detaining authority to send; the representation of the detunue to the Central Government amounts to denial of the right conferred on him under Art. 22(5) of the Constitution and hence the order of detention made under Section 14 of the National Security Act, 1980 would become illegal and was liable to be struck down. When the representation was addressed to the Central Government it was incumbent on the part of the detaining authority to forward the same to the Central Government and not to take pre-emptive action thereupon of its own.[46]

Whether the representation has been disposed off expeditiously or not will be determined by the Court on the facts and circumstances of each case. Thus where the State Government receives detenue's representation only one day before the expiry of 30 days from the date of his detention within which the Government has to refer his case to the Advisory

Board under Section 10 of the West Bengal (Prevention of Violent Activities) Act, 1970 stogether with his representation it is practically impossible for the State Government to consider the representation properly and bona fide arrive at its decision thereon before it refers the case to the Advisory Board.[47] But where in a case under Section 5 of COFEPOSA the detaining

44. *Ashok Kumar* v. *Delhi Administration,* AIR 1982 SC 1143
45. *Satya Deo Prasad* v. *State of Bihar,* AIR 1957 SC 367.
46. *Prem Lata Sharma* v. *District Magistrate Mathura,* AIR 1998 SC 2212.
47. *J.N. Roy* v. *State of W.B.,* AIR 1972 SC 2143.

authority supplied the copies of documents which formed the basis of the grounds of detention after long delay of 32 days after they were demanded by the detenu and the detenu had forwarded his representation to the Board it was held that there was denial of opportunity to make representation as the copies were of no use to the detenu in making effective representation and therefore the detention was held to be illegal.[48]

Similarly, it has been held that where there is unexplained long delay in disposal of representation the order of detention will be invalid. In *T.D. Abdul Rahman* v. *State of Kerala*,[49] the court held that the delay of 72 days in the absence of satisfactory explanation was too long a period for ignoring the indolence on the part of the concerned authority and hence the order of detention was invalid. The explanation given that delay had occurred in seeking the comment of the Collector of Customs etc. was held to be not at all convincing and acceptable.

Thus there is dual obligation on the appropriate Government and the dual right in favour of the detenu, namely, (1) to have his representation considered by the appropriate authority, and (2) to have once again the representation considered by the Advisory Board.[50] If in the light of that representation the Board finds that there is no sufficient cause for detention, the Government has to revoke the order of detention and set the detenu at liberty. Thus whereas the Government considers the representation to ascertain whether the order is in conformity with its power under the relevant law, the Board considers such representation from the point of view of arriving at its opinion whether there is sufficient cause for detention. The obligation of the appropriate Government to afford to the detenu the opportunity to make representation and to consider that representation is distinct form the Government's obligation to constitute a Board and to communicate the representation amongst other materials to the Board to enable it to form its opinion. The above conclusion is strengthened by the provisions of the Preventive Detention Act, 1950, made in conformity with clauses (4) and (5) of Article 22.

---

48. AIR 1981 SC 92; *Khatoon Begum v. Union of India*, AIR 1981 SC 1077.
49. AIR 1990 SC 434.
50. Punkaj Kumar v. Sate of W.B., AIR 1970 SC 97.

Consequently, the detenu has a constitutional right and there is, on the Government, corresponding constitutional obligation to consider his representation irrespective of whether it is made before or after his case is referred to the Advisory Board.

Thus, where the State Government waited till the receipt of the Advisory Board's opinion and there was an unexplained period of 24 days of non-consideration of the representation and there was no independent consideration of the representation by the State Government, it was held that there was clear non-compliance of Article 22(5) and consequently, the detention was liable to be quashed.[51]

In *Jaynarain Sukul* v. *State of West Bengal*,[52] the Court held that the language of Article 22(5) of the Constitution makes it obligatory for the State Government to consider the representation of the detenu as soon as it is received by it. The opinion of Advisory Board is no substitute for the consideration of the representation by the Government. The Court has enunciated the following four principles to be followed in regard to the representation of the detenu: (1) The appropriate authority is bound to give an opportunity to the detenu to make representation and to consider the representation as early as possible. (2) The consideration of the representation of the detenu by the appropriate authority is entirely independent of any action by the Advisory Board, including the consideration of the representation by the Board. (3) There should not be any delay in the matter of consideration. (4) The appropriate Government is to exercise its opinion and judgment on the representation before sending the case along with the detenu's representation to the Advisory Board. If the appropriate Government will release the detenu it will not send the matter to the Advisory Board. If the Government will not release, it will send the case along with detenu's representation to the Board. If the Board reports in favour of release the Government will release. If the Board expresses its opinion against the representation the Government may still exercise the power to release the detenu.

51. *Rahmatullah* v. *State of Bihar,* AIR 1981 SC 2069.
52. AIR 1979 SC 675; see also *S.K. Sakawat* v. *State of W.B., AIR 1975 SC 64.*

Thus where the detenu made a representation against the order of his detention and the State Government without considering the representation confirmed the order of detention it was held that the State Government failed in its obligation and that the confirmation of detention was in violation of Section 7 of the MISA, and Article 22(5) of the Constitution and therefore invalid. The subsequent consideration and rejection of the representation could not scure such invalidity of the confirmation of the order of detention and consequently the detention was illegal and void.[53]

In *Balchand Chorasia* v. *Union of India*,[54] the representation was filed by the detenu through his counsel. The Government did not consider the representation and approved the detention on the ground that it was not filed by the detenu. The Court held that the High Court was wrong in construing that the representation was not made by the detenu himself but by his counsel. The lawyer had filed the representation on the instruction of the detenu. The Supreme Court said that *in matters where the liberty of the individual is concerned and a highly cherished right is involved the representation should be construed liberally and not technically so as to frustrate or defeat the concept of liberty which is guaranteed by Article 21 of the Constitution*. As the representation was not considered at all by the Government which it was duly bound to consider the detention order was vitiated and detenu is to be released forthwith.

In *Kamla* v. *State of Maharshtra*,[55] the Supreme Court has expressed great concern about the non-compliance of the constitutional safeguards contained in Article 22(5) by the detaining authorities. Despite repeated warnings of the court in a series of decision, the detaining authorities do not take care to comply these requirements. When the detaining authority applies its mind to the documents and materials which form basis of the detention, there could be no difficulty in getting photo state copies of the same and attached the same along with the grounds of detention, if he is really serious in passing a valid order of detention. Unfortunately, these requirements are not

53. *S.K. Sakawat* v. *State of W.B.*, AIR 1975 SC 64.
54. AIR 1978 SC 297.
55. AIR 1981 SC 814.

complied with resulting in the orders of detention being set aside by the court, even though on merits they might have been justified in suitable cases. The Court, suggested that whenever a detention is struck down by the courts, *the detaining authority or officer concerned who are associated with the preparation of the grounds of detention must be held personally responsible and action should be taken against them for not complying with the constitutional requirements contained in Article 22(5).* It is high time, the Court suggested, that the Government should impress on the detaining authority the desirability of complying with above constitutional safeguard. In the instant case, the order of detention was declared void on the ground that the documents and materials were not supplied along with the detention order and also there was an unexplained delay of 25 days in disposing of the representation of the detenu. Similarly, the detention was declared to be void on the ground that there was undue delay of 75 days in disposal of the representation' by the Central Government.[56]

In *Sheela Devi* v. *Mohan Sarup*[57] the grounds of detention communicated to the detenu were not legible, The legible copies of documents were supplied to him later on. The detention order was confirmed before the supply of legible copies of document. The Court held that this was violative of Article 22 as he was denied the opportunity of making representation and hence entitled to be released.

Conservation of Foreign Exchange, Prevention of Smuggling Activities Act, 1974 and Article 22(5)

Parliament has passed the COFEPOSA to provide for preventive detention for preventing smuggling and conserving foreign exchange. The constitutional safeguards embodied in Article 22(5) of the Constitution are available to a person detained under the Conservation of Foreign Exchange, Prevention of Smuggling Activities Act, 1974 (COFEPOSA). Merely because there is no express provision in Section 8(b) of the (COFEPOSA) Act placing an obligation to forward the

56. *Raghavendra Singh* v. *Superintendent, District Jail, Kanpur,* AIR 1986 SC 356.
57. (1987) 3 SCC 234.

representation made by the detenu along with the reference to the Advisory Board, unlike those contained in Section 9 of the Preventive Detention Act, 1950; and Section 10 of the MIS A, 1971, it cannot be said that there is no obligation cast on the Government to consider the representation made by the detenu before forwarding it to the Advisory Board. The repeal of MISA and retention of the COFEPOSA does not imply that preventive detention can be freely used without any power of judicial review and without any checks and balances against persons engaged in anti-social and economic offences. The courts have always viewed with disfavour the detention without trial whatever be the nature of offence.[58] The Court re-affirmed its view expressed in its earlier decisions that the Government is bound to consider the representation made by the detenu without waiting for the opinion of the Advisory Board.

In a landmark judgment in *Attorney General of India* v. *Amrit Lal Prajivandas*[59] a nine judges Constitution Bench of the Supreme Court unanimously has held that during the period of emergency the President is empowered to suspend fundamental rights of people and a detenue has no locus standi to question the reasons or grounds of his detention. During that period the Presidential order suspending enforcement of certain fundamental rights was in operation, the State was empowered to make any law or to take any executive action inconsistent with such rights.

The Court upheld the validity of the two enactments of 1975 period—The Conservation of Foreign Exchange and Prevention of Smuggling Act (COFEPOSA) and Smugglers and Foreign Exchange Manipulator (Forfeiture of Property) Act, 1976 (SAFEMA) as they were passed to meet the threat to the security of India and had to be implemented effectively. The Court also upheld Section 12-A of COFEPOSA which had done away with the requirements of supply of grounds of detention and the consultation with Advisory Board during the emergency. The Court also upheld the provisions of SAFEMA which empowers the government to forfeit the illegally acquired properties of such smugglers and foreign exchange

58. *Narendra* v. *B.B. Gujral*, AIR 1979 SC 420.
59. (1994) 5 SCC 54.

manipulators (the detenues) in whom so ever's name they may have been held.

After the emergency was over on March 21, 1977 the detenues challenged the validity of their detention and seizure of their property on the ground both the Act violate Arts. 14, 19 and 22 of the Constitution.

The ruling of the court is as follows :

(1) Parliament was perfectly competent to enact both the COFEPOSA and the SAFEMA.
(2) An order of detention under Section 3 of COFEPOSA is also an order of detention for the purpose of and within the meaning of Section 2(2) of SAFEMA.
(3) An order of detention to which Section 12-A is applicable as well as an order of detention to which Section 12-A was not applicable can serve as the foundation, as the basis, for applying SAFEMA to such detenu and to his relatives and associates provided such order of detention does not attract any of the sub-clauses in proviso to Section 2(2)(b).
(4) If such detenu did not choose to question the said detention before the court during when such order of detention was in force or is unsuccessful in his attack-he, or his relatives and associates cannot attack or question its validity when it is made the basis for applying SAFEMA to him or to his relatives 'or associates.
(5) The definition of "illegally acquired properties" in clause (c) of Section 3 of SAFEMA is not invalid or ineffective.
(6) The application of SAFEMA to the relatives and associates is equally valid in as much as the purpose and object of bringing such persons within the net of SAFEMA is to reach the properties of the detenu or convict as the case may be, wherever they are, however, they are held and by whomsoever they are held. But the SAFEMA provisions would not affect the independent properties of such relatives and associates.

(7) Section 5-A of COFEPOSA is not void. It is not violative of clause 5 of Art. 22 of the Constitution.
(8) The petitioners have failed to establish that the provisions of SAFEMA are violative of Arts. 14, 19 and 21 of the Constitution.

This is a very important judgment of the Supreme Court. By upholding the validity of the above Acts the court has struck a heavy blow on economic offenders by depriving them of their ill-gotten gains. Both the Acts were enacted to check activities of smugglers and foreign exchange manipulators who were out to frustrate the regulations and restrictions of the government governing imports and exports. The COFEPOSA is a law relating to preventive detention and it seeks to deter them by means of preventive detention. On the other hand, SAFEMA is a measure designed to protect the economy of the country and also a measure to discourage law breaking-in particular-economic violaters who have illegally acquired property either themselves or other persons on their behalf.

In *Kamlesh Kumar Ishwardas Patel* v. *Union of India*[60] it has been held that where an officer specially empowered by the Central Government under the COFEPOSA and the Prevention of Illicit Traffic in Narcotic Drugs and Psychotropic Substance Act, 1988 (PITNDPS Act) has passed an order of detention the detenue has a right to make a representation to the said officer and the said officer is obliged to consider the said representation and the failure on this part to do so results in denial of the right conferred on the person detained against order of detention. This right of the detenue is in addition to his right to make representation to the State Government. This right to make a representation necessarily implies that the person detained must be informed of his right to make a representation to the authority that has made the order of detention and failure to do so will result in denial of the right of the person to make the representation. Thus the specially empowered officer can independently consider the representation. Failure to take independent decision on revocation of detention order will result in non-compliance with Art 22(5) and render the

60. (1995) 4 SCC 51.

detention illegal. It is to be noted that the provisions of COFEPOSA Act and PITNDPS Act are different from those of NSA, MIS A and PDA Acts.

In *Rajammal* v. *State of Tamil Nadu*[61] a the Government received remarks from different authorities and submitted the relevant files on the next day. The Under Secretary forwarded it to the deputy Secretary on the next working day. Thereafter the file was submitted before the Minister who received it while he was on tour. The Minister passed the order after five days and there was no explanation whatever as for the delay which occurred thereafter. It was held that the unexplained delay of five days in considering and disposing detenu's representation vitiated detention. Merely stating that the minister was on tour and hence he could pass orders only after five days was not a justifiable explanation when the liberty of citizen guaranteed under Art. 21 of the Constitution is involved.

Exception

Under Article 22(6) disclosure of facts which are considered to be against public interest may not be fUJIlished to the detenu. Hence it follows that both the obligations to furnish particulars and the duty to consider whether the disclosure of any facts involved therein is against public interest are vested in the detaining authority, not in any other.[62]

Subjective Satisfaction of Detaining Authority

The language used in the preventive detention laws make it clear that the power of detention was to be exercised on the subjective satisfaction of the detaining authority. The court will not normally interfere With the decision of the detaining authority whether the grounds given in the detaining order are sufficient or not.[63] However, the subjective satisfaction of the detaining authority is not wholly immune from judicial scrutiny. The Courts have, by judicial decision, carved out an area, limited though it be, within which the validity of the subjective

61. AIR 1999 SC 684.
62. *Puran Lal Lakhan Lal* v. *Union of India* AIR 1958 SC 163.
63. *Saraswathi Seshagiri* v. *State of Kerala*, AIR 1982 SC 1165; *Khudiram Das v. State of W.B.*, AIR 1975 SC 550.

satisfaction can yet be subject to judicial scrutiny. The basic postulate on which the courts have proceeded is that subjective satisfaction begin a condition precedent for the exercise of the power conferred on the Executive the courts can always examine whether the requisite satisfaction is arrived at by the authority, if it is not the condition precedent to the exercise of the power would not be fulfilled and the exercise of power would be bad.[64]

The subjective satisfaction of the detaining authority can be challenged on the following grounds, namely, mala fide or vagueness, and irrelevant or non-existent grounds or mechanical application of mind of detaining authority.

However, the recent amendments in the NSA have considerably limited the scope of judicial review of the subjective decision of the detaining authority. The amendments provides that the validity of the preventive detention order cannot be challenged on the ground that one of the several grounds of detention is vague, or non-existent or unconnected or invalid.

The Act thus gives an extraordinary power of high potency to the Executive. If these powers are exercised with due discretion and care it may prove to be an effective weapon for fighting social evils, encompassed by the statute that are eating into the vitals of the nation and pose a threat to its stability. But if wielded casually and capriciously, the power may turn into an engine of oppression posing a threat to the democratic way of life itself. The need for utmost good faith and caution in exercise of this power, therefore, cannot be over-emphasised.[65]

In Srilal Shaw v. State of West Bengal,[66] the petitioner was detained under the provisions of the Maintenance of Internal Security Act, 1975, for unlawful possession of railway. property. The detenu was prosecuted under the Railway Property (Unlawful Possession) Act, 1966. But the case was not proceeded with because according to District Magistrate, the witnesses did not dare to give witness against detenu for fear of

64. *S.N. Sarkar* v. *Union of India*, AIR 1973 SC 1425.
65. *Bankatlal* v. *State of Rajasthan*, AIR 1975 SC 522.
66. AIR 1975 SC 393; see also *Abdul Gaffar* v. *State of West Bengal*, AIR 1975 SC 1496.

their lives and therefore the case was dropped. The Supreme Court held the detention invalid. However, the Court made an important observation. It said, "this is typical case in which for no apparent reason a person who could easily be prosecuted and punished under the punitive law is being preventively detained. The Railway Property Act confers extensive powers to bring to book persons who are found in unlawful possession of railway property.

But the courts will upheld the detention valid even on isolated grounds if they are so serious to effect the whole community. In *Babulal* v. *State of West Bengal*,[67] the Court upheld the detention of detenues under MISA valid on the ground that they were members of a gang which committed an organised dacoity in a running train equipped with firearms and putting innocent passengers to peril of life and property.

In *Habeas Corpus Case*,[68] the constitutional validity of Section 16-A of the MISA (now repealed) was challenged. It was contended on behalf of the detenu that it was violative of Article 226 inasmuch as it prevented the High Court from exercising the jurisdiction under the Article to issue writ of *habeas corpus* and examining whether the detention under the Act was based on proper satisfaction of executive authority or not. The Court by 4 : 1 majority, (Khanna, J., not expressing any opinion on the question) held that Section 16-A, was constitutionally valid. The Court held that it was a rule of evidence and it was not open either to the detenu or to the Court to ask for grounds of detention". Section 16-A did not affect the jurisdiction of High Court under Art. 226. The jurisdiction to issue writs was neither abrogated nor abridged. It is a rule of evidence. Therefore, when detaining authority was bound by Section 16-A and forbade absolutely from disclosing grounds of arrests no question could arise for adverse inference against the authority that the power was exercised *mala fide* or not on subjective satisfaction. Even if a detenu makes out a *prima facie* case that the detention was *mala fide* the affidavit of the authority will be the answer and judicial inquiry will be closed. The Courts cannot insist on the

67. AIR 1973 SC 606 : see also *Abdul Sattar Ibrahim Manik* v. *Union of India* AIR 1991 SC 2261.
68. *A.D.M. Jabalpur* v. *Shukla, AIR 1976 SC 1207.*

production of the file or hold that the case of detenu stands unrebutted by reason of non-disclosure of grounds of arrest.

The effect of the decision in *Habeas Corpus* case was that courts were barred from examining the question of *mala fide* of the order of detention or *ultra vires* character of the orders of detention or that the order was not passed on the subjective satisfaction of the detaining authority. The decision of the Supreme Court overrules impliedly a number of earlier decisions in which it had claimed that it could examine the validity of the detention order on the ground either that the order was not passed on the subjective satisfaction of the detaining authority or the detention was made mala fide or the detention was made not for the purposes of the preventive detention laws.[69]

It is interesting to note that Section 14 of the Preventive Detention Act, 1951 which was similar to the present Section 16-A of the MIS A, was struck down as unconstitutional by the Supreme Court in the case of *A.K. Gopalan* v. *State of Madras*,[70] on the ground that it foreclosed the judicial inquiry of the legality of the detention under the said Act.

In view of the 42nd Amendment the decision of the Habeas Corpus case is no longer a good law.

C. CIVIL LIBERTIES AND EMERGENCY

One of the chief-characteristics of the Indian Constitution is the way in which the normal federal Constitution can be adapted to emergency situation. It is the merit of the Constitution that visualises the circumstances when the strict application of the federal principles might destroy the basic assumptions on which our Constitution is built.

The Constitution of India provides for three types of emergency:

A. *National Emergency* : due to war, external and internal aggression or armed rebellion (Art. 352).

69. *Makhan v. State of Punjab*, AIR 1964 SC 381.
70. AIR 1950 SC 27.

B. *State Emergency* : due to the failure of constitutional machinery in States (Art. 356).

C. *Financial Emergency* : (Art. 360).

National Emergency

Art. 352 provides that if the President is satisfied that a grave emergency exists whereby the security of India or any part of India is threatened, either by war or external aggression or *armed rebellion*.[71] he may make a Proclamation of Emergency in respect of the whole of India or any part of India as may be specified in the Proclamation. The Proclamation of Emergency made under clause (1) may be varied or revoked by the President by a subsequent Proclamation [Cl. (2)].

A Proclamation of Emergency can be made even before the actual occurrence of event contemplated in Art. 352 have taken place if the President is satisfied that there is imminent danger of war or external aggression or armed rebellion. Thus actual occurrence of the events mentioned in Art. 352 is not essential. An imminent danger of war or external aggression or armed rebellion is enough for the proclamation of emergency.

The President shall not issue a Proclamation under clause (1) or a Proclamation varying such Proclamation unless the decision of the Union Cabinet (i.e. the Council consisting of the Prime Minister and other Ministers of Cabinet rank appointed under Art. 75) that such a Proclamation may be issued has been communicated to him in writing. This means that the emergency can be declared only on the concurrence of the Cabinet, and not merely on the advice of the Prime Minister as was done by the Prime Minister Smt. Indira Gandhi in June, 1975. She had advised the President to proclaim emergency without consulting her Cabinet.

The Proclamation of Emergency must be laid before each House of Parliament and it shall cease to be in operation at the expiration of one month (prior to the 44th amendment two months) unless before the expiry of one month it has been approved by resolutions of both Houses of Parliament. If the Proclamation of emergency is issued at a time when the Lok Sabha has been dissolved or the dissolution of the Lok Sabha

71. Inserted by the 44th Amendment.

takes place during the period of one month referred to above, without approving the Proclamation but the Proclamation has been approved by the Rajya Sabha, the Proclamation shall cease to operate at the expiration of 30 days from the date on which the Lok Sabha sits after fresh election, unless before the expiry of the above period of thirty days a resolution, approving the Proclamation has been passed by the Lok Sabha [Cl. (4)]. A resolution approving the Proclamation must be passed by special majority. that is by a majority of the total members of each House and also by a majority of not less then 2/3 of the members present and voting in each House. Prior to the 44th amendment, such resolution could be passed by Parliament by a simple majority.

A Proclamation of Emergency once approved by Parliament shall remain in force for a period of six months from the date of the passing of the second resolution approving it under clause (4), unless revoked earlier. For the further continuance of the emergency beyond the period of six months' approval by Parliament would be required every six months. If the dissolution of the Lok Sabha takes place during the period of six months without approving the further continuance of emergency, but it has been approved by the Rajya Sabha, the Proclamation shall cease to operate at the expiry of 30 days after the Lok Sabha sits after fresh election unless before the expiry of the above period, it is approved by the Lok Sabha (CI. 5). Here also the resolution is required to be passed by the special majority referred to above.

The President shall revoke a Proclamation of Emergency or a Proclamation varying such proclamation if the Lok Sabha passes a resolution disapproving it or disapproving its continuance. Where a notice in writing signed by not less than 1/10th of the total number of members of the Lok Sabha have been given their intention to move a resolution for disapproving the continuance of a Proclamation of Emergency—(a) to the Speaker, if the House is in session; or (b) to the President, if the House is not in session; a special sitting of the Lok Sabha shall be held within 14 days from the date on which such a notice is received by the Speaker or the President for the purpose of considering the resolution. (Cls. 7 and 8). In such a case the session must be convened for considering the resolution. Now, it is not left to the discretion of the Government to convene or not a session of the Lok Sabha, for considering whether continuance of emergency is necessary or not.

The power conferred on the President by this Article shall include the power to issue different Proclamations on different grounds, either war or external aggression or armed rebellion or imminent danger thereof, whether or not there is a Proclamation already issued by the President under clause (1) and such Proclamation is in operation (Cl. 9).

Grounds

The President can proclaim emergency if he is satisfied that the security of India or any part thereof is threatened either by war or external aggression or armed rebellion. Prior to the 44th amendment one of the ground on which emergency could be declared under Cl. (1) was "internal disturbance". These words "internal disturbance" were vague and gave wide discretion to the Executive to declare emergency even on flimsy grounds. In 1975, the emergency was declared on the ground of internal disturbance by the then P.M. Indira Gandhi because the opposition parties had given a call to .launch a movement with a view to compelling the P.M. to resign from her post as her election to the Lok Sabha was declared void by the Allahabad High Court. The 44th Amendment has now substituted the words "armed rebellion" for the words "internal disturbance" which will exclude the possibility of a situation which arose in 1975.

The "*satisfaction*" that the security of India is threatened or there is an imminent danger of its being threatened by war or internal aggression or armed rebellion is the "subjective satisfaction" of the President and cannot be challenged in a court of law and even on ground that the opinion of the President had been actuated by mala fides. The question whether emergency exists is essentially a political question entrusted by the Constitution to the Union Executive and therefore not justiciable before the Court. The President is the sole judge to decide whether circumstances exist justifying the Proclamation of Emergency.

In *Minerva Mills Ltd.* v. *Union of India*,[72] Bhagwati, J. has held that there is no bar to judicial review of the validity of a Proclamation of Emergency issued by the President under Article 352 (I). Merely because a question has a political complexion, it is no ground why the court should shrink from performing its duty under the Constitution if it raises an issue of Constitutional' determination. The Court's power, however, is limited only to examining whether the limitations conferred by the Constitution have been observed or not. The Court cannot go into question of correctness or adequacy of the facts and circumstances on which the satisfaction of the Government is based. The satisfaction of the President is a condition precedent and if it can be shown that there is no satisfaction of the President at all, the exercise of the power would be constitutionally invalid. Where at all, the satisfaction is *absurd or perverse or mala fide* or based by wholly extraneous and irrelevant ground, it would be no satisfaction at all and it would be liable to be challenged before a court of law.

It is to be, however, noted that the word 'satisfaction' used in Art. 352 does not mean the personal satisfaction of the President, but it is satisfaction of the Cabinet. The power to declare emergency can be exercised by the President only on the advice of the Council of Ministers. The provisions has further been strengthened by the addition of the new clause (3) to Art. 352 by the 44th Amendment Act, 1978. It makes it clear that the President shall declare emergency only on the written advice of the Cabinet and not merely on the advice of Prime Minister as was done by the Prime Minister Smt. Indira Gandhi in June, 1975. She had advised the President to proclaim emergency without consulting her Cabinet. The Cabinet was simply informed about the proclamation of emergency which was a fait accompli. The object of clause (3) is to prevent the recurrence of such a situation in future.

Emergency provisions vest a very great power in the Executive. In the Constituent Assembly certain members had expressed the view that this power might be misused by the Executive. Dr. Ambedkar, however, said that the possibility that the emergency power might be abused furnishes no ground for

72. AIR 1980 SC 1789.

denial of emergency powers to the Executive. The power of Executive is not unbriddled. He pointed out that Constitution itself provides certain safeguards against the abuse of emergency powers by the Executive. First, it is to be exercised on the advice of the Council of Ministers who are representatives of the people. Secondly, it must be laid before the Parliament and cannot remain in force beyond one month without its approval. A review of the past events, however, have amply made it clear that in spite of the several safeguards incorporated in the Constitution the emergency provisions were misused. In 1975 emergency provisions were used to perpetuate the rule of one party which was in power,[73] It is submitted that effective safeguards against the abuse of emergency powers by the Executive are not constitutional provisions (even after the 44th Amendment, 1978) but the existence of an enlightened and vigilant public opinion. As promised to the electorate, the Janata Government enacted the 44th Amendment and incorporated certain safeguards in the Constitution with a view to checking the abuse of emergency powers by Government in future.

Territorial Extent of Proclamation

Article 352 enables the President to make a proclamation of emergency either "in respect of the whole of India or of such part of the territory thereof as may be specified". These words were added by the 42nd Amendment Act, 1976, which now enables the President to confine the declaration of emergency to any part of the territory of India. If the situation becomes normal in any part of the country emergency could be revoked from that part of the country, but it may continue to operate in other parts of the country.

Duration of Emergency

Prior to the 44th Amendment a Proclamation of Emergency could remain in force in the first instance for "two" months. But once approved by Parliament emergency could remain in force indefinitely i.e., as long as the Executive wanted it to continue. The 44th Amendment has curtailed the power of the Executive

73. D.K. Singh, Emergency and the Constitution of India, Indian Constitution Trends Constitution Trends and Issues, 288 (iii).

to prolong the operation of emergency unnecessarily. After the 44th Amendment, a Proclamation of Emergency may remain in force in the first instance for "one" month. Such a Proclamation, if approved by Parliament, shall remain in force for the period of "six months" unless revoked earlier. The resolution approving the Proclamation of Emergency must be passed by either House of Parliament by the special majority, that is by majority of the total membership of that House present and voting. For the further continuance of emergency beyond the period of six months' approval by Parliament would be required after every six months. Thus after this Amendment the continuance of emergency does not depend upon the discretion of the Executive. It can now be done only with the approval of Parliament and that too by a special majority of the House.

Effects of Proclamation of Emergency

The following are the consequences of the Proclamation of Emergency.

1. *Extension of Centre's Executive Power (Art. 353)*

During the operation of a Proclamation of Emergency the executive power of the Union extends to giving of directions to any State as to the manner in which the executive power of the State is to be exercised. The 42nd amendment made a consequential change in Art. 353 following the amendment made in Article 352. It provides that the executive power of the Union to give directions under clause (a) and the power to make laws under clause (b) shall also extend to any State other than the State where emergency is in force, if the security of India or any part of the territory is threatened by activities in or in relation to that part of the territory of India in which the Proclamation of Emergency is in operation.

In normal time, the executive power does not extend to give such direction subject to certain exceptions.

2. *Parliament Empowered to Legislate on State Subjects [Art. 353 (b)]*

While the Proclamation of Emergency is in operation, the Union Parliament is empowered to make laws with respect to any of the matters in the State List. The distribution of legislative power is thus fundamentally changed during emergency. The law-making power of the State is not suspended during the emergency. The State can make law but it is subject to the overriding power of the Union Parliament.

3. *Centre Empowered to Alter Distribution of Revenue between the Union and the State (Art. 354)*

The President may, while a Proclamation of Emergency is in operation by the order after the Financial arrangement between the State and the Union as provided in Articles 268 to 279. Every such order is to be laid before each House of Parliament and will come to an end by the end of the financial year in which the Proclamation of Emergency ceases to operate.

4. *Extension of Life of Lok Sabha [Art. 83 (2)]*

While the Proclamation of Emergency is in operation, the President may extend the normal life of the Lok Sabha by a year each time upto a period not exceeding beyond six months after Proclamation ceases to operate.

5. *Suspension of Fundamental Rights Guaranteed by Art. 19*

Article 358 provides for suspension of the six freedoms guaranteed to the citizens by Article 19 of the Constitution. It says that while a Proclamation of Emergency is in operation nothing in Article 19 shall restrict the power of the State to make any law or to take any executive action abridging or taking away the rights guaranteed by Article 19 of the Constitution. It means that as soon as the Proclamation of Emergency is made the freedoms guaranteed by Art. 19 are automatically suspended.

Normally, the rights guaranteed by Article 19 cannot be taken away or abridged by any law of Parliament or State Legislature. But Article 19 ceases to restrict the legislative or the executive power of the Centre or the States for the period of emergency and any law made by the Legislature or any action taken by the Executive cannot be challenged on the ground that they are inconsistent with the rights guaranteed by Article 19. As soon as the Proclamation of Emergency cease to operate Article 19 which remains suspended during emergency, automatically comes into life and begins to operate and any law inconsistent with Article 19 made during emergency ceases to have effect to the extent of the inconsistency except as respect things done or omitted to be done before the law so ceases have effect. But no action will lie for anything done during the emergency even after the emergency is over.

The 44th Amendment Act, 1978, has made two important changes in Article 358 : First, Article 19 will be suspended only when a Proclamation of Emergency is declared on the ground of war or external aggression and not when emergency is declared on the ground of armed rebellion. Secondly, it has inserted a new clause (2) in Article 358 which says that nothing in clause (1) shall apply to—(a) any law which does not contain a recital to the effect that such law is in relation to the Proclamation of Emergency, or (b) to any executive action taken otherwise than under a law containing such recital. This clause makes it clear that Article 358 will only protect emergency laws from being challenged in a court of law and not other laws which are not related to the emergency. Prior to this, the validity of even other laws, which were not related to emergency, could not be challenged under Article 358.

The *59th Amendment* has amended Art. 358 and has inserted the words "or by armed rebellion, or that the integrity of India is threatened by internal disturbance in the whole or any part of the territory of Punjab" after the words" or by external aggression". This means that, in cases of Punjab, the rights guaranteed by Art. 19 will be suspended also when emergency is declared on the ground of "armed rebellion or internal disturbance".

This amendment will apply only in case Punjab and shall cease to be in operation after the expiry of two years from the commencement of this Act i.e., 30 March, 1988.

The Proclamation of Emergency, however, does not invalidated a law which was valid before the Proclamation of Emergency.[74]

In *M.M. Pathak* v. *Union of India,*[75] the Supreme Court had an occasion to consider the effect of the expression "the things

74. *Bennett Coleman & Co.* v. *Union of India,* AIR 1973 SC 106.
75. AIR 1978 SC 803.

done or omitted to be done" in Article 358 after the Proclamation of Emergency ceases. In that case a settlement was arrived at between the LIC of India and its employees in 1971 under which the LIC had agreed to pay in cash bonus to its employees. In 1977, however, by the LIC (Modification of Settlement) Act, 1976 passed by Parliament during emergency the settlement was made ineffective and therefore the employees could not demand their bonus while the emergency was in force. The employees of the LIC challenged the constitutional validity of the above Act. The Supreme Court held that the effect of Proclamation of Emergency on fundamental rights is that the rights guaranteed by Articles 14 and 19 are not suspended during emergency but only their operation is suspended. This means that only the validity of an attack based on Articles 14 and 19 is suspended during the emergency. But once this embargo IS lifted Articles 14 and 19 of the Constitution, whose use was suspended, would strike down any legislation which would have been invalid. In other words, it means that the declaration of validity is stayed during the emergency. The expression "the things done or omitted to be done" occurring in Article 358 does not mean that the right conferred under the settlement is washed off completely. The expression is to be interpreted very narrowly. Therefore, as soon as the emergency was over, the settlement would revive and what could not be demanded during the period of emergency would become payable even for the period of emergency for which payment was suspended. In other words, the enactment will have effect even after the emergency had ceased. Thus valid claims cannot be washed off by the emergency per se. They can only be suspended by a law passed during the operation of Articles 358 and 359 (1).

Suspension of Right of Enforcement of Fundamental Rights (Art. 359)

Article 359 empowers the President to suspend the right to enforce fundamental right guaranteed by Part III of the Constitution. It says that while the Proclamation of Emergency is in operation, the President may by order declare that the right to move any court for the enforcement of such of the fundamental rights as may be mentioned in the order (except

Articles 20 and 21)[76] and all proceedings pending in any court for the enforcement of such rights shall remain suspended for the period during the Proclamation is in force or for such shorter period as may be specified in the order. An order suspending the enforcement of fundamental rights may extend to the whole or any part of the territory of India. An order made under clause (1) shall, as soon as possible, be laid before each House of Parliament.

The Constitution (38th Amendment) Act, 1975, added a new clause (1-A) in Art. 359 which provides that while an order under clause (1) is in operation, nothing in Part III shall restrict the power of the State to make any law or to take any executive action. Any such law shall cease to have effect to the extent of incompetency, as soon as the order ceased to operate except as respects things done or omitted to be done before the law so ceased to have effect.

The 44th amendment has made two significant changes in Art. 359 : First, it provides that under Article 359 the President does not have the power to suspend the enforcement of the fundamental rights guaranteed in Arts. 20 and 21 of the Constitution. Secondly, it provides that suspension of any fundamental right under Article 359 will not apply in relation to any law which does not contain a declaration that such a law is in relation to the Proclamation of Emergency in operation when it is made or to any executive action taken otherwise than under a law containing such a recital. Thus laws not related to the emergency can be challenged in a court of law even during the emergency. This amendment was a sequel to the decision of the Supreme Court in the Habeas Corpus case. The amendment is intended to remove the recurrence of such a situation in future.

It is to be noted that unlike Art. 358 under Article 359 the suspension of right to move any court for the enforcement of fundamental rights is not automatic. It can only be brought about by a Presidential order.

In September 1962, China attacked India. On 26th October, 1962, the President of India issued a Proclamation of Emergency under Article 352 (1) declaring that a grave emergency exist

76. *Added by the 44th Amendment Act, 1978.*

whereby the security of India is threatened by 'external aggression'.

On 3rd November, 1962, the President issued an order under Article 359 (1) which ran thus:

> "In exercise of the powers conferred by clause (1) of Article 359 of the Constitution, the President hereby declares that the right of any person to move any court for the enforcement of the rights conferred by Arts. 14, 21 and 22 of the Constitution shall remain suspended for the period during which the emergency issued under Article 352(1) on 26th October, 1962 was in force, if such person has been deprived of any such rights under the Defence of India Act, 1962 or any rule or order made thereunder."

In *Makhan Singh v. State of Punjab,*[77] Makhan Singh and other were detained under the Defence of India Act, 1962. They applied to the High Court under Section 491(1)(b) of the Criminal Procedure Code and alleged that they had been improperly and illegally detained because the Defence of India Act and the rules made thereunder contravence their Fundamental Rights under Articles 14, 21 and 22. Their petitions were dismissed by the High Court on the ground that the Presidential Order issued under Article 359 created a bar, which precluded them from moving the High Court under Section 491(1)(b), Criminal Procedure Code. They went in appeal to the Supreme Court. The two important questions for decision by the Supreme Court were: (1) What is the true scope and effect of the Presidential Order issued under Article 359(1)? (2) Does the bar created by the Presidential Order operate in respect of the applications made by the detenues under Section 491(1)(b) of the Criminal Procedure Code? In construing Article 359 the Court considered it relevant and useful to compare and contrast the provisions of Articles 358 and 359.

(1) Under Article 358, as soon as the Proclamation of Emergency is issued under Article 352 and so long as it lasts, Article 19 is suspended, and the power of the

77. AIR 1964 SC 381.

Legislatures as well as the Executive to that extent is made wider. Although Article 19 will revive and become operative as soon as the Proclamation ceased to operate, but Article 358 expressly provides that "things done or omitted to be done during the emergency" cannot be challenged even after the emergency is over. Thus suspension of Article 19 is completed during the period of emergency and Legislative and Executive action which contravenes Article 19 cannot be questioned even after the emergency is over. Article 359, on the other hand, does not suspend any Fundamental Right, but merely authorise the President to issue an order declaring that the right to move any court for the enforcement of such Fundamental Rights as may be mentioned in the order, shall remain suspended for the period during which the Proclamation is in force or for such shorter period as may be specified in the order. The rights are not suspended, but the citizens is deprived of his right to move any court for their enforcement. The said rights are theoretically alive. The right to seek remedy is suspended.

(2) While the suspension of Article 19 under Article 358 applies to the whole country and so covers all Legislatures and States, the order under Article 352(1) may extend to the whole of India or may be confined to any part of the territory of India..

(3) While the suspension of Article 19 under Article 359 continues for the entire period of emergency, the suspension of the right to move any court will ensure for the period of the emergency, or for a shorter period, if so specified by the Presidential Order.

(4) While Article 358 provides that things done or omitted to be done during the emergency cannot be challenged even after the emergency is over, the position under Article 359 is different. As soon as the order issued under Article 352 ceases to be operative, any information made by the Legislative or Executive action is liable to challenge on the basis that those rights were in operation even during the pendency of

the Presidential Order, unless an appropriate Act of Indemnity is passed by Parliament.

Coming to the true scope and effect of Article 359, the Court held that it was impossible to accept the contention that only right that can be suspended by an Order made under Article 359(1) was the right guaranteed by Article 32(1) to move the Supreme Court for the enforcement of any of the Fundamental Rights, and a citizen would be free to seek relief from a High Court under Article 226. Article 359 uses the words "any court", which does not mean only the Supreme Court but must include all courts of competent jurisdiction. The use of the expression "any Court" cannot be justified by a reference to Article 32(3) which enables Parliament to empower any other court to exercise all or any of the powers exercisable by the Supreme Court under Article 32(2). Article 32(3) clearly shows that the other courts empowered by the Parliament cannot have the same status as the Supreme Court to which alone Article 32(1) is applicable. Hence the words "any court" in Article 359(1) would include the Supreme Court as well as the High Courts before whom the specified right can be e-nforced by citizens.

The Supreme Court, however, took the precaution of pointing out that a citizen would not be deprived of his right to move the appropriate court for a writ of habeas corpus if his detention had been ordered mala fide—The detention can also be challenged on the grounds of infringement of those rights conferred by Part III which have not been mentioned in the Presidential Order. Similarly, if the detenu contends that the provisions of Defence of India Act and the Ordinance under which he is detained suffer from excessive delegation his plea raised cannot be barred by the Presidential Order because it is plea which does not relate to the fundamental rights mentioned in the order.

In *Maharashtra State* v. *Prabhakar*[78] the Supreme Court held that if a person was deprived of his personal liberty not under the Defence of India Act, or any rule made thereunder but the contravention thereof, his right to move the said courts in that

78. AIR 1966 SC 424.

regard would not be suspended. Similarly, in *Ram Manohar Lohia* v. *State of Bihar*,[79] the Supreme Court held the order of detention under the Defence of India Rules illegal on the ground that the order of detention was inconsistent with the conditions laid down in the Defence of India Rules. In this case Dr. Ram Manohar Lohia was detained by an order of District Magistrate to whom the power was delegated by the Government under Section 40(2) of the Defence of India Act, 1962—The order stated that the D.M. was satisfied that with a view to prevent the petitioner from acting in any manner prejudicial to the "public safety and the maintenance of law and order" it was necessary to detain him. The expression used "for this purpose" under the Defence of India Rules was "public safety and maintenance of public order".

The Court held that the order of the President did not form a bar to all applications for release from detention under the Act or the Rules. Where a person was detained in violation of the mandatory provisions of the Defence of India Act his right to move the court was not suspended. The petitioner contended that the order of detention was not justified under the Act or Rules and was, against the provisions of the Act. The petitioner was therefore entitled to be heard. The order detaining the petitioner would not be in terms of the Rule unless it could be said that the expression "law and order" meant the same thing as "public order". What was meant by maintenance of public order was the prevention of disorder of a grave nature, a disorder which the authorities thought was necessary to prevent in view of the emergent situation created by external aggression, whereas the expression maintenance of law and order may mean prevention of disorder of comparatively lesser gravity and of local significance only.

In *Mohd. Yaqub* v. *State of Jammu and Kashmir*,[80] the Supreme Court held that an order by the President under Article 359(I) was not 'law' within the meaning of Article 13(2) and therefore, its validity could not be challenged with reference tolft1e provisions of Part III. Thus if the order suspends the

79. AIR 1966 SC 740.
80. AIR 1968 SC 765 (overruling *Ghulam Sarwar* v. *Union of India*, AIR 1968 SC. 1335).

enforcement of Article 14, if cannot be challenged on the ground that it is discriminatory under Article 14. The validity of the order cannot be tested under the very fundamental rights, i.e., Article 14, which it is suspended. The Supreme Court thus overruled its own decision in *Ghulam Sarwar* v. *Union of India*,[81] wherein it had held that the Presidential Order issued under Article 359(1) could be challenged as being discriminatory.

The Emergency proclaimed in 1962 continued upto January 10, 1968. Emergency was again proclaimed in 1971 when Pakistan attacked India, and continued in operation up to March 1977. On 26th June, 1975, the President declared emergency on the ground that security of India was threatened due to "internal.disturbance". This Proclamation of Emergency was in addition to the Emergency declared in 1971 relating to external aggression which continued upto March 1977.

On June 27, 1975 the President issued an order under Article 359(I) as follows :

> "In exercise of powers conferred by clause (I) of Article 359 the President hereby declares that the right of any person (including a foreigner) to move any court for the enforcement of the rights conferred by Articles 14, 21 and 22 and all proceedings pending in any court for the enforcement of the above-mention rights shall remain suspended for the period during which the Proclamation of Emergency made under clause (1) of Article 352 on the 3rd December and 25th June and both in force".

In *A.D.M. Jabalpur* v. *Shukla*,[82] popularly known as the habeas corpus case the respondents challenged the validity of the Proclamation of Emergency by the President under Article 352 made on 25th June, 1975, and the order of detention made against them thereunder. The respondents were detained under Section 3 of the MISA. They filed applications in different High Courts for the issue of writ of habeas corpus. A preliminary objection was raised on behalf of the State that the President's

81. AIR 1968 SC 1335.
82. AIR 1976 SC 1207.

Order was a bar to invoke writ jurisdiction of the High Courts. The High Courts held that notwithstanding the continuance of emergency and the Presidential Order suspending the enforcement of rights conferred by Articles 19, 21, and 22 the High Court could examine whether an order of detention was in accordance with the provisions of the MIS A or whether the order was mala fide or was made on the basis of relevant materials by which the detaining authority could have satisfied that the order was necessary. The State appealed to the Supreme Court.

The main questions for the consideration of the Supreme Court were two: First, whether in view of the Presidential Order, dated 27th June, 1975 and 8th January, 1976 made under clause (1) of Article 359 any writ-petition under Article 226 would lie in a High Court for habeas corpus to enforce the right to personal liberty of a person detained under the Act on the ground that the order of detention was not in compliance with the Act. Secondly, if such a petition was maintainable what the scope of judicial security particularly in view of the Presidential order mentioning Art. 22 and Section 16-A of the MISA. Section 16-A of MIS A prohibited the detaining authority to communicate grounds of detention to the detenu.

The Supreme Court by a 4 : 1 majority (A.N. Ray, D.J., Beg, Chandrachud and Bhagwati, JJ.-(Khanna, J., dissenting) held that in view of the Presidential Order dated 27th June, 1975 no person had any locus standi (legal right) to move any writ-petition under Article 226 before a High Court for habeas corpus or any other writ or order or direction to challenge the legality of an order of detention on the ground that the order was not under or in compliance with the Act or was illegal, or was vitiated by mala fides factual or legal or has based on extraneous considerations.

The respondents had argued that the present appeal should be decided in the light of the Court's rulings in the Makhan Singh's case. In Makhan Singh's case the court had held that if a detenu challenged his detention on the ground that it violated statutory provisions or the detention was vitiated with malice the challenge could not be barred because of the Presidential Order under Article 359(1). The Court, however, held that the decision in Makhan Singh's case did not apply in the present case. The 1962 Presidential Order was a conditional order as it related to only those persons who had been detained under Defence of India Act. The Presidential Order of June 27, 1975 was a "blanket" order and was not confined to persons detained under a particular law. Mr. Justice Khanna, in his dissenting judgment, however, held that the difference in phraseology in Presidential Order dated June 27, 1975 and that of the 1962 Presidential Order could not justify the conclusion that because of the new Presidential Order a detention order need not comply with the requirement of the law providing for preventive detention.

It was also argued that the object of Article 359 (1) was to bar moving the Supreme Court under Art. 32 for the enforcement of fundamental rights without affecting in any manner the enforcement of common law and statutory right to personal liberty under Article 226 before the High Court. In brief, the contention was that Article 21 was not the sole repository of the right to personal liberty. The Court, however, rejected this argument and held that Art. 21 was the sole repository of the right to life and personal liberty. The moment the right to move any Court for enforcement of the Article 21, was suspended, no one could move any court for any redress.

In view of the 44th Amendment the law laid down in Habeas Corpus case is no longer a good law. Henceforth, Arts. 21 and 22 cannot be suspended during the Proclamation of Emergency. Consequently, a person will be entitled to challenge the validity of his detention even during the operation of emergency.

Duty of the Union to Protect States

Article 355 imposes a duty on the Union to protect every State against external aggression and internal disturbance and ensure that the Government of every State is carried on in accordance with the provisions of the Constitution. Article 355 thus imposes the following two obligations on the Central Government:

(1) The duty to protect States from internal disturbance and external aggression. Such provisions are also found in other federal Constitutions, i.e. America,

Australia. But in America and Australia the Center acts only when the request is made by States, while there is no such pre-condition under Article 355. The Centre can thus interfere even without the State's request.

(2) The duty to see that Government of every State is carried on in accordance with the provisions of the Constitution. The Constitutions of U.S.A. and Australia also contain such provisions. It is this duty in performance of which the Centre takes over the Government of State under Art. 356 in case of failure of the constitutional machinery in the State. In other federations, however, the Centre cannot do so.

6

National Security Laws and Judiciary

The role of judges during times of war—whether it be a traditional war or a "war on terrorism"—is essentially no different than during times of peace: it is to interpret the law to the best of our ability, consistent with our constitutionally mandated role and without regard to external pressure. Among the differences in wartime for the judiciary, however, is one that involves a principle that is essential to the proper operation of the federal courts—judicial independence. In wartime, the need for judicial independence is at its highest, yet the very concept is at its most vulnerable, imperiled by threats both within and without the judiciary. Externally, there is pressure from the elected branches, and often the public, to afford far more deference than may be desirable to the President and Congress, as they wage wars to keep the nation safe. Often this pressure includes threats of retribution, including threats to strip the courts of jurisdiction. Internally, judges may question their own right or ability to make the necessary, potentially perilous judgments at the very time when it is most important that they exercise their full authority. This concern is exacerbated by the fact that the judiciary is essentially a conservative institution and judges are generally conservative individuals who dislike controversy, risk taking, and change.

As Professor Stone can tell you, the history of judicial responses to threats to our liberties in wartime is mixed at best.[1] Now, in the first years of the twenty-first century, the threat to judicial independence is proving particularly troublesome, and I am not referring just to those demagogues who rush to the steps of the Capitol to call for legislation stripping the federal courts of jurisdiction every time they do not like a decision bolstering the Bill of Rights. Rather, I refer to the chilling reality that, as we enter the fifth year of the so-called "Global War on Terror", we are faced with a conflict with no projected or foreseeable end, and, thus, with the prospect that the war-related challenges to constitutional rights and to judicial independence, which typically subside with the end of a conflict, will continue unabated into the indefinite future. In an era of "war without end," any inclination of judges to lessen the necessary constitutional vigilance will not only seriously jeopardize basic rights to privacy and liberty, but also will make it more difficult to fend off other, non-war-related challenges to judicial independence, and as a result cause harm to all of our fundamental rights and liberties.

Archibald Cox—who knew a thing or two about the necessity of government actors being independent—emphasized that an essential element of judicial independence is that "there shall be no tampering with the organization or jurisdiction of the courts for the purposes of controlling their decisions upon constitutional questions." [2] Applying Professor Cox's precept to current events, we might question whether some recent actions and arguments advanced by the elected branches constitute threats to judicial independence. Congress, for instance, recently passed the Detainee Treatment Act. [3] The

1. *See generally* Geoffrey R. Stone, *Civil Liberties* v. *National Security in the Law's Open Areas*, 86 B.U. L. REV. 1315 (2006).
2. Archibald Cox, *The Independence of the Judiciary: History and Purposes*, 21 U. Dayton L. REV. 565, 566 (1996).
3. Pub. L. No. 109-148, 119 Stat. 2739 (2005) (to be codified at 10 U.S.C. § 801, 28 U.S.C. § 2241, 42 U.S.C. § 2000dd).

Graham-Levin Amendment, which is part of that legislation, prohibits any court from hearing or considering habeas petitions filed by aliens detained at Guantanamo Bay.[4] The Supreme Court has been asked to rule on whether the Act applies only prospectively, or whether it applies to pending habeas petitions as well. It is unclear at this time which interpretation will prevail.[5] But if the Act is ultimately construed as applying to pending appeals, one must ask whether it constitutes "tampering with the . . . jurisdiction of the courts for the purposes of controlling their decisions," which Professor Cox identified as a key marker of a violation of judicial independence. All of this, of course, is wholly aside from the question of whether Congress and the President may strip the courts of such jurisdiction prospectively. And it is, of course, also wholly apart from the *Padilla* case,[6] in which many critics believe that the administration has played fast and loose with the courts' jurisdiction in order to avoid a substantive decision on a fundamental issue of great importance to all Americans.

Another possible threat to judicial independence involves the position taken by the administration regarding the scope of its war powers. In challenging cases brought by individuals charged as enemy combatants or detained at Guantanamo, the administration has argued that the President has "inherent powers" as Commander in Chief under Article II and that actions he takes pursuant to those powers are essentially not reviewable by courts or subject to limitation by Congress.[7] The administration's position in the initial round of Guantanamo cases was that no court anywhere had any jurisdiction to consider any claim, be it torture or pending execution, by any individual held on that American base, which is located on territory under American jurisdiction, for an indefinite period.[8] The executive branch has also relied on sweeping and often

4. *Id.* § 1005(e)-(h), 119 Stat. at 2741-44 (to be codified at 10 U.S.C. § 801).
5. Following the presentation of these remarks at the symposium, the Supreme Court ruled that the Act did not apply to pending petitions. Hamdan v. Rumsfeld, 126 S. Ct. 2749, 2769 n. 15 (2006).
6. Padilla v. Hanft, 423 F.3d 386 (4th Cir. 2005), *cert. denied*, 126 S. Ct. 1649 (2006).
7. *See, e.g.*, Hamdi v. Rumsfeld, 542 U.S. 507, 516 (2004).
8. See, e.g., Rasul v. Bush, 542 U.S. 466, 475-76 (2004).

startling assertions of executive authority in defending the administration's domestic surveillance program, asserting at times as well a congressional resolution for the authorization of the use of military force. To some extent, such assertions carry with them a challenge to judicial independence, as they seem to rely on the proposition that a broad range of cases—those that in the administration's view relate to the President's exercise of power as Commander in Chief (and that is a broad range of cases indeed)—are, in effect, beyond the reach of judicial review. The full implications of the President's arguments are open to debate, especially since the scope of the inherent power appears, in the view of some current and former administration lawyers, to be limitless. What is clear, however, is that the administration's stance raises important questions about how the constitutionally imposed system of checks and balances should operate during periods of military conflict, questions judges should not shirk from resolving.

The fundamental question, I suppose, is whether the role of the judge should change in wartime. The answer is that while our function does not change, the manner in which we perform the balancing of interests that we so often undertake in constitutional cases does. In times of national emergency, we must necessarily give greater weight in many instances to the governmental, more specifically the national security, interest than we might at other times. As courts have often recognized, the government's interests in protecting the nation's security are heightened during periods of military conflict. Accordingly, particular searches or detentions that might be unconstitutional during peacetime may well be deemed constitutional during times of war—not because the role of the judge is any different, and not because courts curtail their constitutionally mandated role, but because a governmental interest that may be insufficient to justify such deprivations in peacetime may be sufficiently substantial to justify that action during times of national emergency. Courts must not, however, at any time allow the balancing to turn into a routine licensing of unbridled and unsupervised governmental power.

Because the courts' balancing of the interests of the government and individuals may produce different results during wartime, the question whether the country is indeed "at war," and if so, the extent to which courts should give the government's interest enhanced weight in wartime, is a critical one. This issue is particularly critical now, when our nation is engaged in a new and wholly unprecedented kind of conflict, one that might very well be a "war without end". In this circumstance, we must ask whether the considerations that have led courts to give governmental interests greater weight during the traditional wars of the past apply with as much force during the present "war on terror," and, if so, how long such a circumstance may endure. Equally important is the question: what is the role of the courts in determining when "the war without end" has ended or reached a state of normalcy such that we should reevaluate the extent to which we must allow wartime concerns to distort the ordinary balancing process?

The judiciary's practice of according the government's interest enhanced weight during wartime is premised, at least implicitly, on the notion that because a state of war is temporary, the curtailment of individual liberty that ensues will also exist for only a limited period. Today, we are faced with a conflict with no foreseeable end and thus with the threat that the scale balancing governmental and individual interests may become permanently tipped in favor of the government. Still, the reason that this conflict is a "war without end" is that we face a nontraditional enemy whose threats may continue unabated for the indefinite future. The rationale that the government requires more latitude in order to keep the country safe during wartime is not any less pressing simply because the conflict has no foreseeable end. This poses an interesting conundrum for those who might be willing to sacrifice some rights in the short run but not indefinitely. During the first years of the twenty-first century, judges will undoubtedly have to consider these and similar novel questions resulting from the radically different world situation we now confront.

One might then ask: are judges capable of making such judgments and do they have the knowledge and expertise to do so? Separate this from the different question: is it appropriate for judges to decide such issues? The answer to the first question is "yes", and to the second "maybe" (as it would take an entire conference on the second question to do the subject justice). As to the first question, I need only refer to the experience of the Israeli Supreme Court. In times of gravest crisis, that court has repeatedly decided critical questions of national security, including some that have directly affected military operations and tactics, as well as questions as essential to Israel's survival as where the wall protecting Israel against terrorist incursions should be located, hectare by hectare.[9] The Israeli court's decisions have not only been forceful and unequivocal, but have been accepted without a whimper, and put into immediate effect, by the government, the military, and the people. Israel, of course, has a different cultural tradition and a different view of the role of the courts. But as to whether judges are capable of making decisions that require balancing the most critical national security interests against basic civil liberties, the Israeli experience clearly demonstrates that the answer is an unqualified "yes".

The task of judging national security issues is, however, more difficult now than in the past as a result of a different factor: the remarkable recent advances in the field of technology that permit previously unimaginable invasions of our privacy rights in the name of national security. For various reasons, I will not discuss the controversies regarding the administration's domestic wiretapping programs. The point I want to stress here is simply that the issues raised by recent breathtaking technological advances pose totally new and different questions, questions with which most judges may have no particular familiarity and which may well require them to master new subjects and develop new skills. Technological knowledge beyond that possessed by the ordinary highly educated citizen may become a necessity for future members of the judiciary.

Let me end where I began. There is nothing fundamentally different about the role of the judge in the twenty-first century, in general or with regard to national security issues. Our job is essentially no different than the role of the judge in the twentieth century—or the nineteenth. And our role with respect to national security cases is essentially no different from our role with regard to any other important or controversial matter—maybe a little more difficult, maybe a little more daunting, maybe a little more perilous, but in the end it is simply a matter

9. *See* HCJ 2056/04 Beit Sourik Vill. Council v. Israel [2004] 43 I.L.M. 1099.

of what good jurists regularly do—weighing, balancing, exercising independent judgment, and safeguarding the Constitution. As in earlier times and as with other issues, our role is to interpret the law to the best of our ability without regard to personal bias or outside pressure. It is to review the actions of the government, particularly as they affect individuals' liberties. Perhaps most important in an era in which civil liberties are inevitably in the greatest

jeopardy, we must view with considerable skepticism any attempt to limit the role of the federal courts or undermine their jurisdiction. As dedicated jurists have repeatedly recognized during previous wars, and as some have recognized during the current crisis, the constitutionally mandated function of the judiciary is at least as important, and, in my view even more important, in times of national emergency than in ordinary times—and that may unfortunately be the case for most, if not all, of the twenty-first century.

(A) UNDER CONSTITUTION

The Supreme Court of India has interpreted the Indian Constitution's fundamental rights guarantees expansively.[10]The Constitution protects "equality before the law" and "equal protection of the laws" under provisions which embody a broad guarantee against arbitrary or irrational state action more generally[11]

Judge, U.S. Court of Appeals for the Ninth Circuit. This publication is a revised text of remarks delivered on April 22, 2006, for a panel on "The Judicial Role in National Security," at a symposium sponsored by the Boston University School of Law on "The Role of the Judge in the Twenty-First Century."

---

10. India Const. pt. III, arts. 12-35; see Pathumma v. State of Kerala, A.I.R. 1978 S.C. 771 (in interpreting fundamental rights provisions, court's approach "should be dynamic rather than static, pragmatic and not pedantic[,] and elastic rather than rigid").
11. India Const. art. 14; see JAIN, supra note 33, at 855-901. Other provisions more specifically prohibit discrimination on the basis of religion, race, caste, sex, or place of birth and guarantee equality of opportunity in public employment. India Const. arts. 15-16. The Constitution also explicitly abolishes and forbids "untouchability" and deems unlawful the enforcement of any disabilities based on untouchability. Id. art. 17.

Indian citizens are guaranteed the rights to speech and expression, peaceable assembly, association, free movement, and residence although Parliament may legislate "reasonable restrictions" on some of these rights in the interests of the "sovereignty and integrity of India", "security of the state", or "public order".[12] As discussed below, the Constitution also authorizes suspension of judicial enforcement of these rights during lawful, formally declared periods of emergency.[13] Specifically in the criminal justice context, the Constitution prohibits ex post facto laws, double jeopardy, and compelled self-incrimination.[14]

Individuals arrested and taken into custody must be provided the basis for arrest "as soon as may be" and produced before a magistrate within 24 hours In its landmark case of

D.K. Basu v. *State of West Bengal,* the Supreme Court extended the Constitution's procedural guarantees further by requiring the police to follow detailed guidelines for arrest and interrogation.[15]

The Constitution also guarantees the right to counsel of the defendant's choice, and the Supreme Court has held that legal assistance must be provided to indigent defendants at government expense, a right that attaches at the first appearance before a magistrate.[16] These guarantees do not apply to laws authorizing preventive detention, which, as discussed below, the Constitution subjects to a more limited set of protections.[17]

---

12. India Const. art. 19(1)(a)-(f); see JAIN, supra note 33, at 1009; India Const. art. 19(2) (qualifications on freedom of speech); India Const. art. 19(3)-(4) (qualifications on freedom of assembly and association).
13. India Const. art. 359; see infra subsection III.B.1.
14. India Const. art. 20; see JAIN, supra note 33, at 1055-77.
15. India Const. art. 22(1)-(2); see also Kelkar's Criminal Procedure, supra note 49, at 74 (Code ofCriminal Procedure §§ 50, 55, and 75 impose higher standard than constitutionally required, since they require grounds of arrest to be communicated "forthwith," or immediately).
16. D.K. Basu *v.* State of West Bengal, A.I.R. 1997 S.C. 610, 623. The National Human Rights Commission has similarly issued extensive guidelines on the rights to be provided at the time of arrest. NAT'L Human Rights Comm'n of India, Guidelines on Arrest, Nov. 22, 1989, http://nhrc.nic.in/Documents/sec-3.pdf.
17. India Const. art. 22(2); see M.H. Hoskot *v.* State of Maharashtra, (1978) 3 S.C.C. 544; Kelkar's Criminal procedure.

While the Constitution does not explicitly protect "due process of law", it does prohibit deprivation of life or personal liberty from any person except according to "procedure established by law", and the Supreme Court has broadly interpreted this guarantee to encompass a range of procedural and substantive rights that approximate the concept of "due process."[18]

Procedures must be "right, just and fair", and not arbitrary, fanciful or oppressive.[19] The Court has held, based on its broad understanding of the right to life and liberty, that the Constitution guarantees the right to privacy[20] and freedom from torture or cruel, inhuman, or degrading treatment.[21]

The Court also has recognized a constitutional right to a fair criminal trial, including among other elements the presumption of innocence; independence, impartiality, and competence of the judge; adjudication at a convenient and non-prejudicial venue; knowledge by the accused of the accusations; trial of the accused and taking of evidence in his or her presence; Judge, U.S. Court of Appeals for the Ninth Circuit. This publication is a revised text of remarks delivered on April 22, 2006, for a panel on "The Judicial Role in National Security," at a symposium sponsored by the Boston University School of Law on "The Role of the Judge in the Twenty-First Century".

(B) UNDER SUBSTANTIVE LAW

121. *Waging or attempting to wage war, or abetting waging of war, against the Government of India.—Whoever wages war against the Government of India, or attempts to wage such war, or abets the waging of such war, shall be punished with death, or imprisonment for life, and shall also be liable to fine.*

18. On preventive detention, see infra subsection III.B.2.
19. *Maneka Gandhi* v. *Union of India*, A.I.R. 1978 S.C. 597; see T.R. Andhyarujina, The Evolution of Duerocess of Law by the Supreme Court, in Supreme but not Infallible: Essays in Honour of the Supreme Court of India (B.N. Kirpal *et. al.*, eds., 2000).
20. *Kartar Singh* v. *State of Punjab*, (1994) 2 S.C.R. 375, 1994 Indlaw SC 525, ¶ 216.
21. *Kharak Singh* v. *State of Uttar Pradesh*, A.I.R. 1963 S.C. 898.

Illustration

A joins an insurrection against the Government of India. A has committed the offence defined in this section.

All States have the same right of self-preservation as their subjects, and State like men have from time immemorial, enacted safeguards for their own preservation and protection At common law the crime of treason was created with that end in view. The fundamental characteristic of high treason consisted in the betrayal of that faith and allegiance which were due from a subject to his sovereign as the supreme head of a State. to constitute this offence no specified number of persons is necessary. So also the manner in which the persons are assembled or armed is also not material to constitute this offence. The true test is the purpose or intention with which the men have assembled. The object of the gathering must be to attain, by force and violence, an object of a general public nature thereby striking directly against the Government's authority.[22]

Ingredients—The following are ingredients of this section—(1) the accused waged or attempted to wage war or abetted the waging of war; and (2) that such war was against the Government of India.

Waging War—Any person taking part in organised armed attack on the consitutional authorities and the object of attack being subversion of Government and the establishments of another in its place would be guilty of the offence of waging war.[23] This offence may be committed by citizens or foreigners. Every citizen is free to have his own political theory and also to propagate and work for its etablishment so long as he does not seek to do so by force or

violence. To try to work out a change by peaceful means in the political system or the kind of a Government does not amount to waging war.[24] But if the accused with the object of overthrowing the Government recruits people and punishes those who refuse to join, he would be guilty of waging war.

---

22. Magan Lal, A.I.R. 1946, Nag. 126.
23. In re Umayyathantagatu Puthen Veetikundi khader v. Emperor, 23 Cr,L,J. 203
24. *R. Basu Nair* v. *T.C. State*, A.I.R. 1955 T.C. 33.

In *Maganlal Radhakrishan* v. *Emperor*,[25] the following characteristics of this offence were pointed out :

(1) No specific number of persons is necessary to constitute this offence;
(2) The number of persons concerned and the manner in which they are equipped is immaterial;
(3) The true criterion is "*Quo Animo*" did the gathering assemble ?
(4) The object of the gathering must be to attain by force and violence an object of a general public nature thereby striking directly against the King's authority.
(5) There is no distinction between principal and accessory and everyone who takes part in the unlawful act incurs the same guilt.

Waging war means waging war in the manner usual in war. In order to support a conviction under this section it would not be enough to show that the persons charged have connived to obtain possession of an armory and have when called upon to surrender it, used the rifles and ammunition so obtained against the State troops. It must also be shown that the seizure of the armory was part and parcel of a planned operation and that their intention in resisting the troops of the State was to overwhelm and defeat the troops and then to go on and crush any further opposition with which they might meet until either the leaders of the movement succeed in obtaining possession of the machinery of Government or until those in possession of it yielded to the demands of their leaders.[26] A deliberate and organised attack upon the crown force could amount to a waging of war if the object of the insurgents was by armed force and vilence to overcome the servants of the Crown and prevent the general collection of capitation tax.[27]

Abets the waging of war—Abetment of waging war is made a special offence. It is not essential that as a result of the abetment the war should in face be waged. Although the

25. A.I.R. 1946 Nag. 126.
26. *Mir Hasan Khan* v. *State,* A.I.R. 1951 Pat, 60.
27. *Aung Hala* v. *Emperor,* A.I.R. 1931 Rang. 235 at p. 239.

general law relating to abetment has made a distinction for purposes of punishment between the abetment which has successed and the abetment which has failed, this section makes no distinction between the two. There is also no distinction between the principal and accessory, and all who take part in the unlawful act incur the same liability.[28]

So long as a man only tries to inflame feeling, to excite a state of mind, he is not guilty of anything more than sedition. One is guilty of instigating and thereby abetting the waging of war only when he definitely and clearly incites to action.[29] For instance, in *Ganesh D. Savarkar*,[30] the accused published a book of poems wherein a spirit of blood-thirstiness and murderous eagerness directed against the Government and "white" rulers ran through the poems; the urgency of taking up the sword was conveyed in unambiguous language, and an appeal of blood-thirsty incitement was made to the people to take up the sword, form secret societies, and adopt guerilla warfare for the purpose of rooting out the demon of foreign rule. It was held that the poems conveyed to the readers an instigation to wage war and the accused was gulty of abetting the waging of war.

121-A. *Conspiracy to commit offences punishable by section 121.*—Whoever within or without India comspires to commit any of the offences punishable by section 121, or conspires to overawe, by means of criminal force or the show of criminal force, the Central Government or any State government, shall be punished with imprisonment for life, or with imprisonment of either description which may extend to ten years, and shall also be liable to fine.

Explanation.—To constitute a conspiracy under this section, it is not necessary that any act or illegal omission shall take place in pursuance thereof.

Comment

Ingredients.—This section deals with two kinds of conspiracies :

28. Magan Lal, A.I.R. 1946 Nag. 126.
29. Ganesh D. Saverker, (1909) 12 Bom . L.R. 105.
30. *Ibid.*

(1) Conspiring within or without India to commit any of the offences punishable by section 121.
(2) Conspiring to overawe by means of criminal force, or the show of criminal force the Central Government or any State Government.

The words 'conspires to overawe, by means of criminal force the show of criminal force, the Central Government, or any State Government' in this section clearly embrace not merely a conspiracy to raise a general insurrection, but also a conspiracy to overawe the Central Government or any State Government by the organisation of a serious riot or a large and tumultuous unlawful assembly.[31] The word 'overawe' means something more than the creation of apprehension or alarm or fear. It connotes the creation of a situation in which the members of the Central or State Government feel themselves compelled to choose between yielding to force or exposing themselves or members of the public to a very serious danger. It is not necessary that the danger should be a danger of assassination or of bodily injury to themselves. The danger might well be a danger of public property or to the safety of members of the general public.[32] Any conspiracy to change the form of Government, even though it may constitute an offence under some other section of the Code, is not an offence under some other section of the Code, is not an offence under this section, unless it is a conspiracy to overawe such Government by means of criminal force, or show of criminal force.[33]

The expression "conspiring to overawe government by means of criminal force or the show of criminal force" was interpreted by the Kerala High Court in *Arbind* v. *State*.[34] The Court observed that the word "overawe" means something more than the mere creation of apprehension, alarm or fear. It connotes the creation of a situation in which the government feels itself compelled to choose between yielding to force or exposing itself or members of the public to a very serious

31. Ramanand, (1950) 30 Pat. 152.
32. Ibid., *Mir Hasan Khan* v. *Emperor*, A.I.R. 1951 Pat. 61.
33. Jhavala, (1933) 55 All. 1040.
34. 1983 Cr. L. J. 1259 (Ker).

danger. Therefore, the slogan that the government can be changed through the force, does not mean that a criminal conspiracy has taken place to change the government through force.

122. *Collecting arms, etc. with intention of waging war against the Government of India*—Whoever collects men, arms or ammunition or otherwise prepares to wage war with the intention of either waging or being prepared to wage war against the Government of India, shall be punished with imprisonment for life or imprisonment of either description for a term not exceeding ten years, and shall also be liable to fine.

123. *Conceaing with intent to facilitate design to wage war.*—Whoever, by any act, or by any illegal omission, conceals the existence of a design to wage war against the Government of India, intending by such concealment to facilitate, or knowing it to be likely that such concealment will facilitate, the waging of such war, shall be punished with imprisonment of either description for a term which may extend to ten years, and shall also be liable to fine.

124. *Assaulting President, Governor, etc. with intent to compel or restrain exercise of any lawful power.*— Whoever, with the intention of inducing or compelling the President of India, or the Governor of any State, to exercise or refrain from exercising in any manner any of the lawful powers of such President or Governor.

Assaults of wrongfully restrains, or attempts wrongfully to restrain, or overawes, by means of criminal force or the show of criminal force, or attempts so to overawe, such President or Governor.

124-A. *Sedition.*—Whoever by words, either spoken or written, or by signs, or by visible representation, or otherwise, bring into hatered or contempt, or excites or attempts to excite disaffection towards the government established by law in India, shall be punished with imprisonment for life, to which fine may be added, or with imprisonment which may extend to three years, to which fine may be added, or with fine.

Explanation 1.—The expression "disaffection" includes disloyalty and all feelings of enmity.

Explanation 2.—Comments expressing disapprobation of the measures of the Government with a view to obtain their alteration by lawful means, without exciting or attempting to excite hatred, contempt or disaffection, do not constitute an offence under this section.

Explanation 3—Comments expressing disapprobation of the administrative or other action of the Government without exciting or attempting to excite hatred, contempt or disaffection, do not constitute an offence under this section.

Comment

Ingredients.—The following are two essentials of sedition:

(1) Bringing or attempting to bring into hatred or contempt or exciting or attempting to excite disaffection towards the Government of India.

(2) Such act or attempt may be done (i) by words, either spoken or written, or (ii) signs, or (iii) visible representation.

History.—Section 124-A was added to the Code in 1870 and at that time it was not in the present form. This section was amended in 1891 and it was not in the present form. During 1870 to 1898 the meaning of the word 'disaffection' was discussed in a number of cases. In *Queen* v. *Jogendra Chandra Bose*,[35] C.J. Petheram explained 'disaffection' to mean as a feeling contrary to affection; in other words dislike or hatred. Disprobation means simply disapproval. If a person uses either spoken or written words calculated to create in the minds of the person to whom they are addressed a disposition not to obey the lawful authority of the government, or to subvert or resist the authority, if and when the occasion should arise and if he does so with the intention of creating such disposition, among his hearers or readers, they will be guilty under the section. In *Queen* v. *Balgangadhar Tilak*,[36] Strachey, J., agreed with the above ruling, holding that a man must not make or try to make other feel enmity of any kind towards the Government. Amount and intensity of disaffection is absolutely immaterial except perhaps in deaing with the question of punishment.

35. I.L.R. 19 Cal 35.
36. I.L.R. 22 Bom. 112.

These decisions were quoted with approval by Allahabad High Court in *Q.E.* v. *Ambika Prasad.*[37] The offence of sedition has been known in England for centuries. Every State whatever its form of government has to be armed with the power to punish those who by their conduct jeopardise the safety or disseminate such feelings of disloyalty as have the tendency to lead the disruption of the State or breach of public order.

In *Niharendra Dutta Majumdar,*[38] Sir Maurice Gawyer said, The first fundamental duty of every government is the preservation of order, since order is the condition precedent to all civilization and advance of human happiness. This duty has no doubt been sometimes performed in such a way as to make the remedy worse than disease, butit does not cease to be a matter of obligation because some on whom the duty rests have performed it well. It is the answer of the State to those who for the purpose of attacking or subverting it try to disturb its tranquility to create public disturbance or to promote disorder or who incite others to do so. Words, deeds and writings constitute sedition if they have this intention or this tendency. Public disorder or the reasonable anticipation or likelihood of public disorder is thus the gist of the offence. The acts or words complained of must either incite to disorder or must be such as to satisfy reasonable men that that is their intention or tendency."

The above statement of law was not approved by their Lordships of the Privy Council in the case of *Emperor* v. *Sada Shiv Narayan,*[39] and they held that the language of section 124-A or of the rules under which the case was tried not justify the statement of law as made by the C.J. The expression "excite did disaffection" did not include "excite disorder". The dicta in *Tilak* and *Bensant's* case was approved.

After coming into force of the Constitution the validity of this section was considered by the Supreme Court in *Ramesh Thapart*[40] and *Brij Bhusan's*[41] cases. As a result of these two decisions Constitution First Amendment Act was passed in

37. I.L.R. 20 All. 55.
38. A.I.R 1942 F.C. 22 at 26.
39. A.I.R 1943 P.C. 82.
40. A.I.R. 1950 S.C. 124.
41. A.I.R. 1950 S.C. 129.

1951. Thereafter, in *Kedar Nath Singh*,[42] case the validity of this section was again questioned on the ground of the provisions of this section being in violation of freedom of speech and expression. The plea was negatived by the court and the sectio was held to be constitutional. The explanation to the section makes it clear that criticism of public measures or comment on Government action, however strongly worded, within reasonable limits and consistent with the fundamental right of freedom of speech and expression is not affected. It is only when the words have the pernicious tendency or intention of creating public disorder or disturbance of law and order that the provisions of the section are attached.

Any act within the meaning of section 124-A which has the effect of subverting the government by bringing that government into contempt or hatred or creating disaffection against it would be within the penal statute because the feeling of disloyalty to the government established by law or enmity to it imports the idea of tendency to public disorder by the use of actual violence or incitement to offence.

In other words, any written or spoken words, etc. which have implicit in them the idea of subverting government by violent means which are compendiously included within the term 'revolution' have been made penal by the section in question.

Exciting disaffection.—To constitute an offence under this section it is not necessary that one should excite or attempt to excite mutiny or rebellion or any kind of actual disturbance, it would be sufficient that one tries to excite feeling of hatred or contempt towards the government.[43] In a case the Federal Court has opined that the essence of the offence of sedition is incitement to violence; mere abusive words are not enough and that "public disorder or the reasonable anticipation or likelihood of public disorder is the gist of the offence." The acts or words complained of must either incite to disorder or must be such as to satisfy reasonable men that it is their intention or tendency.[44] But in a later case this view was overruled by the

42. A.I.R. 1962 S.C. 955.
43. *Balgangadhar Tilak* (1867) 22 Bom. 112.
44. *Niharendra Dutta Majumdar*, (1942) F.C.R 38.

Privy Council.[45] The offence under this section does not require an intention to incite violence of public disorder.[46] The essence of the offence under this section consists in the intention with which the language is used. The intention of a speaker, writer or publisher may be inferred from the particular speech, article or letter. The intention is gathered from the articles. The requisite intention cannot be attributed to a person if he was not aware of the contents of the seditious publication.[47]

In *B.G. Tilak's* case,[48] it was pointed out that if, on reading the articles or speeches, the reasonable, natural and probable effect of the articles or speeches on the minds of those who read them or to whom they were addressed appears to be that feelings of hatred, contempt or disaffection, would be excited towards the government, the offence is committed. But in considering the intention of the accused, and the effect his writings are likely to produce, it is necessary to take into consideration the state of the country and of the public mind at the date or publication.[49] Not only the time but the place, the circumstances and the occasion of publication are material. Regard must also be had to the character and description of that part of the public who are expected to read the words.[50] To sum up, the time, the place, the circumstances and the occasion of publicatin all are important.

Attempt.—A Person may be charged not only with exciting but also with attempting to excite and both successful and unsuccessful attempts to excite disaffection were placed on the same footing. So even if a person had only tried to excite the feeling he could be convicted.[51] In *Surendra Narayan Adicharya,*[52] it was held that sending through the post of a packet containing a copy of a manuscript of a seditious publication with a covering letter requesting the addressee to circulate it to others, when the same was intercepted by another person and never

45. *Sadashiv Narayan, (1947) 49 Bom. L.R. 526.*
46. *Ram Nnandan* v. *State, A.I.R. 1959 All. 101.*
47. *Chunnilal, (1931) 12 Lah. 483.*
48. I.L.R. 22 Bom. 112.
49. Per Lord Fitzgerald in *Sulivan, 11 Cox. 50 at p. 59.*
50. *Satendra Nath Majumdar* v. Emp., A.I.R. 1931 Cal. 337.
51. *B.G. Tilak (1867) I.L.R. 22 Bom. 112.*
52. *(1911) 39 Cal. 522.*

reached the addressee, constitutes an attempt to commit an offence under this section.

Government established by law in India.—The expression "Government established by law in India" includes the executive power in action and does not mean merely the constitutional framework. It includes the State Government as well as the Central Government.[53] Government does not mean the person or persons for the time being. It means the person or persons collectively, in succession, who are authorised to administer Government for the time being. One particular set of persons may be open to objection, and to assail them and to attack them and excite hatred against them is not necessarily exciting hatred against the government because they are only individuals and are not representatives of that abstract conception which is Government.[54] To suggest a change in the form of Government cannot be said to be causing disaffection towards the Government established by law or to bring present Government into hatred or contempt.[55] A general criticism of certain officers cannot be deemed to be a criticism of Government established by law in India. Similarly an attempt to remove from power the ministers in office in any State or any agitation for the repeal of an Act of Parliament cannot fall under the section if no unlawful means are employed.[56]

Various Forms of Excitement.—Disaffection may be excited in a number of ways. Writing of any kind, poem, drama, story, novel or essays may be used for the puspose of exciting disaffection. But seditious writing, if it remains in the hands of the author or unpubished does not constitute this offence because publication of some kind is necessary.[57] Sending of seditious matter by post addressed to someone not by name but by designation as the representative of a large body (such as of students or teachers) amounts to publication if it is opened by anybody.[58]

53. Kshiteesh Chandra Roy *v.* Emp. A.I.R. 1932 Cal. 547.
54. Bhaskar, (1906) 8 Bom. L.R. 421
55. Arjun Arora *v.* Emp. A.I.R. 1937 All. 295.
56. Dhirendra Nath Sen (1938). 2 Cal. 672.
57. Foster 198.
58. Suresh Chandra Sanyal, (1912) 39 Cal. 606.

Not only the author of seditious matter but whosoever uses in any way words or printed matter for the purpose of exciting feelings of disaffection to the Government is liable under this section.[59] The gravamen of the offence consists in the publication and not in the authorship of the seditious matter.

The printer, the publisher, the editor or the owner or proprietor of the press of a seditious publication is also liable like the author unless he proves that he was absent and was not aware of the contents of the paper beyond the fact that he was the declared proprietor and keeper of the press.[60] In order to escape liability such printer or publisher etc. must prove lack of knowledge on his part. Sedition does not necessarily consist of written matter; it may be evidenced by a woodcut or engraving of any kind[61] or by exhibition of flags.

Explanation 1.—Explanation 1 makes it clear that the word "disaffection" includes disloyality and all feelings of enmity. Disaffection means anything which is 'contrary to affection'. It is very much nearer to 'hatred or dislike'. To urge people to rise against the Government is tantamount to trying to excite feelings of disloyalty in their minds.[62] 'Feelings of enmity' includes ill-will, hostility, feelings of dislike amounting to enmity, and anything of a similar class or character which can be summarised under the expression 'disloyalty' and 'feelings of enmity'.[63]

Explanation 2 and 3.—This section has taken care to indicate clearly that strong words used to express disapprobation of the measures of government with a view to their improvements or alternatively lawful means would not come within the section. Similarly, comments however strongly worded expressing disapprobation of actions of government without inciting those feelings which generate the inclination to cause public disorder by acts of violence would not be penal.

In other words, disloyalty to government established by law is not the same thing as commenting in strong-terms upon mesures or acts of government or its agencies so as to

59. B.G. Tilak, (1867) I.L.R. 22 Bom. 112.
60. Chunni, *et. al.* (1931) 12 Lah. 483.
61. Alexander, M. Sullivan, (1868) 11 Cox. 44 at 51.
62. Per Fawcent, J. in Phillip, S. Pratt, 1927 (Unrep, Bom.).
63. B.G. Tilak, (1867) 22 Bom. 112.

ameliorate the conditions of the peple or to secure cancellation or alteration of those acts or measures by lawful means, that is to say, "without exciting those feelings of enmity and disloyalty which imply excitement to public disorder or use of violence."

Disapprobation.—Disapprobation means disapproval. One may disapprove of man's sentiments or actions and yet he may like him.[64]

Liability of editor's etc.—The editor of a paper will be liable for unsigned seditious letters appearing in the newspaper.[65] Where extracts of foreigh newspapers are published as a news item, it may attract the provisions of this section if such writings are seditious libels.[66] Republication of seditious articles from another newspaper, one of which only was field as an exhibit by the prosecution and used in the case against the editor of that paper on his trial for sedition, is not a report of the Court of Justice, and is, therefore, punishable.[67]

Dramatic Performance.—Any dramatic performance likely to excite feelings of disaffection to the Government may be prohibited by the Government and persons taking part in any such performance may be punished.

125. *Waging was against any Asiatic power in aliance with the Government of India.*—Whoever wages war against the government of any Asiatic power in alliance or at peace with the Government of India or attempts to wage such war, or abets the waging of such war, shall be punished with improsonment for life, to which fine may be added, or with improsonment of either description for a term which may extend to seven years, to which fine may be added, or with fine.

126. *Committing depredation on territories of power at peace with the Government of India.*—Whoever commits depredation, or makes preparation to commit depredation, on the territories of any power in alliance or at peace with the Government of India, shall be punished with imprisonment of either description for a term which may extend to seven years, and shal also be liable to fine and to forfeiture of any property used or intended to be

64. B.G. Tilak, (1867) 22 Bom. 112.
65. Apurba Krishna Bose (1907) 35 Cal. 141.
66. Alexender, M. Sullivan, (1868) 11 Cox. 44.
67. Apurba Krishna Bose, (1907) 35 Cal. 141.

used in committing such depredation, or acquired by such depredation.

128. *Pubic servant voluntarily allowing prisoner of State or of war to escape.*—Whoever, being a public servant and having the custody of any State prisoner or prisoners of war, voluntarily allows such prisoner to escape from any place in which such prisoner is confined, shall be punished with imprisonment for life, or imprisonment of either description for a term which may extend to ten years, and shall also be liable to fine.

State Prisoner.—State prisoner is a prisoner whose confinement is necessary in order to preserve the security of India from foreign hostility or from internal commotion, and who has been confined by the order of the Government of India.

Prisoner of War.—Prisoner of war is an enemy taken in arms who is according to the law of civilised war to be treated as prisoner till the termination of hostilities, and not slain.

Comment

This section deals with the Government servant, who has the custody of the prisoner, acting negligently in allowing prisoner to escape.

Ingredients.—The following are ingredients of this section:

1. The accused must be a public servant;
2. The accused had in his custody a State prisoner to escape from place where he was confined.
3. The accused negligently allowed such a prisoner to escape from place where he was confined.

130. *Aiding escape of rescuing or harbouring such prisoner.*—Whoever, knowingly aids or assists any State prisoner or prisoner of war in escaping from lawful custody, or rescues or attempts to rescue any such prisoner, or harbours or conceals any such prisoner who has escaped from lawful custody, or offers or attempts to offer any resistance to the recapture of such prisoner, shal be punished with imprisonment for life, or with imprisonment of either such prisoner, shal be punished with imprisonment for life, or with imprisonment of either description for a term which may extend to ten years, and shall also be liable to fine.

Explanation.— A State prisoner or prisoner of war, who is permitted to be at arge on his parole within certain limits in India, is said to escape from lawful custody if he goes beyond the limits within which he is allowed to be at large.

Comment

Ingredients.—The following are ingredients of this section:

1. The State prisoner or the prisoner of war in question must be in lawful custody.
2. The accused aided or assisted the escape of such prisoner;
3. The accused must have done so knowingly;
4. The accused rescued or attempted to rescue any such prisoner;
5. He must have harboured or concealed any such prisoner; or
6. He must have resisted or attempted to resist the recapture of such prisoner.

The accused must know that the person assisted is a State prisoner or a prisoner of war. The use of the word 'whoever' in this section implies that the accused need not be a Government servant.

(C) UNDER PROCEDURAL LAW

The Constitution requires pretrial detention to be as short as possible, and a number of statutory provisions implement this principle.[68] Under the Code of Criminal Procedure, detention in police custody beyond the constitutional limit of 24 hours must be authorized by a magistrate. When the accused is initially produced before the magistrate, the magistrate must release the accused on bail unless it "appears that the investigation cannot be completed" within 24 hours and the accusation is well-founded—in which case the accused may be

68. The Supreme Court has held that unjust or harsh bail conditions are unconstitutional and has raised concerns about unreasonable denial of bail where it has not been available as of right. *Babu Singh* v. *State of Uttar Pradesh*, A.I.R. 1978 S.C. 527.

remanded to police custody for up to 15 days, although in principle remand is disfavored.[69]

Bail is meant to be the rule and continued detention the exception.[70] For minor, so-called "bailable" offenses, release on bail is available as of right, while for most serious or "non-bailable" offenses, the accused may be released on bail at the discretion of the court.[71] Under the Criminal Procedure Code, Parliament may designate certain offenses as "bailable"; all other offenses are "non-bailable." Most serious offenses carrying potential prison sentences of at least three years are non-bailable. Id. at 270-74, 279-80; India Code Crim. Proc. §§ 436-37. If there are "reasonable grounds" for believing the accused is guilty of an offense punishable by death or life imprisonment, or if the accused's criminal history meets certain statutory criteria, bail may not be granted unless the accused is female, sick or infirm, or under age sixteen. Kelkar's Criminal Procedure, supra note 49, at 283-85. The factors the court must consider in deciding whether to grant bail include the severity of the charged offense and potential punishment; the alleged factual circumstances and the nature of the evidence supporting the charge; the risk of flight; the risk of witness tampering; the ability of the accused to prepare their defense and access counsel; the health, age, sex, and criminal history of the accused; and the likelihood that the defendant might pose a danger to public safety. Id. If denied by the lower courts, bail may be sought from the High Court.Before ordering remand to police custody, the magistrate must record the reasons for continued detention. Upon finding "adequate grounds"to do so, the magistrate may order detention beyond the fifteen day period for up to 60 days, or in a case involving a potential prison

69. India Code Crim. Proc. §§ 57, 167; see Kelkar's Criminal Procedure. In practice, remand to police custody "is routine" except for individuals who can afford to pay for counsel to appear before the magistrate and for bail itself. Human rights advocates have also documented periods of police custody beyond what is legally permissible. See Human Rights Watch, Prison Conditions in India 7-8 (1991) [hereinafter HRW, Prison Conditions In India].

70. Kelkar's Criminal Procedure.

71. Under Criminal Procedure Code. India Code Crim. Proc. § 439; Kelkar's Criminal Procedure.

sentence of at least 10 years or the death penalty, for up to 90 days. This extended period of detention, however, must take place in judicial custody, rather than police custody.[72] The police must file with the magistrate a "charge sheet" setting forth the particulars of their allegations "without unnecessary delay."[73] If the charge sheet is not filed upon expiration of the 60- or 90-day extended detention period, the individual must be released on bail, regardless of the seriousness of the offense alleged.[74] However, if the charge sheet is filed before that period expires, and the magistrate decides to charge the accused, the decision to grant bail must be determined based on the contents of the charge sheet. The investigation may continue even after filing of the charge sheet, which may subsequently be amended. Once the accused actually has been charged by the court, the court may not drop the charges, but rather must either convict or acquit the accused.[75] Indian law sharply limits the use of statements given to the police or while in police custody. Under the Indian Evidence Act, confessions made to police officers are inadmissible as substantive evidence against the accused, and confessions made to others while in police custody must be made in the immediate presence of a magistrate to be admissible.[76] More generally, the Code of Criminal Procedure prohibits statements made to the police in the course of an investigation by any person, if reduced to writing, to be signed by the individual or used for any purpose during proceedings concerning the offense under investigation, except to impeach that person's subsequent testimony.[77] These rules, which date to the colonial period, are intended to reduce the incentive for police to engage in torture and other coercive interrogation practices, in recognition that torture by the Indian police has

72. India Code Crim. Proc. § 167(2), (4); Kelkar's Criminal Procedure.
73. India Code Crim. Proc. § 173(2).
74. Kelkar's Criminal Procedure, supra note 49, at 165-66, 274-75; see Matabar Parida v. State of Orissa, (1975) 2 S.C.C. 220 ("If it is not possible to complete the investigation within a period of 60 days (or 90 days, as the case may be), then even in serious and ghastly types of crimes the accused will be entitled to release on bail").
75. Kelkar's Criminal Procedure.
76. *Ibid.*
77. India Code Crim. Proc. § 162; Kelkar's Criminal Procedure.

been a longstanding problem.[78] However, these limitations are not unqualified. If part of a confession or other statement given to the police leads to the discovery of admissible evidence, that portion of the statement may be admitted as corroborative evidence.[79]

(D) UNDER OTHER SPECIAL LAWS— POTA, TADA, NSA, COFEPOSA etc.

History of Anti-terrorism Laws in India

Terrorism has immensely affected India. The reasons for terrorism in India may vary vastly from religious to geographical to caste to history. The Indian Supreme Court took a note of it in *Kartar Singh v. State of Punjab [1994] 3 SCC 569,* where it observed that the country has been in the firm grip of spiraling terrorist violence and is caught between deadly pangs of disruptive activities. Apart from many skirmishes in various parts of the country, there were countless serious and horrendous events engulfing many cities with blood-bath, firing, looting, mad killing even without sparing women and children and reducing those areas into a graveyard, which brutal atrocities have rocked and shocked the whole nation decisively rejected that proposal, but instead proposed that the rule be strengthened in some respects, noting that the use of such confessions by the police would lead to "gross abuse of power" and a strong likelihood that innocent people would be coerced into making confessions. *Andrew H.L. Fraser et. al., Report of the Indian Police Commission and Resolution of the Government of India,* 1902-03, p. 163 (1905); see Bayley, (discussing Fraser Commission's conclusion that police services were insufficiently trained and supervised and regarded by public as corrupt and oppressive).

78. Ved Marwah, A Citizen Friendly Force?, Seminar, Nov. 1999, at 14, available at http://www.indiaseminar. com/1999/483/483%20ved%20marwah.htm (rule against admissibility originated because "torture, in order to extract confessions was so endemic in our land"). These longstanding concerns about the police were sufficiently apparent during the colonial period that when considering in the 1900s whether to permit confessions to police officers to be admissible, the Fraser Commission not only.
79. Indian Evidence Act § 27.

Deplorably, determined youths lured by hard-core criminals and underground extremists and attracted by the ideology of terrorism are indulging in committing serious crimes against the humanity. Anti-terrorism laws in India have always been a subject of much controversy. One of the arguments is that these laws stand in the way of fundamental rights of citizens guaranteed by Part III of the Constitution. The anti-terrorist laws have been enacted before by the legislature and upheld by the judiciary though not without reluctance. The intention was to enact these statutes and bring them in force till the situation improves. The intention was not to make these drastic measures a permanent feature of law of the land. But because of continuing terrorist activities, the statutes have been reintroduced with requisite modifications. At present, the legislations in force to check terrorism in India are the National Security Act, 1980 and the Unlawful Activities (Prevention) Act, 1967. There have been other anti-terrorism laws in force in this country a different points in time. Earlier, the following laws had been in force to counter and curb terrorism. The first law made in independent India to deal with terrorism and terrorist activities that came into force on 30 Dec. 1967 was

The Unlawful Activities (Prevention) Act 1967

The UAPA was designed to deal with associations and activities that questioned the territorial integrity of India. When the Bill was debated in Parliament, leaders, and cutting across party affiliation, insisted that its ambit be so limited that the right to association remained unaffected and that the executive did not expose political parties to intrusion. So, the ambit of the Act was strictly limited to meeting the challenge to the territorial integrity of India. The Act was a self-contained code of provisions for declaring secessionist associations as unlawful, adjudication by a tribunal, control of funds and places of work of unlawful associations, penalties for their members etc. The Act has all along been worked holistically as such and is completely within the purview of the central list in the 7th Schedule of the Constitution.

Terrorist and Disruptive Activities (Prevention) Act, 1987 (TADA)

The second major act came into force on 3 September 1987 was The Terrorist & Disruptive Activities (Prevention) Act 1987 this act had much more stringent provisions then the UAPA and it was specifically designed to deal with terrorist activities in India. When TADA was enacted it came to be challenged before the Apex Court of the country as being unconstitutional. The Supreme Court of India upheld its constitutional validity on the assumption that those entrusted with such draconic statutory powers would act in good faith and for the public good in the case of Kartar Singh vs State of Punjab (1994) 3 SCC 569. However, there were many instances of misuse of power for collateral purposes. The rigorous provisions contained in the statute came to be abused in the hands of law enforcement officials. TADA lapsed in 1995. Other major Anti-terrorist law in India is The Maharashtra Control of Organised Crime Act, 1999 which was enforced on 24th April 1999. This law was specifically made to deal with rising organized crime in Maharashtra and specially in Mumbai due to the underworld. For instance, the definition of a terrorist act is far more stretchable in MCOCA than under POTA. For, POTA did not take note of organised crime as such while MCOCA not only mentions that but, what is more, includes 'promotion of insurgency' as a terrorist act. Again, the onus to prove a person guilty under POTA lies on the prosecution while under the Maharashtra law a person is presumed guilty unless he is able to prove his innocence. MCOCA does not stipulate prosecution of police officers found guilty of its misuse. But POTA did.

(E) POTA

Analysis of Some Important Sections of Pota

In the case of *People's Union for Civil Liberties* v. *Union of India (UOI)*[80] the constitutional validity of the Prevention of Terrorism Act, 2002 was discussed. The court said that the Parliament possesses power under Article 248 and entry 97 of list I of the Seventh Schedule of the Constitution of India to

80. (2004) 9 SCC 580.

legislate the Act. Need for the Act is a matter of policy and the court cannot go into the same. Once legislation is passed, the Govt. has an obligation to exercise all available options to prevent terrorism within the bounds of the constitution. Mere possibility of abuse cannot be a ground for denying the vesting of powers or for declaring a statute unconstitutionally. Court upheld the constitutional validity of the various provisions of the Act.

1. *Section 3(1)—Defining Terrorist Act*

(1) Whoever,—

(a) with intent to threaten the unity, integrity, security or sovereignty of India or to strike terror in the people or any section of the people does any act or thing by using bombs, dynamite or other explosive substances or inflammable substances or firearms or other lethal weapons or poisons or noxious gases or other chemicals or by any other substances (whether biological or otherwise) of a hazardous nature or by any other means whatsoever, in such a manner as to cause, or likely to cause, death of, or injuries to any person or persons or loss of, or damage to, or destruction of, property or disruption of any supplies or services essential to the life of the community or causes damage or destruction of any property or equipment used or intended to be used for the defense of India or in connection with any other purposes of the Government of India, any State Government or any of their agencies, or detains any person and threatens to kill or injure such person in order to compel the Government or any other person to do or abstain from doing any act;

(b) is or continues to be a member of an association declared unlawful under the Unlawful Activities (Prevention) Act, 1967 (37 of 1967), or voluntarily does an act aiding or promoting in any manner the objects of such association and in either case is in possession of any unlicensed firearms, ammunition, explosive or other instrument or substance capable of causing mass destruction and commits any act resulting in loss of human life or grievous injury to any person or causes significant damage to any property, commits a terrorist act.

Explanation.—For the purposes of this sub-section, "a terrorist act" shall include the act of raising funds intended for the purpose of terrorism.

Case Law—Devender Pal Singh v. *State of N.C.T. of Delhi*,[81] In a case where 9 person had died and several other injured on account of perpetrated acts, The court said that such terrorist who have no respect for human life and people are killed due to their mindless killing. So any compassion to such person would frustrate the purpose of enactment of Tada and would amount to misplaced and unwarranted sympathy. Thus they should be given death sentence.

Argument against—Trade union activity would be affected because whoever disrupts essential supplies would be covered under POTA.

Argument in favour—At least our trade union leaders are nationalist leaders. Nobody has ever suggested that when our trade union leaders go on strike, they threaten the unity, integrity, security and sovereignty of India.

2. Section 4—Possession of Certain Unauthorized Arms

Where any person is in unauthorized possession of any—

(a) arms or ammunition specified in columns (2) and (3) of Category I or Category III (a) of Schedule I to the Arms Rules, 1962, in a notified area,

(b) bombs, dynamite or hazardous explosive substances or other lethal weapons capable of mass destruction or biological or chemical substances of warfare in any area, whether notified or not, he shall be guilty of terrorist act notwithstanding anything contained in

81. 2002 (1) SC (Cr.) 209.

any other law for the time being in force, and be punishable with imprisonment for a term which may extend to imprisonment for life or with fine which may extend to rupees ten lakh or with both.

Explanation.—In this section, "notified area" means such area as the State Government may, by notification in the Official Gazette, specify.

Case Law—Sanjay Dutt v. *State through C.B.I.*[82] The expression possession though that of section 5 of Tada has been stated to mean a conscious possession introducing thereby involvement of a mental element, i.e. conscious possession and not mere custody without awareness of nature of such possession and as regards unauthorized means and regards without any authority of law.

Argument against—That an offence coming under the Arms Act has been brought under POTA, irrespective of whether a person carrying such arms has any nexus with a terrorist.

Argument in favour—Firstly the section clearly says that any person who has unauthorized possession of arms that is does not possess a proper license for the arms. This section is only making the law stringent by stating that anybody who possesses arms should also possess proper license from the proper authority.

Secondly.it also states weapons should be capable of mass destruction or biological or chemical substances of warfare so why would any person without any reason possess such kind of weapons and that to unauthorized

3. *Section 7—Powers of investigating officers and appeal against order of Designated Authority*

(1) If an officer (not below the rank of Superintendent of Police) investigating an offence committed under this Act, has reason to believe that any property in relation to which an investigation is being conducted, represents proceeds of terrorism, he shall, with the prior approval in writing of the

82. 1994 SCC 410.

Director General of the Police of the State in which such property is situated, make an order seizing such property and where it is not practicable to seize such property, make an order of attachment directing that such property shall not be transferred or otherwise dealt with except with the prior permission of the officer making such order, or of the Designated Authority before whom the properties seized or attached are produced and a copy of such order shall be served on the person concerned.

(2) For the removal of doubts, it is hereby provided that where an organization is declared as a terrorist organization under this Act and the investigating officer has reason to believe that any person has custody of any property which is being used or is intended to be used for the purpose of such terrorist organization, he may, by an order in writing, seize or attach such property.

(3) The investigating officer shall duly inform the Designated Authority within forty-eight hours of the seizure or attachment of such property.

(4) It shall be open to the Designated Authority before whom the seized or attached properties are produced either to confirm or revoke the order of attachment so issued:

Provided that an opportunity of making a representation by the person whose property is being attached shall be given.

(5) In the case of immovable property attached by the investigating officer, it shall be deemed to have been produced before the Designated Authority, when the investigating officer notifies his report and places it at the disposal of the Designated Authority.

(6) The investigating officer may seize and detain any cash to which this Chapter applies if he has reasonable grounds for suspecting that—

(a) it is intended to be used for the purposes of terrorism;

(b) it forms the whole or part of the resources of an organization declared as terrorist organization under this Act:

Provided that the cash seized under this sub-section by the

investigating officer shall be released not later than the period of forty-eight hours beginning with the time when it is seized unless the matter involving the cash is before the Designated Authority and such Authority passes an order allowing its retention beyond forty-eight hours.

Explanation.—For the purposes of this sub-section, "cash" means—

(a) coins and notes in any currency;
(b) postal orders;
(c) traveller's cheques;
(d) banker's drafts; and
(e) such other monetary instruments as the Central Government or, as the case may be, the State Government may specify by an order made in writing.

(7) Any person aggrieved by an order made by the Designated Authority may prefer an appeal to the Special Court and the Special Court may either confirm the order of attachment of property or seizure so made or revoke such order and release the property.

Argument against—The petition articulates the fear that permitting a police officer to act on the basis of his belief will be "draconian and unguided".

Argument in favour—Case Law—*T.T. Anthony* v. *State of Kerala.*[83] This plenary power of police to investigate a cognizable offence is not unlimited. It is subject to certain limitations such as if no cognizable offence is disclosed and still more if no offence of any kind is disclosed the police would have no authority to undertake an investigation.

4. *Section 21—Offence relating to support given to a terrorist organization*

(1) A person commits an offence if—

(a) he invites support for a terrorist organization, and

83. 2001 Cri LJ 3329.

(b) the support is not, or is not restricted to, the provision of money or other property within the meaning of section 22.

(2) A person commits an offence if he arranges, manages or assists in arranging or managing a meeting which he knows is—

(a) to support a terrorist organization, or
(b) to further the activities of a terrorist organization, or
(c) to be addressed by a person who belongs or professes to belong to a terrorist organization.

(3) A person commits an offence if he addresses a meeting for the purpose of encouraging support for a terrorist organization or to further its activities.

(4) A person guilty of an offence under this section shall be liable on conviction, to imprisonment for a term not exceeding ten years or with fine or with both.

Explanation.—For the purposes of this section, the expression "meeting" means a meeting of three or more persons whether or not the public are admitted.

Case Law—Vaiko's Case One of the petitions in this regard admitted by the Supreme Court has been filed by Vaiko, the general secretary of the (MDMK), a constituent of the ruling National Democratic Alliance at the Centre. Vaiko had defended POTA in Parliament during the debate on it. Therefore his petition challenging the validity of Section 21 of the Act assumes particular significance. Under this Section, a person commits an offence if he invites support for a terrorist organization, and even if the support is not confined to the provision of money or other property. He is guilty if he arranges or addresses a meeting which he knows is meant to support a terrorist organization or to further its activities. Vaiko was arrested under this Section on the basis of certain remarks saying that *"I was a supporter of LTTE once. I was a supporter of LTTE yesterday; I am a supporter of LTTE today and I will be a supporter of LTTE tomorrow."* Then, he asked his audience whether the LTTE had engaged in terrorism for the sake of violence or had taken up arms to suppress a culture. Mr. Vaiko, was in detention for 17 months, did not choose to seek bail on a matter of principle.

When we looked at various chapters internationally, it was found that as far as membership of a terrorist group is concerned, the British law has an exclusive chapter on banning terrorist organizations. After banning a terrorist organization, membership of a terrorist organization, ipso facto, becomes a punishable act.

5 *Section 22—Fund raising for a terrorist organization to be an offence*

(1) A person commits an offence if he—

(a) invites another to provide money or other property, and
(b) intends that it should be used, or has reasonable cause to suspect that it may be used, for the purposes of terrorism.

(2) A person commits an offence if he—

(a) receives money or other property, and
(b) intends that it should be used, or has reasonable cause to suspect that it may be used, for the purposes of terrorism.

(3) A person commits an offence if he—

(a) provides money or other property, and
(b) knows or has reasonable cause to suspect that it will or may be used for the purposes of terrorism.

(4) In this section, a reference to the provision of money or other property is a reference to its being given, lent or otherwise made available, whether or not for consideration.

(5) A person guilty of an offence under this section shall be liable on conviction, to imprisonment for a term not exceeding fourteen years or with fine or with both.

The clause 1(b) that was not there in TADA is, if you try and earn money through a crime, that is, through terrorism, there are two offences which flow out of that. Whoever funds terrorism is also held guilty. By funding terrorism you are abetting terrorism. You are giving resources to terrorism. The old terrorist laws the world over never had a chapter on funding of terrorists. But now you must create a fear and scare in the minds of those who fund terrorists.

What you earn out of crime is not your private property, it is against public interest and must belong to the state. The UN passed a draft *Money Laundering Bill* which all of us have been debating. The whole concept of money laundering is that profits out of crime must be confiscated because they cannot belong to an individual. Is it the argument today that since India is now to have a provision where profits from terrorism will be confiscated, it is a draconian provision?

6. *Section 27—Powers to direct for samples, etc.*

(1) When a police officer investigating a case requests the Court of a Chief Judicial Magistrate or the Court of a Chief Metropolitan Magistrate in writing for obtaining samples of handwriting, finger-prints, foot-prints, photographs, blood, saliva, semen, hair, voice of any accused person, reasonably suspected to be involved in the commission of an offence under this Act, it shall be lawful for the Court of a Chief Judicial Magistrate or the Court of a Chief Metropolitan Magistrate to direct that such samples be given by the accused person to the police officer either through a medical practitioner or otherwise, as the case may be.

(2) If any accused person refuses to give samples as provided in sub-section (1), the Court shall draw adverse inference against the accused.

Case Law—*S. Srinivasa* v. *M/s Deccan Petroleum Ltd.*[84] The most important part of the section says that the power to take samples is not given to the police authorities but when a police officer investigating a case requests a Chief Metropolitan Magistrate to obtain samples of any accused person reasonably suspected to be involved in the commission of this act and then

84. 2001 Cri LJ 659.

if only the Chief Metropolitan Magistrate gives the order to obtain such samples its only then he can force the accused to give such samples. If any accused person refuses to give such samples the court shall only then draw adverse inference against the accused.

7. *Section 32—Certain confessions made to police officers taken into consideration*

(1) Notwithstanding anything in the Code or in the Indian Evidence Act, 1872 (1 of 1872), but subject to the provisions of this section, a confession made by a person before a police officer not lower in rank than a Superintendent of Police and recorded by such police officer either in writing or on any mechanical or electronic device like cassettes, tapes or sound tracks from out of which sound or images can be reproduced, shall be admissible in the trial of such person for an offence under this Act or the rules made there under.

(2) A police officer shall, before recording any confession made by a person under sub-section (1), explain to such person in writing that he is not bound to make a confession and that if he does so, it may be used against him:

Provided that where such person prefers to remain silent, the police officer shall not compel or induce him to make any confession.

(3) The confession shall be recorded in an atmosphere free from threat or inducement and shall be in the same language in which the person makes it.

(4) The person from whom a confession has been recorded under sub-section (1), shall be produced before the Court of a Chief Metropolitan Magistrate or the Court of a Chief Judicial Magistrate along with the original statement of confession, written or recorded on mechanical or electronic device within forty-eight hours.

(5) The Chief Metropolitan Magistrate or the Chief Judicial Magistrate, shall, record the statement, if any, made by the person so produced and get his signature or thumb impression and if there is any complaint of torture, such person shall be directed to be produced for medical examination before a

Medical Officer not lower in rank than an Assistant Civil Surgeon and thereafter, he shall be sent to judicial custody.

A confession made by a person before a police officer not lower in rank than a S.P. and recorded by him out of whom sound or images could be reproduced shall be admissible in trial of such person for the offence under this act.

Case Law—*Devender Pal Singh* v. *State of N.C.T. of Delhi*[85] The court said that it is entirely to the court trying the offence to decide the question of admissibility or reliability of a confession in its judicial wisdom strictly adhering to law, it must while so deciding the question should satisfy itself that there was no trap. 'No track and no importance seeking evidence during the custodial interrogations and all the conditions required are fulfilled. If the court is satisfied then the confessional statement will be a part of the statement.

Confessions could be made admissible evidence—

> In respect of confessions, we have given the facility of video recording. After that, within 48 hours, the person should be produced before a magistrate. The magistrate will ask whether it was voluntary or not. If the accused says that it was not voluntary, that he had been assaulted and coerced, the magistrate will have a medical examination done. So, a safeguard has been put in.

Case Law—*State (N.C.T. of Delhi)* v. *Navjot Sandhu @ Afsan Guru*[86] this was an appeal against convictions in view of attacks made on parliament. The matter was relating to admissibility and evidentiary value of evidence that retracted confessions cannot be acted upon by Court unless it is voluntary and can be corroborated by other evidence. Confession of accused can be used against co-accused only if there is sufficient evidence pointing to his guilt confession made under POTA cannot be used against co-accused as POTA operates independently of Indian Evidence Act and Indian Penal Code. Section 10 of Evidence Act has no applicability as confessionary statement has not been relied on for rendering conviction.

85. 2002 (1) SC (Cr.) 209.
86. (2005) 11 SCC 600.

Admissibility of intercepted phone calls, intercepted phone calls are admissible piece of evidence under ordinary laws even though provisions of POTA cannot be invoked as it presupposes investigation to be set in motion on date of its interception. Confession made involuntary is inadmissible evidence. If procedural safeguards have not been complied it will affect admissibility and evidentiary value of evidence.

8. *Section 45—Admissibility of evidence collected through the interception of communication*

Notwithstanding anything in the Code or in any other law for the time being in force, the evidence collected through the interception of wire, electronic or oral communication under this Chapter shall be admissible as evidence against the accused in the Court during the trial of a case:

Provided that, the contents of any wire, electronic or oral communication intercepted pursuant to this Chapter or evidence derived therefrom shall not be received in evidence or otherwise disclosed in any trial, hearing or other proceeding in any court unless each accused has been furnished with a copy of the order of the Competent Authority, and accompanying application, under which the interception was authorized or approved not less than ten days before trial, hearing or proceeding:

Provided further that, the period of ten days may be waived by the judge trying the matter, if he comes to the conclusion that it was not possible to furnish the accused with the above information ten days before the trial, hearing or proceeding and that the accused will not be prejudiced by the delay in receiving such information.

It is said that TADA was misused. Probably it was misused. I would like to point out that one of the great weaknesses in TADA *'a structural defect'* was its dependence on witnesses; eyewitnesses and humble citizens appearing against terrorist groups. Anybody from Punjab, Mumbai or Kashmir will testify that the average citizen is scared of coming and honestly deposing before these institutions. This is a threat that the witnesses face against terrorist acts. So how can a normal person be able to give a statement before the court?

So there is a need bring in a provision that when terrorist gangs communicate with each other, intercepts of their communication should be allowed and these intercepts should become admissible evidence in court. So, when you arrest terrorists, you do not need a humble citizen to come and give evidence against them. You produce the recording of that intercept. At that moment, it becomes admissible evidence. Under normal law it is not admissible evidence. We examined the suggestion and accepted it. One of the strengths of this law is actually on the question of intercepts becoming admissible evidence. It is one reason why in Maharashtra, the conviction rate has reached 75% plus under MCOCA.

9. *Bail provision: Section 49—Modified application of certain provisions of the Code*

(5) That no person will be released on bail unless the public prosecutor has an opportunity or where he opposes the application, there is a reasonable opportunity of believing that the person is innocent and shall not commit an offence. This was the language under TADA. (5) Nothing in section 438 of the Code shall apply in relation to any case involving the arrest of any person accused of having committed an offence punishable under this Act.

(6) Notwithstanding anything contained in the Code, no person accused of an offence punishable under this Act shall, if in custody, be released on bail or on his own bond unless the Court gives the Public Prosecutor an opportunity of being heard.

(7) Where the Public Prosecutor opposes the application of the accused to release on bail, no person accused of an offence punishable under this Act or any rule made there under shall be released on bail until the Court is satisfied that there are grounds for believing that he is not guilty of committing such offence:

Provided that after the expiry of a period of one year from the date of detention of the accused for an offence under this Act, the provisions of sub-section (6) of this section shall apply.

10. *Action against police officer*

There is a provision that in case any police officer misuses this law for his own personal purposes or for collateral reasons, he will be prosecuted under POTA itself. Several safeguards have been incorporated in the Act to minimize the possibility of its misuse. Some of the main safeguards are as follows:

(i) Investigation of an offence under the Act is to be done by an officer not below the rank of Deputy Superintendent of Police.
(ii) No court can take cognizance of an offence under the Act unless sanction of the State.
(iii) The Act provides safeguards against abuse of the provision relating to admissibility of confession made before a police officer.
(iv) Intimation of arrest of the accused will have to be provided to a family member immediately after arrest and this fact is to be recorded by the police officer.
(v) Provision for prosecution of police officers for malafide actions under the Act and compensation to affected persons in such cases.

The State Government/UT Administrations were advised to ensure that the provisions of this law are used only against the terrorists and not against the innocent. They were also advised to sensitize the police officers and others concerned with the implementation of POTA on the need to ensure its fair and transparent operation and to also install a mechanism to oversee the implementation of the Act.

MCOCA does not stipulate prosecution of police officers found guilty of its misuse. But POTA did. Under POTA a police officer found guilty of malafide action could be jailed for up to two years but MCOCA offers no such protection. Finally the law extended to the state of JandK unlike other laws.

Consequences of Repeal of POTA

Finally on September 17, 2004 the Union Cabinet in keeping with the UPA government's Common Minimum Program, approved ordinances to repeal the controversial Prevention of Terrorism Act, 2002 and amend the Unlawful Activities (Prevention) Act, 1967. By the promulgation of—

1. Ordinance No. 1 of 2004, it repealed POTA, a law specially designed to deal with the menace of terrorism with its repeal, the state apparatus combating terrorism has been debilitated.
2. By Ordinance No. 2 promulgated on the same day, virtually all the penal provisions of Pota concerning terrorist organizations and activities were transferred to the pre-existing milder sounding Unlawful Activities (Prevention) Act, 1967 (UAPA). By Ordinance No. 2, the definition of "unlawful association" has been expanded to also include *"any association which has for its object any activity which is punishable under Section 153A of the Indian Penal Code, or which encourages or aids persons to undertake any such activity, or of which the members undertake any such activity."* Section 153A is about promoting enmity between different groups on grounds of religion, race, place of birth, residence, language, etc.
3. There would be no arrests made after the ordinance is promulgated.
4. Among the special provisions dropped are those restricting release on bail and allowing longer periods of police remand for the accused. Now suspected terrorists may roam free under the *bail a rule, jail an exception dictum.* The police will not get sufficient time to interrogate the accused to investigate the cases which, by their very nature, are complex. In Pota, as in Tada earlier, confessions made before a police officer of the rank of superintendent were admitted as evidence.
5. All terrorist organizations banned under POTA would continue to remain banned, under the Unlawful Activities Act, after the repeal of the Act.
6. Some of the clauses contained in POTA, which will be completely dropped in the amended Unlawful Activities Act, are: the onus on the accused to prove his innocence, compulsory denial of bail to accused and admission as evidence in the court of law the confession made by the accused before the police officer.

7. In another major departure from Pota, the government has removed all traces of strict liability. Meaning, the burden of proof has shifted from the accused to the police. There is no presumption of guilt under UAPA. Like under any other ordinary criminal law, the police will have to establish that the accused person had a criminal intention for committing the offence in question.
8. But beware; these concessions from the internal security establishment have not come without a price. As reported recently in the Indian Express, UAPA is more draconian than Pota when it comes to the admissibility in evidence of telephone and e-mail intercepts. The police can now produce intercepts in the court without abiding by any of the elaborate safeguards provided by the repealed law. Thus, if the police cannot anymore extract a confession in custody, they have been given more scope than before to plant evidence in the form of interceptions.
9. Another glaring shortcoming in the new law pertains to the dichotomy in the provision for banning terrorist organizations and unlawful organizations. UAPA was originally meant only for banning unlawful organizations. Now it has a separate chapter for banning terrorist organizations as well. Thus, the procedures prescribed by the same law for the two kinds of bans are different. *But the problem is that the procedure for banning a group on the charge of terrorism is easier than to ban it on the milder charge of unlawful activities.* The government cannot, for instance, ban any group for unlawful activities without having its decision ratified within six months by a judicial tribunal headed by a sitting high court judge. There is no such requirement if the ban is on the charge of terrorism. This anomaly has arisen because of the strategy adopted by the UPA government to hide special provisions in an ordinary law.

So What Remains on the Statute Books?

The UAPA was designed to deal with associations and activities that questioned the territorial integrity of India. When the Bill was debated in Parliament, leaders, cutting across party affiliation, insisted that its ambit be so limited that the right to association remained unaffected and those political parties were not exposed to intrusion by the executive. So, the ambit of the Act was strictly limited to meeting the challenge to the territorial integrity of India.

The Changes by UAPA, 2004

The Act does not define the word *terrorist* in its definition clause but defines a *terrorist act*. The word terrorist is to be construed according the definition of the terrorist act. Terrorist act is defined in the Act as—*Whoever, with intent to threaten the unity, integrity, security or sovereignty of India or to strike terror in the people or any section of the people in India or in any foreign country, does any act by using bombs, dynamite or other explosive substances or inflammable substances or firearms or other lethal weapons or poisons or noxious gases or other chemicals or by any other substances (whether biological or otherwise) of a hazardous nature, in such a manner as to cause, or likely to cause, death of, or injuries to any person or persons or loss of, or damage to, or destruction of, property or disruption of any supplies or services essential to the life of the community in India or in any foreign country or causes damage or destruction of any property or equipment used or intended to be used for the defence of India or in connection with any other purposes of the Government of India, any State Government or any of their agencies, or detains any person and threatens to kill or injure such person in order to compel the Government in India or the Government of a foreign country or any other person to do or abstain from doing any act, commits a terrorist act*—(Section 15).The above definition did not exist in the 1967 Act. The previous Act only defined and dealt with unlawful activity. An unlawful activity includes an activity which intends to bring about cession of a part of the territory of India or the secession of a part of the territory of India from the Union, or which incites any individual or group of individuals to bring about such cession or secession; or which disclaims, questions, disrupts or is intended to disrupt the sovereignty and territorial integrity of India, or which causes or is intended to cause disaffection against India—*Section 2(o)*.

Whether an association is unlawful is to be declared by the Central government by giving the grounds for such a declaration—Section 3. Thereafter; it is referred to the Tribunal—Section 4. A notice is issued by the Tribunal to the association concerned to show cause why it should not be declared unlawful. To ascertain whether there is sufficient cause for declaring the association unlawful.

For taking cognizance of any offence under this Act prior sanction of the Central or the State government, as the case may be, is necessary. Criminal Procedure Code, 1973, is made applicable in matters of arrest, bail, confessions and burden of proof. Those arrested are to be brought before a magistrate within 24 hours, confessions are no longer admissible before police officers and bail need not be denied for the first three months. The presumption of innocence leaving the burden of proof on the prosecution has also been restored.

The evidence collected through interception of wireless, electronic or oral communication under the provisions of the Indian Telegraph Act or the Information Technology Act or any law being in force has been made admissible as evidence against the accused in the court—Section 46.

The Stringent Provisions of UAPA, 2008

The POTA favourites of pretrial imprisonment till 180 days, 30 days police custody, denial of bail if a prima facie case exists and the denial of bail to foreigners (including, perforce, suspect Bangladeshis) is back (Sections 43A to 43F). So, also, are the provisions—if there is recovery of arms, explosives and other substances, suspected to be involved, including finger prints on them. Second, the definition of 'terrorist act' includes not just radioactive and nuclear material, but anything that may threaten India or overawe or kidnap constitutional and other functionaries listed by the government (Section 53). This list is potentially endless.

New offences for organising terrorist training camps or recruiting terrorists attract punishment (Section 18A and 18B).

There are salutary provisions against raising funds likely to be for terrorist use (Section 17). All these can be frozen (Section 51A). Criminalising intent to aid terrorists and terrorist organisations is extended to aid to terrorist gangs (Section 23). The magnum Sections 43A to 43F that modify our Criminal Code. We have already noted the pre-trial custody, denial of bail provisions and adverse inference provisions. To these may be added arrest and search and seizure on suspicion authorised by general or special orders by officers designated by the state and Union governments (Section 43A). All offences mentioned in the new legislation will permit arrest without warrant (Section 43D). There is an obligation to disclose any information which a superintendent of police thinks is relevant.

Other Highlights of the UAPA, 2008

Use of bombs, dynamite, poisons or noxious gases, biological radioactive nuclear substances are terror act.—*Section 15.*

Aiding, abetting or committing a terrorist act shall be punishable with imprisonment up to ten years. Funding terror activities, organising training camps and recruiting persons for committing terror acts shall be punishable with at least five years' imprisonment.—*Section 17.*

Detention of accused upto 180 days if investigation not completed.—Section 43D (2).

No bail shall be granted if accused is not an Indian citizen and has entered the country unauthorisedly.—*Section 43D (7).*

No accused, if in custody, to be released on bail or on his own bond.—*Section 43D (5).*

Court shall presume, unless contrary is shown, that accused has committed offence.—*Section 43 E.*

(F) UNLAWFUL ACTIVITIES (PREVENTION) AMENDMENT ACT, 2004

It would however be simplistic to suggest, as some critics did, that the new law has retained all the operational teeth of Pota or it has made only cosmetic changes. The difference between Pota and UAPA is substantial even as a lot of provisions are in common.

A Brief Outline of the Amended Act

The Act does not define the word terrorist in its definition clause but defines a terrorist act. The word terrorist is to be construed according the definition of the terrorist act. Terrorist act is defined in the Act as - Whoever, with intent to threaten the unity, integrity, security or sovereignty of India or to strike terror in the people or any section of the people in India or in any foreign country, does any act by using bombs, dynamite or other explosive substances or inflammable substances or firearms or other lethal weapons or poisons or noxious gases or other chemicals or by any other substances (whether biological or otherwise) of a hazardous nature, in such a manner as to cause, or likely to cause, death of, or injuries to any person or persons or loss of, or damage to, or destruction of, property or disruption of any supplies or services essential to the life of the community in India or in any foreign country or causes damage or destruction of any property or equipment used or intended to be used for the defence of India or in connection with any other purposes of the Government of India, any State Government or any of their agencies, or detains any person and threatens to kill or injure such person in order to compel the Government in India or the Government of a foreign country or any other person to do or abstain from doing any act, commits a terrorist act (Section 15). The above definition did not exist in the 1967 Act. The previous Act only defined and dealt with unlawful activity. An unlawful activity includes an activity which intends to bring about cession of a part of the territory of India or the secession of a part of the territory of India from the Union, or which incites any individual or group of individuals to bring about such cession or secession; or which disclaims, questions, disrupts or is intended to disrupt the sovereignty and territorial integrity of India, or which causes or is intended to cause disaffection against India Section 2(o). Whether an association is unlawful is to be declared by the Central government by giving the grounds for such a declaration. Section 3 Thereafter; it is referred to the Tribunal Section 4. A notice is issued by the Tribunal to the For taking cognizance of any offence under this

Act prior sanction of the Central or the State government, as the case may be, is necessary. Criminal Procedure Code, 1973, is made applicable in matters of arrest, bail, confessions and burden of proof. Those arrested are to be brought before a magistrate within 24 hours, confessions are no longer admissible before police officers and bail need not be denied for the first three months. The presumption of innocence leaving the burden of proof on the prosecution has also been restored.

The evidence collected through interception of wireless, electronic or oral communication under the provisions of the Indian Telegraph Act or the Information Technology Act or any law being in force has been made admissible as evidence against the accused in the court Section 46.The amended Act provides for following penalties: Offence Includes Penalty .Being a member of an unlawful association A person who is and continues to be a member of such association, takes part in meetings, contributes to, or receives or solicits any contribution for the purposes of the association or in any way assists the operations of such association. If such person is in possession of unlicensed firearms, ammunition, explosive, etc, capable of causing mass destruction and commits any act resulting in loss of human life or grievous injury to any person or causes significant damage to any property, and if such act has resulted in the death of any person. In any other case Imprisonment for a term which may extend to two years and fine.

Death or Imprisonment for Life

Imprisonment for not less than five years. Dealing with funds of an unlawful association Includes an association declared unlawful by the central government. Such association is prohibited from dealing in any manner with moneys, securities or credits pays. Imprisonment upto three years, or fine, or both. Contravention of an order made in respect of a notified place Includes use of articles for unlawful activities found in a notified place (i.e. a place used for unlawful association and so notified by the central government). Imprisonment upto one year. Unlawful activities Includes taking part in or committing an unlawful act, advocating, abetting, advising or inciting the commission of any unlawful activity. Assisting an unlawful organization in its activities. A term of seven years and fine.Imprisonment upto five years or fine, or both. The amended law now contains new provisions dealing with terrorist acts, the offences and their punishments. Chapter IV, sections 15-22. The following table summarises these provisions:Offence Punishment Terrorist act Resulting in death of any person In any other case Death or imprisonment for life.A term for not less than five years.Raising funds for a terrorist act Term not less than five years. Conspiracy Term not less than five years. Harbouring Imprisonment for not less than three years. Being a member of a terrorist organization The term may extend upto imprisonment for life.Holding proceeds of terrorism May extend to imprisonment for life. Threatening witnesses Imprisonment upto three years. There is a provision in the Act which provides for enhanced penalties. Any person aiding a terrorist or acting in contravention to Explosives Act, 1884, the Explosive Substances Act, 1908 or the Inflammable Substances Act, 1952 or the Arms Act, 1959, or has unauthorized possession of bombs, explosives, etc, will be punished with a term not less than three years and may extend for life (Section 23). The Act also gives power to the Central and the State Governments, as the case may be, to forfeiture the proceeds of terrorism. The investigating officer is empowered to seize the concerned property with the prior approval of the Director General of the police of the State (Section 24 and 25). Cash (including monetary instruments) can also be seized if it is intended to be used for purposes of terrorism. The Court confirms the seized property and orders its forfeiture Section 26. An appeal to the High Court against the forfeiture is allowed within one month from the date of receipt of such order.Chapter VI of the amended Act gives power to the Central government under section 35 to add or remove an organization in the schedule as a terrorist organization. Under section 36, an application can also be made to remove an organization from the schedule. Such an application can be made by an organization or any affected person. The offences and penalties under this chapter as given below :

Offences Punishment Membership of a terrorist organization (S. 38) Imprisonment not exceeding ten years. Supporting a terrorist organization (S. 39) Imprisonment not exceeding ten years. Raising funds for terrorist organization (S. 40) A term not exceeding fourteen years.The Act also provides for protection of witnesses under section 44 such as keeping the their identities secret even in orders, judgments and records of the Court, issuing directions to secure the identity of the witnesses and by imposing punishment for contravention of any such directions.

(G) COFEPOSA—THE CONSERVATION OF FOREIGN EXCHANGE AND PREVENTION OF SMUGGLING ACTIVITIES ACT, 1974 (ACT 52 OF 1974)

AN Act to provide for preventive detention in certain cases for the purposes of conservationand augmentation of foreign exchange and prevention of smuggling activities and formatters connected therewith.Whereas violating of foreign exchange regulations and smuggling activities are having anincreasingly deleterious effect on the national economy and thereby a serious adverse effecton the security of the State:And whereas having regard to the persons by whom and the manner in which such activitiesor violations are organised and carried on, and having regard to the fact that in certain areas which are highly vulnerable to smuggling, smuggling activities of a considerable magnitude are clandestinely organised and carried on, it is necessary for the effective prevention of such activities and violations to provide for detention of persons concerned in any manner therewith:Be it enacted by Parliament in the Twenty-fifth Year of the Republic of India as follows:

1. Short Title, Extent and Commencement

(1) This Act may be called the Conservation of Foreign Exchange and Prevention ofSmuggling Activities Act, 1974.

(2) It extends to the whole of India.

(3) It shall come into force on such date (being a date not later than the twentieth day of December, 1974), as the Central Government may, by notification in the Official Gazette,appoint.

2. Definitions

In this Act, unless the context otherwise requires,

(a) "appropriate Government" means, as respects a detention order made by the Central Government or by an officer of the Central Government or a person detained under such order, the Central Government, and as respects a detention order made by a State Government or by an officer of a State Government or a person detained under such order, the State Government;

(b) "detention order" means an order made under section 3;

(c) "foreigner" has the same meaning as in the Foreigners Act, 1946 (31 of 1946);

(d) "Indian customs waters" has the same meaning as in clause (28) of section 2 of theCustoms Act, 1962 (52 of 1962);

(e) "smuggling" has the same meaning as in clause (39) of section 2 of the Customs Act,1962 (52 of 1952), and all its grammatical variations and cognate expressions shall be construed accordingly;

(f) "State Government " in relation to a Union territory, means the administrator thereof;

(g) any reference in this Act to a law which is not in force in the State of Jammu and Kashmir shall, in relation to that State, be construed as a reference to the corresponding law, if any, in force in that State.

3. Power to make Orders Detaining Certain Persons

(1) The Central Government or the State Government or any officer of the Central Government, not below the rank of a Joint Secretary to that Government, specially empowered for the purposes of this section by that Government, or any officer of a State Government, not below the rank of a Secretary to that Government, specially empowered for the purposes of this section by that Government, may, if satisfied, with respect to any person (including a foreigner), that, with a view to

preventing him from acting in any manner prejudicial to the conservation or augmentation of foreign exchange or with a view to preventing him from—

(i) smuggling goods, or
(ii) abetting the smuggling of goods, or
(iii) engaging in transporting or concealing or keeping smuggled goods, or
(iv) dealing in, smuggled goods otherwise than by engaging in transporting or concealing or keeping smuggled goods, or
(v) harbouring persons engaged in smuggling goods or in abetting the smuggling of goods, It is necessary so to do, make an order directing that such person be detained.

(2) When any order of detention is made by a State Government or by an officer empowered by a State Government, the State Government shall, within ten days, forward to the Central Government a report in respect of the order.

(3) For the purposes of clause (5) of Article 22 of the Constitution, the communication to a person detained in pursuance of a detention order of the grounds on which the order has been made shall be made as soon as may be after the detention, but ordinarily not later than five days, and in exceptional circumstances and for reasons to be recorded in writing not later than fifteen days, from the date of detention.

4. Execution of Detention Orders

A detention order may be executed at any place in India in the manner provided for the execution of warrants of arrest under the Code of Criminal Procedure, 1973 (2 of 1974).

5. Power to Regulate Place and Conditions of Detention

Every person in respect of whom a detention order has been made shall be liable—

(a) to be detained in such place and under such conditions including conditions as to maintenance, interviews or communication with the appropriate Government may, by general or special order, specify; and

(b) to be removed from one place of detention to another place of detention, whether within the same State or in another State by order of the appropriate Government: Provided that no order shall be made by a State Government under clause (b) for the removal of a person from one State to another State except with the consent of the Government of that other State.

5A. Grounds of detention severable

Where a person has been detained in pursuance of an order of detention under sub-section (1) of section 3 which has been made on two or more grounds, such order of detention shall be deemed to have been made separately on each of such grounds and accordingly (a) Such order shall not be deemed to be invalid or inoperative merely because one or some of the grounds is or are:

(i) vague,
(ii) non-existent,
(iii) not relevant,
(iv) not connected or not proximately connected with such person, or
(v) invalid for any other reason whatsoever, and it is not therefore possible to hold that the Government or officer making such order would have been satisfied as provided in subsection (1) of section 3 with reference to the remaining ground or grounds and made the order of detention; (b) The Government or office making the order of detention shall be deemed to have made the order of detention under the said sub-section (1) after being satisfied as providedin that sub-section with reference to the remaining ground or grounds.

6. Detention Orders not to be Invalid or Inoperative on Certain Grounds

No detention order shall be invalid or inoperative merely by reason—

(a) that the person to be detained thereunder is outside the limits of the territorial jurisdiction of the Government or the office making the order of detention, or

(b) that the place of detention of such person is outside the said limits.

7. Powers in Relation to Absconding Persons

(1) If the appropriate Government has reason to believe that a person in respect of whom a detention order has been made has absconded or is concealing himself so that the order cannot be executed, that Government may:

(a) make a report in writing of the fact to a Metropolitan Magistrate of or a Magistrate of the first class having jurisdiction in the place where the said person ordinarily resides; and thereupon the provisions of sections 82, 83, 84 and 85 of the Code of Criminal Procedure, 1973 (2 of 1974), shall apply in respect of the said person and his property as if the order directing that he be detained were a warrant issued by the Magistrate; (b) by order notified in the Official Gazette direct the said person to appear before such officer, at such place and within such period as may be specified in the order; and if the said person fails to comply with such direction, he shall , unless he proves that it was not possible for him to comply therewith and that he had, within the period specified in the order, informed the officer mentioned in the order of the reason which rendered compliance therewith impossible and of his whereabouts, be punishable with imprisonment for a term which may extend to one year or with fine or with both.

(2) Notwithstanding anything contained in the Code of Criminal Procedure, 1973 (2 of 1974), every offence under clause

(b) of sub-section (1) shall be cognisable.

8. Advisory Boards

For the purposes of sub-clause (a) of clause (4), and sub-clause (c) of clause (7), of Article 22 of the Constitution:

(a) the Central Government and each State Government shall, whenever necessary, constitute one or more Advisory Boards each of which shall consist of a chairman and two other persons possessing the qualifications specified in sub-clause (a) of clause (4) of Article 22 of the Constitution;

(b) save as otherwise provided in section 9, the appropriate Government shall, within five weeks from the date of detention of a person under a detention order make a reference in respect thereof to the Advisory Board constituted under clause (a) to enable the Advisory Board to make the report under sub-clause (a) of clause (4) of Article 22 of the Constitution; the advisory board to which a reference is made under clause (b) shall after considering the reference and the materials placed before it and after calling for such further information as it may deem necessary from, the appropriate Government or from any person called for the purpose through the appropriate Government or from the person concerned, and if, in any particular case, it considers it essential so to do or if the person concerned desired to be heard in person, after hearing him in person, prepare its report specifying in a separate paragraph thereof its opinion as to whether or not there is sufficient cause for the detention of the person concerned and submit the same within eleven weeks from the date of detention of the person concerned;

(c) when there is a difference of opinion among the members forming the Advisory Board, the opinion of the majority of such members shall be deemed to be the opinion of the board;

(c) a person against whom an order of detention has been made under this Act shall not be entitled to appear by any legal practitioner in any matter connected with the reference to the Advisory Board, and the proceedings of the Advisory Board and its report, excepting that part of the report in which the opinion of the Advisory Board is specified, shall be confidential;

(d) in every case where the Advisory Board has reported that there is in its opinion sufficient cause for the detention of a person, the appropriate Government may confirm the detention order and continue the detention of the person concerned for such period as it thinks fit and in every case where the Advisory Board has reported that there is in its opinion no sufficient cause for the detention of the person concerned, the appropriate Government shall revoke the detention order and cause the person to be released forthwith.

9. Cases in which and circumstances under which persons may be detained for periods longer than three months without obtaining the opinion of Advisory Board.

(1) Notwithstanding anything contained in this Act, any person (including a foreigner) in respect of whom an order of detention is made under this Act at any time before the [31st day of July, 1999], may be detained without obtaining, in accordance with the provisions of sub-clause (a) of clause (4) of Article 22 of the Constitution, the opinion of an Advisory Board for a period longer than three months but not exceeding six months from the date of his detention, where the order of detention has been made against such person with a view to preventing him from smuggling goods or abetting the smuggling of goods or engaging in transporting or concealing or keeping smuggled goods and the Central Government or any officer of the Central Government, not below the rank of an Additional Secretary to that Government, specially empowered for the purposes of this section by the Government, is satisfied that such person

(a) smuggles or is likely to smuggle goods into, out of or through any area highly vulnerable to smuggling; or (b) abets or is likely to abet the smuggling of goods into, out of or through any area highly vulnerable to smuggling; or (c) engages or is likely to engage in transporting or concealing or keeping smuggled goods in any area highly vulnerable to smuggling, and makes a declaration to that effect within five weeks of the detention of such person. Explanation 1 In this sub-section, "area highly vulnerable to smuggling" means (i) the Indian customs waters contiguous to the States of Goa, Gujarat, Karnataka, Kerala,Maharashtra and Tamil Nadu and the Union territories of Daman, Diu and Pondicherry; (ii) the inland area fifty kilometres in width from the coast of India falling within the territories of the States of Goa, Gujarat, territories of Daman, Diu and Pondicherry; (iii) the inland area fifty kilometres in width from the India-Pakistan border in the States of Gujarat, Jammu and Kashmir, Punjab and Rajasthan; (iv) the customs airport of Delhi; and (v) such further or other Indian customs waters, or inland area not exceeding one hundred kilometres in width from any other coast or border of India, or such other customs station, as the Central Government may, having regard to the vulnerability of such waters, area or customs station, as the case may be, to smuggling, by notification in the Official Gazette, speecify in this behalf. Explanation 2(1) For the purposes of Explanation 1, "customs airport" and "customs station" shall have the same meaning as in clauses (10) and (13) of section 2 of the Customs Act, 1962 (52 of1962), respectively. 2) In the case of any person detained under a detention order to which the provisions ofsub-section (1) apply, section 8 shall have effect subject to the following modifications, namely: (i) in clause (b), for the words "shall, within five weeks", the words, "shall, within four months and two weeks" shall be substituted; (ii) in clause (c), (1) for the words "the detention of the person concerned", the words "the continued detention of the person concerned" shall be substituted; (2) for the words "eleven weeks", the words "five months and three weeks" shall besubstituted; (iii) in clause (f), for the words "for the detention", as both the places where they occur, the words "for the continued detention" shall be substituted.

10. Maximum Period of Detention

The maximum period for which any person may be detained in pursuance of any detentionorder to which the provisions of section 9 do not apply and which has been confirmed underclause (f) of section 8 shall be one year from the date of detention and the maximum period for which any person may be detained in pursuance of any detention order to which the provisions of section 9 apply and which has been confirmed under clause (f) of section 8 read with sub-section (2) of section 9 shall be two years from the date of detention: Provided that nothing contained in this section shall affect the power of the appropriate Government in either case to revoke or modify the detention order at any earlier time.

11. Revocation of Detention Orders

(1) Without prejudice to the provisions of section 21 of the General Clauses Act, 1897 (10 of1897), a detention order may, at any time, be revoked or modified- (a) notwithstanding that the order has been made by an officer of a State Government, by that State Government or by the Central Government; (b) notwithstanding that the order has been made by an officer of the Central Government or by a State Government, by the Central Government;

(2) The revocation of a detention order shall not bar the making of another detention order under section 3 against the same person.

12. Temporary Release of Persons Detained

(1) The Central Government may, at any time, direct that any person detained in pursuance of a detention order made by that Government or an office subordinate to that Government or by a State Government or by an officer subordinate to a State Government, may be released for any specified period either without conditions or upon such conditions specified in the direction as that person accepts, and may, at any time, cancel his release.(1A) A State Government may, at any time, direct that any person detained in pursuance of a detention order made by that Government or by an officer subordinate to that Government may be released for any specified period either without conditions or upon such conditions specified in the

directions as that person accepts, and may, at any time, cancel his release. (2) In directing the release of any person under sub-section (1) or sub-section (1A), the Government directing the release may require him to enter into a bond with sureties for the due observance of the conditions specified in the direction. (3) Any person released under sub-section (1) or sub-section (1A) shall surrender himself at the time and place, and to the authority specified in the order directing his release or cancelling his release, as the case may be. (4) If any person fails without sufficient cause to surrender himself in the manner specified in sub-section (3); he shall be punishable with imprisonment for a term which may extend to two years, or with fine, or with both. (5) If any person released under sub-section (1) or sub-section (1A) fails to fulfil any of the conditions imposed upon him under the said sub-section or in the bond entered into by him, the bond shall be declared to be forfeited and any person bound thereby shall be liable to pay the penalty thereof. (6) Notwithstanding anything contained in any other law and save as otherwise provided in this section, no person against whom a detention order made under this Act is in force shall be released whether on bail or bail bond or otherwise.

12A. Special Provisions for Dealing with Emergency

(1) Notwithstanding anything contained in this Act or any rules of natural Justice, the provisions of this section shall have effect during the period of operation of the Proclamation of Emergency issued under clause (1) of Article 352 of the Constitution on the 3rd day of December 1971, or the Proclamation of Emergency issued under that clause on the 25th day of June, 1975, or a period of twenty-four months from the 25th day of June, 1975, whichever period is the shortest. (2) When making an order of detention under this Act against any person after the commencement of the Conservation of Foreign Exchange and Prevention of Smuggling Activities (Amendment) Act, 1975, the Central Government or the State Government or, as the case may be, the office making the order of detention shall consider whether the detention of such person under this Act is necessary for dealing effectively with the emergency in respect of which the Proclamations referred to in sub-section (1) have been issued (hereafter in this section referred to as the

emergency) and if, on such consideration, the Central Government or the State Government or, as the case may be, the officer is satisfied that it is necessary to detain such person for effectively dealing with the emergency, that Government or officer may make a declaration to that effect and communicate a copy of the declaration to the person concerned: Provided that where such declaration is made by an officer, it shall be reviewed by the appropriate Government within fifteen days from the date of making of the declaration and such declaration shall cease to have effect unless it is confirmed by that Government, after such review, within the said period of fifteen days. (3) The question whether the detention of any person in respect of whom a declaration has been made under sub-section (2) continues to be necessary for effectively dealing with the emergency shall be reconsidered by the appropriate Government within four months from the date of such declaration and thereafter at intervals not exceeding four months, and if, on such reconsideration, it appears to the appropriate Government that the detention of the person is no longer necessary for effectively dealing with the emergency, that Government may revoke the declaration. (4) In making any consideration, review or reconsideration under sub-section (2) or (3), the appropriate Government or officer may, if such Government or officer considers it to be against the public interest to do otherwise, act on the basis of the information and materials in its or his possession without disclosing the facts or giving an opportunity of making a representation to the person concerned. (5) It shall not be necessary to disclose to any person detained under a detention order to which the provisions of sub-section (2) apply, the grounds on which the order has been made during the period the declaration made in respect of such person under that subsection in is force, and, accordingly, such period shall not be taken into account for the purpose of sub-section (3) of section 3. (6) In the case of every person detained under a detention order to which the provisions of sub-section (2) apply, being a person in respect of whom a declaration has been made there under, the period during which such declaration is in force shall not be taken into account for the purpose of computing- (i) the periods specified in clauses (b) and (c) of section 8;(ii) the periods of "one year" and "five weeks" specified in sub-section (1), the period of n"one year" specified in sub-section (2)(i), and the period of "six months" specified in subsection (3) of section 9.

13. Protection of Action Taken in Good Faith

No suit or other legal proceeding shall lie against the Central Government or a State Government, and no suit prosecution or other legal proceedings shall lie against any person, for anything in good faith done or intended to be done in pursuance of this Act.

14. Repeal

The Maintenance of Internal Security (Amendment) Ordinance, 1974 (11 of 1974) shall, on the commencement of this Act, stand repealed and accordingly the amendments made in the Maintenance of Internal Security Act, 1971 (26 of 1971), by the said Ordinance shall, on such commencement, cease to have effect.

The National Security Act, 1980 Enactment Date: [27th December, 1980.]

Act Objective: An Act to provide for preventive detention in certain cases and for matters connected therewith. BE it enacted by Parliament in the Thirty-first Year of the Republic of India as follows: 2. Definitions. In this Act, unless the context otherwise requires, (a) "appropriate Government" means, as respects a detention order made by the Central Government or a person detained under such order, the Central Government, and as respects a detention order made by a State Government or by an officer subordinate to a State Government or as respects a person detained under such order, the State Government; (b) "detention order" means an order made under section 3;(c) "foreigner" has the same meaning as in the Foreigners Act, 1946 (31 of 1946);(d) "person" includes a foreigner;

(e) "State Government", in relation to a Union territory, means the administrator thereof.

3. Power to make orders detaining certain persons. (1) The Central Government or the State Government may,—(a) if satisfied with respect to any person that with a view to preventing him from acting in any manner prejudicial to the

defence of India, the relations of India with foreign powers, or the security of India, or (b) if satisfied with respect to any foreigner that with a view to regulating his continued presence in India or with a view to making arrangements for his expulsion from India, it is necessary so to do, make an order directing that such person be detained.

(2) The Central Government or the State Government may, if satisfied with respect to any person that with a view to preventing him from acting in any manner prejudicial to the security of the State or from acting in any manner prejudicial to the maintenance of Public order or from acting in any manner prejudicial to the maintenance of supplies and services essential to the community it is necessary so to do, make an order directing that such person be detained.

Explanation.—For the purposes of this sub-section, "acting in any manner prejudicial to the maintenance of supplies and services essential to the community" does not include "acting in any manner prejudicial to the maintenance of supplies of commodities essential to the community" as defined in the Explanation to sub-section (1) of section 3 of the Prevention of Black-marketing and Maintenance of Supplies of Essential Commodities Act, 1980 (7 of 1980), and accordingly, no order of detention shall be made under this Act on any ground on which an order of detention may be made under that Act.(3) If, having regard to the circumstances prevailing or likely to prevail in any area within the local limits of the jurisdiction of a District Magistrate or a Commissioner of Police, the State Government is satisfied that it is necessary so to do, it may, by order in writing, direct, that during such period as may be specified in the order, such District Magistrate or Commissioner of Police may also, if satisfied as provided in sub-section (2), exercise the powers conferred by the said sub-section: Provided that the period specified in an order made by the State Government under this sub-section shall not, in the first instance, exceed three months, but the State Government may, if satisfied as aforesaid that it is necessary so to do, amend such order to extend such period from time to time by any period not exceeding three months at any one time.(4) When any order is made under this section by an officer mentioned in sub-section (3), he shall forthwith report the fact to the State Government to which he is subordinate together with the grounds on which the order has been made and such other particulars as, in his opinion, have a bearing on the matter, and no such order shall remain in force for more than twelve days after the making thereof unless, in the meantime, it has been approved by the State Government: Provided that where under section 8 the grounds of detention are communicated by the officer making the order after five days but not later than ten days from the date of detention, this sub-section shall apply subject to the modification that, for the words "twelve days", the words "fifteen days" shall be substituted. (5) When any order is made or approved by the State Government under this section, the State Government shall, within seven days, report the fact to the Central Government together with the grounds on which the order has been made and such other particulars as, in the opinion of the State Government, have a bearing on the necessity for the order.

4. Execution of detention orders. A detention order may be executed at any place in India in the manner provided for the execution of warrants of arrest under the Code of Criminal Procedure, 1973 (2 of 1974).

5. Power to regulate place and conditions of detention. Every person in respect of whom a detention order has been made shall be liable— (a) to be detained in such place and under such conditions, (b) including conditions as to maintenance, discipline and punishment for breaches of discipline, as the appropriate Government may, by general or special order, specify; and (c) to be removed from one place of detention to another place of detention, whether within the same State or in another State, by order of the appropriate Government: Provided that no order shall be made by a State Government under clause (d) for the removal of a person from one State to another State except with the consent of the Government of that other State.

6. Detention orders not to be invalid or inoperative on certain grounds. No detention order shall be invalid or inoperative merely by reason—(a) that the person to be detained thereunder is outside the limits of the territorial jurisdiction of the Government or officer making the order, or (b) that the place of detention of such person is outside the said limits.

7. Powers in relation to absconding persons. (1) If the Central Government or the State Government or an officer mentioned in sub-section (3) of section 3, as the case may be, has reason to believe that a person in respect of whom a detention order has been made has absconded or is concealing himself so that the order cannot be executed, that Government or officer may— (a) make a report in writing of the fact to a Metropolitan Magistrate or a Judicial Magistrate of the first class having jurisdiction in the place where the said person ordinarily resides; (b) by order notified in the Official Gazette direct the said person to appear before such officer, at such place and within such period as may be specified in the order.

(2) Upon the making of a report against any person under clause (a) of sub-section (1), the provisions of sections 82, 83, 84 and 85 of the Code of Criminal Procedure, 1973 (2 of 1974), shall apply in respect of such person and his property as if the detention order made against him were a warrant issued by the Magistrate.

(3) If any person fails to comply with an order issued under clause (b) of sub-section (1), he shall, unless he proves that it was not possible for him to comply therewith and that he had, within the period specified in the order, informed the officer mentioned in the order of the reason which rendered compliance therewith impossible and of his whereabouts, be punishable with imprisonment for a term which may extend to one year, or with fine, or with both.

(4) Notwithstanding anything contained in the Code of Criminal Procedure, 1973 (2 of 1974), every offence under sub-section (3) shall be cognizable.

8. Grounds of order of detention to be disclosed to persons affected by the order. (1) When a person is detained in pursuance of a detention order, the authority making the order shall, as soon as may be, but ordinarily not later than five days and in exceptional circumstances and for reasons to be recorded in writing, not later than ten days from the date of detention, communicate to him the grounds on which the order has been made and shall afford him the earliest opportunity of making a representation against the order to the appropriate Government.

(2) Nothing in sub-section (1) shall require the authority to disclose facts which it considers to be against the public interest to disclose.

9. Constitution of Advisory Boards. (1) The Central Government and each State Government shall, whenever necessary, constitute one or more Advisory Boards for the purposes of this Act.

(2) Every such Board shall consist of three persons who are, or have been, or are qualified to be appointed as, Judges of a High Court, and such persons shall be appointed by the appropriate Government.

(3) The appropriate Government shall appoint one of the members of the Advisory Board who is, or has been, a Judge of a High Court to be its Chairman, and in the case of a Union territory, the appointment to the Advisory Board of any person who is a Judge of the High Court of a State shall be with the previous approval of the State Government concerned.

10. Reference to Advisory Boards. Save as otherwise expressly provided in this Act, in every case where a detention order has been made under this Act, the appropriate Government shall, within three weeks from the date of detention of a person under the order, place before the Advisory Board constituted by it under section 9, the grounds on which the order has been made and the representation, if any, made by the person affected by the order, and in case where the order has been made by an officer mentioned in sub-section (3) of section 3, also the report by such officer under sub-section (4) of that section.

11. Procedure of Advisory Boards. (1) The Advisory Board shall, after considering the materials placed before it and, after calling for such further information as it may deem necessary from the appropriate Government or from any person called for the purpose through the appropriate Government or from the person concerned, and if, in any particular case, it considers it essential so to do or if the person concerned desires to be heard, after hearing him in person, submit its report to the appropriate Government within seven weeks from the date of detention of the person concerned.

(2) The report of the Advisory Board shall specify in a separate part thereof the opinion of the Advisory Board as to whether or not there is sufficient cause for the detention of the person concerned.

(3) When there is a difference of opinion among the members forming the Advisory Board, the opinion of the majority of such members shall be deemed to be the opinion of the Board.

(4) Nothing in this section shall entitle any person against whom a detention order has been made to appear by any legal practitioner in any matter connected with the reference to the Advisory Board; and the proceedings of the Advisory Board and its report, excepting that part of the report in which the opinion of the Advisory Board is specified, shall be confidential.

12. Action upon the report of the Advisory Board. (1) In any case where the Advisory Board has reported that there is, in its opinion, sufficient cause for the detention of a person, the appropriate Government may confirm the detention order and continue the detention of the person concerned for such period as it thinks fit.

(2) In any case where the Advisory Board has reported that there is, in its opinion, no sufficient cause for the detention of a person, the appropriate Government shall revoke the detention order and cause the person concerned to be released forthwith.

13. Maximum period of detention. The maximum period for which any person may be detained in pursuance of any detention order which has been confirmed under section 12 shall be twelve months from the date of detention: Provided that nothing contained in this section shall affect the power of the appropriate Government to revoke or modify the detention order at any earlier time.

14. Revocation of detention orders. (1) Without prejudice to the provisions of section 21 of the General Clauses Act, 1897 (10 of1897), a detention order may, at any time, be revoked or modified,—(a) notwithstanding that the order has been made by an officer mentioned in sub-section (3) of section 3, by the State Government to which that officer is subordinate or by the Central Government; (b) notwithstanding that the order has been made by a State Government, by the Central Government.

15. Temporary release of persons detained. (1) The appropriate Government may, at any time, direct that any person detained in pursuance of a detention order may be released for any specified period either without conditions or upon such conditions specified in the direction as that person accepts, and may, at any time, cancel his release.

(2) In directing the release of any person under sub-section (1), the appropriate Government may require him to enter into a bond with or without sureties for the due observance of the conditions specified in the direction.

(3) Any person released under sub-section (1) shall surrender himself at the time and place, and to the authority, specified in the order directing his release or cancelling his release, as the case may be.

(4) If any person fails without sufficient cause to surrender himself in the manner specified in sub-section (3), he shall be punishable with imprisonment for a term which may extend to two years, or with fine, or with both.

(5) If any person released under sub-section (1) fails to fulfil any of the conditions imposed upon him under the said sub-section or in the bond entered into by him, the bond shall be declared to be forfeited and any person bound thereby shall be liable to pay thepenalty thereof.

16. Protection of action taken in good faith. No suit or other legal proceeding shall lie against the Central Government or a State Government, and no suit, prosecution or other legal proceeding shall lie against any person, for anything in good faith done or intended to be done in pursuance of this Act.

17. Act not to have effect with respect to detentions under State laws. (1) Nothing in this Act shall apply or have any effect with respect to orders of detention, made under any State law, which are in force immediately before the commencement of the National Security Ordinance, 1980 (11 of 1980), and accordingly every person in respect of whom an order of detention made under any State law is in force immediately before such commencement, shall be governed with respect to such detention by the provisions of such State law or where the State law under which such order of detention is made is an Ordinance (hereinafter referred to as the State Ordinance) promulgated by the Governor of that State and the State

Ordinance has been replaced—(i) before such commencement, by an enactment passed by the Legislature of that State, by such enactment; or (ii) after such commencement, by an enactment which is passed by the Legislature of that State and the application of which is confined to orders of detention made before such commencement under the State Ordinance, by such enactment, as if this Act had not been enacted.

(2) Nothing in this section shall be deemed to bar the making under section 3, of a detention order against any person referred to in sub-section (1) after the detention order in force in respect of him as aforesaid immediately before the commencement of the National Security Ordinance, 1980 (11 of 1980), ceases to have effect for any reason whatsoever.

Explanation.—For the purposes of this section, "State law" means any law providing for preventive detention on all or any of the grounds on which an order of detention may be made under sub-section (2) of section 3 and in force in any State immediately before the commencement of the said Ordinance.

18. Repeal and saving. (1) The National Security Ordinance, 1980 (11 of 1980), is hereby repealed.

(2) Notwithstanding such repeal, anything done or any action taken under the said Ordinance shall be deemed to have been done or taken under the corresponding provisions of this Act, as if this Act had come into force on the 23rd day of September, 1980, and, in particular, any reference made under section 10 of the said Ordinance and pending before any Advisory Board immediately before the date on which this Act receives the assent of the President may continue to be dealt with by that Board after that date as if such Board had been constituted under section 9 of this Act.

IN PRESENT SCENARIO

On 26 March 2002, the controversial anti-terror law, the Prevention of Terrorism Act (POTA) was passed with 425 votes for the Act and 296 against, after a 10-hour debate in the parliament. The intensity of the effects of the bill could be seen very clearly by the rejection of the bill by the upper house of the Indian Parliament leading to a Joint Session of Parliament, a measure that had taken place only the third time in the past. The

Indian Ministry of Home Affairs justified the initial Ordinance after the September 11,2001 terror attacks by claiming an upsurge of terrorist activities, intensification of cross border terrorism, and insurgent groups in different parts of the country, despite the fact that the state of Jammu and Kashmir witnessed a decrease in the terrorist incidents taking place in that state.POTA, though now has been repealed, lives as an example showing the bold step taken by India in its fight against terrorism. The POTA had during its days and even after its downfall, has made India a silent spectator to serous ongoing debates between political parties, the media, social activists and NGOs on certain provisions seen to be draconian, within POTA.Two years from the enactment of the POTA, a number of issues as to the possibilities of misuse of the provisions of the anti terror law including the targeting of minorities and using it against political opponents had arisen. In Gujarat, all except one of the POTA detainees are from the Muslim minority and in Tamil Nadu and UP too the ostensible anti-terror law has been abused to book, without lucidity and accountability, political opponents and underprivileged communities respectively.A decade long experience with a previous national anti-terror law, the infamous Terrorist and Disruptive Activities Prevention (TADA) that was in force between 1985-1995 gives legitimacy to the fear that the misuse of such laws evoke among human rights activists, political dissenters and minorities. Under the TADA, the conviction rate was less than 1%, despite the fact that the confessions made to the police, even though being given under torture, were admissible as evidence.The developments after the enactment of the POTA, including the responses received by the POTA review committee show that the POTA is worse then TADA. POTA provides for criminal liability for mere association or communication with suspected terrorists without the possession of criminal intent (Section 3(5) of the POTA). Section 4 of POTA is similar to Section 5 of TADA in laying out a legal presumption that if a person is found in unauthorized possession of arms in a notified area, he/she is automatically linked with terrorist activity. Section 48(2) provides for the option of pre-trial police detention for up to 180 days. As under the TADA, where 98% of the cases never reached the trial stage, this Section 48(2) could also be misused by the police by keeping an accused for long periods of detention without charge or trial. Special courts for trials are established under POTA which are given the discretion to hold trials in non-public places, like prisons, and to withhold ! trial records from public scrutiny, thus preventing the independent monitoring of special court sessions. Section 32 provides that confessions made to police officers are to be admissible in trial, which has increased the possibility of coercion and torture in securing confessions.The developments after the enactment of the POTA, including the responses received by the POTA review committee show that the POTA is worse then TADA. POTA provides for criminal liability for mere association or communication with suspected terrorists without the possession of criminal intent (Section 3(5) of the POTA). Section 4 of POTA is similar to Section 5 of TADA in laying out a legal presumption that if a person is found in unauthorized possession of arms in a notified area, he/she is automatically linked with terrorist activity. Section 48(2) provides for the option of pre-trial police detention for up to 180 days. As under the TADA, where 98% of the cases never reached the trial stage, this Section 48(2) could also be misused by the police by keeping an accused for long periods of detention without charge or trial. Special courts for trials are established under POTA which are given the discretion to hold trials in non-public places, like prisons, and to withhold ! trial records from public scrutiny, thus preventing the independent monitoring of special court sessions. Section 32 provides that confessions made to police officers are to be admissible in trial, which has increased the possibility of coercion and torture in securing confessions.But these provisions could not act as an effective shield to protect the Act from the criticism it received for its other provisions abusing human rights. Those opposed to POTA had argued that existing laws were sufficient to deal with terrorism. Within a year POTA had already built up a dubious record and in some states it was already dreaded as its predecessor. State governments, including opposition-ruled ones, had not hesitated to use POTA to fix political opponents.

At the Peoples Tribunal on POTA and Other Security Legislation at the Press Club in New Delhi on July 16,2004 a 629-page report based on depositions made before the Tribunal by victims and their families from ten states in India, as well as expert depositions by lawyers and activists, showed that such security legislations grant sweeping powers to authorities, which has led to misuse of these powers and severe restriction of basic rights. At the same time, such legislations do not address the political, social and economic roots of the problem.

The tribunal concluded that the review of victim and expert testimony showed that the misuse of the Act is inseparable from its normal use. The tribunal stated that the statute meant to terrorise not so much the terrorists as ordinary civiliansand particularly the poor and disadvantaged such as dalits, religious minorities, adivasis, and working people. Thus the tribunal recommended that POTA be repealed and that too in such a manner that the POTA charges are deleted from all existing investigations and trials. But, if the state so desires, these may continue under other laws and charges.

Finally on September 17, 2004 the Union Cabinet in keeping with the UPA government's Common Minimum Programme, approved ordinances to repeal the controversial Prevention of Terrorism Act, 2002 (POTA) and amend the Unlawful Activities (Prevention) Act, 1967. Home Minister Shivraj Patil said that the government would provide a sunset period of one year during which all cases pertaining to POTA would be reviewed by the Central POTA Review Committee. He added, There would be no arrests made after the ordinance is promulgated. To fill the lacuna that have been created due to the repeal of the Act, adequate amendments were being brought to the Unlawful Activities (Prevention) Act, 1967 to define a terrorist act and provide for banning of terrorist organisations and their support systems, including funding of terrorism, attachment and forfeiture of proceeds of terrorism, etc. All terrorist organisations banned under POTA would continue to remain banned, under the Unlawful Activities Act, after the repeal of the Act. Some of the clauses contained in POTA, which will be completely dropped in the amended Unlawful Activities Act, are: the onus on the accused to prove his innocence, compulsory denial of bail to accused and admission as evidence in the court of law the confession made by the accused before the police officer.The BJP government has slammed the Cabinet decision to repeal POTA as politically motivated and compromising of the essentials of national security. BJP spokesperson and former Law Minister Arun Jaitley said if the amendments brought out under the existing laws after the repeal of POTA are found to be inadequate, the BJP-ruled states would be asked to come out with their own legislations filling up the lacuna. But till such a step is taken many innocent victims of the POTA can take a sign of relief and thank their stars that the reign of terror under the stringent anti terror law POTA has come to an end.

Critical Analysis of National Security Laws

It came as a shock to the citizens of the country that in spite of the tall claims of not having implemented the draconian POTA in Bihar , the government, administration and police in the state have been using the lapsed law TADA, to imprison and victimise political activists and agrarian poor. These violations could be carried out because the government did not withdraw the TADA cases after it lapsed but instead allowed the states to apply their own discretion. This left ample scope for the rich and the powerful to escape while allowing the police and administration to crackdown upon the asserting poor and those organising them.

Since the NDA government introduced POTA through an unprecedented joint session of the parliament, several political parties have expressed their opinion against POTA. Though no action has been taken as yet, the UPA government after assuming power has announced the withdrawal of POTA. However this also been announced prospectively and not with retrospective effect as has been the demand of dozens of civil liberty organisation and human rights groups who have pointed out violations in case after case. The fate of thousands of innocents across the country, who have been booked under POTA, continues to hang in uncertainty, particularly in the light of the fate of the TADA prisoners of Bihar, who found no justice even after the law that they had been booked under had long lapsed, since the cases against them were never withdrawn.

If 9 years after TADA has lapsed, activists, children and agrarian poor can be picked up and tried under the law, what is there to assure that a child booked under POTA would not be tried under the law 20 years from now? Why is it that black laws are being served on a platter to the police and administration, for strangling the democratic voices of those engaged in the struggle for social change? Addressing these questions a broad spectrum of political leaders from the Left and prominent citizens from all walks of life including jurists, advocates, human rights activists, academicians, artists, writers, journalists and students joined the convention, called on 6 August 2004, in New Delhi by Forum for Democratic Initiatives (FDI). The convention endorsed by the speakers and participants called for a nationwide movement against the murder of democracy through black laws like TADA and POTA. Speaker after speaker demanded the repeal of POTA and TADA retrospectively and condemned the Bihar Government for not withdrawing the TADA charges against activists and agrarian labourers of Jehanabad, Bihar. The convention also discussed the situation in Manipur and passed a resolution demanding the repeal of AFSPA, which has left the North Eastern states under the terror of Army rule.

The convention was chaired by eminent journalist and human rights activist Kuldeep Nayyar and addressed by a host of political leaders and prominent citizens from Delhi. The meeting was addressed by CPI-ML General Secretary Dipankar Bhattacharya, CPI-M Parliamentarian Dipankar Mukherjee, RSP leader and MP Abani Roy, Forward Bloc leader Devararjan, CPI leader Atul Anjan, Justice Rajinder Sachar, writer and activist Arundhati Roy, Editor of Mainstream Sumit Chakravarty, Supreme Court lawyers Nandita Haksar and Prashant Bhushan, Associate Editor of EPW Gautam Navlakha, JNU Professor Kamal Mitra Chenoy, Delhi University teacher Tripta Wahi and those battling POTA, TADA and AFSPA like DU lecturer SAR Geelani, CPI-ML activist from Jehanabad, Mahanand Prasad and a representative of Manipuri Students Association of Delhi, Seram Rojesh. The Convention was conducted by Radhika Menon, Convenor of FDI.

Initiating the discussion, eminent jurist, Rajinder Sachar said that the UPA government's failure to repeal POTA retrospectively and its attempt to retain some of its clauses through other laws is an instance of its 'hypocrisy in politics'.

CPI-ML activist and leader from Jehanabad, Mahanand Prasad presented a detailed account of the repression of agricultural labourers by the feudal-kulak-criminal-police nexus which was enjoying the protection of the state government. He said that this nexus led to the conviction for life of 14 activists of CPI-ML and implication of 17 others who are still awaiting trial, in a case where the dalits and agricultural labourers led a wage struggle and resisted the tyranny of a landlord who forced a dalit youth to lick spit. He described the Arwal TADA case of 1988, in which a dispute over the harvest of water-chestnut pond became an excuse for booking leaders of agrarian and democratic struggles under TADA. The main accused in this case is Shah Chand, who along with 13 others have been sentenced to life imprisonment imposing TADA on innocent citizens arrested at random which included two children aged 13 and 14 years, as well as local by a TADA court. Shah Chand, is the founding secretary of Inquilabi Muslim Conference, and a former mukhiya of Bhadasi village, whose work to introduce innovations in canal irrigation and free development work from corruption was hailed by the official quarters as the "Chand Model". Shah Chand and 13 others are in jail today, after the Supreme Court upheld the TADA court judgement in which possession of easily available Marxist and Kisan Sabha literature was cited as the sole 'evidence' for their being "terrorists"! Mahanand narrated the events that led to another case from Jehanabad, where 17 agricultural labourers are facing trial today, under TADA. They had been charged under TADA in 1989, when they complained to a labour inspector and led an agitation against a landlord, who had planted a dead cow outside the house of a dalit labourer, and forced another to "lick spit" in public. He questioned the intent of the "social justice" government of RJD, a key ally of the UPA, which had chosen to open TADA cases against the likes of Shankar Mehtar, a sweeper, Vijay Paswan and other dalit labourers, whose only crime was that of protesting against humiliations and paltry wages imposed by feudal landlords- a matter of shame for independent India. Mahanand notably pointed out that the

TADA case, in that very district of Bihar, against the notorious Ramadhar Singh, the chief of 'Sawarn Liberation Front', a private army of upper caste landlords and the prime accused in the Sawanbigha massacre was withdrawn by the same RJD government.

CPI-ML General Secretary Dipankar Bhattacharya hailed the people of Manipur and the rural poor of Bihar and others, who had paid with their blood, their liberty and their lives to make laws like TADA, POTA, AFSPA a national issue. He said it was sustained protests alone that have made violations a matter of national concern. He recalled the unrelenting struggle of the people of Bihar, including those who are today imprisoned under TADA, that made the police firing on labourers in Arwal a national issue. He said that today it was the protests sparked by Manorama Devi's killing that has forced the horrors of AFSPA onto the consciousness of the nation. He said that the democratic forces in the country, who had made POTA an issue in the elections, were now being taken for granted and stressed the need for mass movements to exert pressure on the govt. He called upon people to participate in the various campaigns to bring justice to the wronged TADA victims and visit Jehanabad to see the situation for themselves first hand.

CPI-M leader Dipankar Mukherjee, Forward Block leader Devarajan, CPI leader Atul Anjan, and RSP parliamentarian Abani Roy expressed solidarity with the struggles against black laws. Abani Roy questioned the definition of terrorism, saying even Bhagat Singh was branded a terrorist by colonialists, and today workers and poor peasants are being booked under "Terror Laws". He said that capitalist states did not consider the masses to be humans and capitalists of the world have united through globalisation and have resorted to newer forms of repression through agreements like WTO. He stressed the need to fight unitedly against TADA and POTA. Dipankar Mukherjee pointed out with examples how ordinary corporate laws were becoming terror laws for workers.

Speaking at the Convention writer Arundhati Roy said that India was showing the world how laws on terrorism can be used. For the US , terrorism replaced communism as a bogey to justify imperialist aggression. In their view, "terrorism" means those who resist colonial occupation. She said all over the world, poverty, too is conflated with "terrorism". She drew attention to the machinations of neo-liberal capitalism and its functioning, which imposes one law after another to suppress those who resist it. Taking a dig at the UPA government's announcements that it would not withdraw POTA retrospectively, she claimed that POTA may go but mota (intending the Hindi pun) would be in. She said that to view these laws as mere "human rights violations" is to wish away their political implications. The machine that assaults the poor, the colonised and the minority cannot be reduced to 'Bush' or 'BJP', said the writer, calling for a movement against the system itself.

Supreme Court lawyer Nandita Haksar cautioned against the trend in the human rights movement to divorce the struggle against such laws from the politics that surround it. She said it is to be remembered, that the ruling political establishment would not guarantee the democratic space for rising in favour of people's interest, even if TADA and POTA were removed. She reiterated the need to unite in the struggle against black laws.

According to DU teacher Tripta Wahi, state atrocities have been directed against minorities, dalits and agrarian labourers in particular, who do not have the ability to fight cases and circumvent loopholes in the act. She pointed out that AFPSA had been brought in during Congress rule under Nehru to suppress the nationality question in North-East. She wondered why the land reform agenda introduced in 1929 was never implemented while those who were asking for its implementation were being repressed. She spoke of how an Exhibition on the State's lies in the Parliament attack case had been banned in Delhi University and raised the issue of the thousands of youth of Punjab , Jammu and Kashmir and North-East who have gone missing.

Gautam Navlakha, Associate editor EPW, pointed out that leaders of landlord armies which massacre dalit poor are never convicted under "Terror Laws", whereas even lapsed laws like

TADA are invoked to sentence dalit landless labourers to life imprisonment and even death. He said, clearly the issue is not merely of 'civil liberties' but one of politics - since such laws had the political intention of snuffing out specific movements. He said the judicial procedures need to be probed as well, as there have been three-judge benches which have given verdicts of death sentence against 4 dalit landless labourers, even when one of the judges has said that the quality of evidence cited before the court was appalling.

DU lecturer SAR Geelani spoke of systematic shrinkage of democratic space in India , saying that India could be considered "free" only if it was truly democratic. He said laws like TADA, POTA, AFSPA were a threat to each citizen, not just Kashmiris, Manipuris or the dalit poor of Andhra and Bihar . Alluding to the criminal nexus between the police and judiciary he said that black laws permitted statements to be taken from the victims in a state of duress.

Prof. Kamal Mitra Chenoy of JNU pointed out that the ruling class always brands class struggles as "anti-national", and uses "national security" as an excuse to crush dissent. When such laws are contested by the civil liberties groups in the Supreme Court they have always been upheld by the latter because of the stated objective of dealing with terrorism. He said that while international agreements like WTO are complied with, there is no conformance to international human rights laws. The AFPSA, which was brought in as a temporary measure continues to be used even 50 years later. It is high time that black laws, which lead to human rights violations, be denounced as anti-national.

Supreme Court lawyer Prashant Bhushan said that most of the cases of TADA were in states like Gujarat , which were not affected by terrorism. The arbitrariness of TADA is evident from the fact that only one percent of the arrested was convicted. Referring to the TADA case where 14 activists of CPI-ML had been given life sentences, he said his study of the case indicated that it was completely unfair. He said that even as talks of repealing POTA were on, there were apprehensions that anti-people provisions of POTA would be included in the Indian

Penal Code to eliminate the need for establishment of a separate draconian law like POTA. He pointed out that the police and law and order machinery in the country is able to undermine democracy even without these laws and emphasised the inherent bias in our criminal jurisprudence, whereby white-collar criminals roam free under bail and have their cases withdrawn by buying witnesses and even judges off, while the poor are implicated in false cases and end up fighting losing legal battles for years.

Seram, a representative of the Manipur Students Association, Delhi while addressing the Convention said that the AFSPA which legitimised state repression is more dangerous than colonial laws. The procedural provisions of the act like detention without formal charges on the basis of suspicion and admitting confessions to the hawaldar as evidence is unjust in regard to the accused. He appealed that the law be repealed in toto and not just withdrawn from the Central part of Manipur.

APPENDIX I

INDIA TIMELINE—TERRORIST ACTIVITIES 2009 (LAST THREE MONTHS ONLY)

August 16: Two persons were seriously injured and a parked scooter was damaged badly in a blast near Grace Church in Margao city in south Goa around 9.45 p.m. (IST). Police sources said that the two injured persons were identified as Melgunda Patil and Yogesh Naik of Sanathan Sangsthan, a right wing Hindu outfit linked to Pragya Singh Thakur, one of the accused of Malegaon bomb blast.

August 17: Malgonda Patil, who was wounded in the October 16 bomb blast in the Margao area of Goa, succumbed to his injuries. The other injured was identified as Yogesh Naik. Police have registered cases under sections 121, 122, 123 of IPC and Section 4 & 5 of explosive substances act against both of them who are members of the Sanatan Sanstha, a Hindu extremist organisation, said the Deputy Inspector General of Police R. S. Yadav. Investigations have revealed that the bag containing one of the IEDs was placed in the scooter, which exploded while the scooter was being parked.

Pakistan's external intelligence agency, the ISI, is actively engaged in reviving militancy in Punjab by providing arms and money to extremists, the Director General of Punjab Police, Paramdeep Singh Gill, said. The Punjab Police will soon deploy five companies of the Indian Reserve Battalion on the lines of the National Security Guard commandos to tackle any disturbance in the State, the DGP said.

August 18: The death toll increased to two in the October 16 Margao bomb blast as the other wounded person, identified as Yogesh Naik, succumbed to his injuries.

October 19: Police in Margao in Goa arrested a man with alleged links to a Hindu extremist group Sanathan Saunstha in connection with the bomb blast on October 16. The man, who is yet to be identified, was arrested from the outfit's office by the ATS personnel from Maharashtra and Goa Police. A search of the outfit's office in Nesai near Margao town was conducted, Police sources confirmed. They said the outfit was suspected to have links with the 2008 Malegaon blast accused Sadhvi Pragya Singh Thakur.

October 20: Prime Minister Manmohan Singh said in New Delhi that regular intelligence reports had warned of "imminent attacks" in the country and the Security Forces needed to be prepared to meet any challenge. "There are both state and non-state actors involved in the business of terrorism. India is a democracy and an open society and is, therefore, sometimes highly vulnerable," said Dr. Singh.

Five SIMI cadres were arrested from Indore city in Madhya Pradesh. Two of the arrested cadres, identified as Mohammad Shafiq and Mohammad Yunus, belonged to Ujjain District, and were wanted by the Police to stand trial for serial bomb blasts in Ahmedabad (Gujarat) on July 26, 2008.

October 22: The Union Government indicated that an apex federal maritime security agency could well be in the offing. The Defence minister A.K. Antony indicated that the Government was trying to work out the modalities for such a body.

SFs were put on high alert in Chennai, capital of Tamil Nadu, and its suburbs following a letter received at the Adyar Police Station that warned of attacks on important targets. Though the letter did not specify any date or time for an attack, it named the Tamil Nadu Police Academy, Chennai Airport, Officers Training Academy and the "American Embassy" (U.S. Consulate) among others as its targets and challenged the Police to avert the sabotage if they could, Police sources said.

October 23: Tamil Nadu Congress Committee headquarters secretary R. Dhamotharan lodged a complaint with the Commissioner of Police that an anonymous caller had on warned of explosions in the TNCC office on Thiru VI Ka Salai and the residence of TNCC president K.V. Thangkabalu at Adyar. The man had claimed he was calling from the Sri Lankan Tamil refugee camp at Gummidipoondi, near Chennai.

Security of the Madhya Pradesh Chief Minister Shivraj Singh Chouhan has been beefed up in wake of a threat letter. Though the letter (written in Hindi) bore no address, the sender's name was stated as LeT, said Inspector General A.K. Soni adding a team has been assigned to probe the matter.

October 25: The Securities and Exchange Board of India (SEBI) has directed all stock exchanges and other securities intermediaries to keep a strict watch on the United Nations-listed terror funding entities, including underworld gangster Dawood Ibrahim. The market regulator has asked the securities intermediaries to inform the MHA within 24 hours if they find any client whose particulars match those of the entries listed by the UN.

Pakistan-based terrorist outfits the LeT, JeM and HM are planning to infiltrate terrorists into India to "create mayhem", the Union Home Minister P. Chidambaram said, asserting that the country's security forces were, however, prepared to meet any external threat. He also said that Pakistan has no will to prosecute and punish the perpetrators of the Mumbai terrorist attacks of November 2008 and voiced concern over the spread of Taliban in that country, apprehending that the danger could spread to the rest of South Asia, including India.

October 27: The Union Government issued a travel advisory alerting Indian pilgrims against visiting Pakistan. "Government of India is of the view that it is not advisable for Indian pilgrims to visit Pakistan in the prevailing situation when frequent terrorist attacks are taking place in Punjab province of Pakistan, where all *Gurudwaras* [Sikh places of worship] are situated," the advisory said.

The Union Home Minister P. Chidambaram said in New Delhi that massive expansion of the Central Paramilitary Forces (CPMFs) is indicative of inadequacies of State Police. Chidambaram said: "The police-population ratio in the country is much lower than the desired level of 220 and there is also wide variation among the States. He also drew the attention to other problems like outdated equipment and lack of training." He expressed concern over the lack of efforts made to fill a large number of vacancies which exist in the State Police at lower as well as higher levels. "Policing in the country has long been neglected and urgent reforms are needed in the State Police system," the Minister added.

Rajdhani Express was Hi-jacked by approx. 500 Naxalaties in Midnapur demanding their youth-leader Chattardhar-Mehto to be released.

October 28: Prime Minister Manmohan Singh said that the Government was willing to talk to anyone for peace in Jammu and Kashmir. The public sentiment was for peace and peaceful resolution of all problems and the era of violence and terrorism was coming to an end, he added.

October 29: Asserting that the offer of dialogue to resolve the Kashmir issue was not under any pressure, Prime Minister Manmohan Singh said that the spirit of his offer for talks to all shades of opinion in Jammu and Kashmir would be reciprocated in the same spirit The Prime Minister said the Centre wanted a peaceful resolution to Kashmir issue on both internal and external fronts. On the Pakistani allegations about India's involvement in fomenting trouble in Balochistan and funding Taliban, Dr. Singh said that these allegations were baseless, false and far from truth.

October 30: A Pakistani boat, which had intruded into Indian waters near Sir Creek area of Kutch District in Gujarat, was seized by the BSF personnel on but its occupants managed to escape. The BSF has heightened vigil in the area after receiving inputs of increased ISI activities in the creek area, they said.

Seven persons were arrested from different parts of the Indore District in Madhya Pradesh over the last seven days and booked under section 188 of IPC on charges of providing shelter to five SIMI cadres, Police said. Referring to the activities of SIMI in the State, Director General of Police S. K. Rout told reporters that so far Police have arrested 13 top SIMI leaders and 63 suspected cadres of the group.

October 31: The Union Home Minister P. Chidambaram warned that any more terrorist attacks like the one on November 26, 2008 in Mumbai would invite serious retaliation. If they carry out any more attacks on India, they will not only be defeated, but we will also retaliate with the force of a sledgehammer," he told a public meeting in Madurai in Tamil Nadu.

Two persons were arrested in Goa for allegedly planting explosives on the eve of the Diwali festival (October 16) at Sancoale in Panjim.

November 3: The Ahmedabad Police submitted 66 charge-sheets filed in 20 cases lodged in connection with the serial blasts of July 26, 2008 which killed over 59 persons in the city, to a special court for trial.

The Surat Police has also reportedly filed numerous charge-sheets in connection with 15 FIRs lodged after 29 unexploded bombs were recovered from various areas in Surat in the week that followed the Ahmedabad bomb blasts.

David Coleman Headley and Tahawwur Hussain Rana, arrested on October 27 by the US FBI, were part of a LeT plan of a major terrorist attack on the facilities of a Danish newspaper and the National Defence College in India, federal prosecutors have said.

Four cadres of the banned SIMI outfit were arrested near a graveyard in the Madra Tekri locality of Jabalpur by personnel of the Madhya Pradesh Police.

November 4: The Union Government said that adequate steps were being taken to protect military installations amid reports that the National Defence College was among prime targets identified for attack by terrorists.

A day after the LeT plot to attack key installations and schools was revealed by the FBI of US, more details were reported about the terror plan directed at India. As per a report obtained by *Zeenews*, the LeT is planning more 26/11 (the November 26, 2008 attack in Mumbai) like attacks in India. FBI inputs suggest that popular tourist spots, international boarding schools and several key installations in India are the prime targets of LeT this time. Two unidentified militants associated with the LeT's Bangladesh module have successfully sneaked into India through the eastern border. The FBI has warned Indian intelligence agencies that they have strong evidence about one of the two militants being in Maharashtra.

November 5: The Vice-Admiral Anil Chopra said in Mumbai that the Coast Guard would be doubling its strength in four years and tripling it in the coming decade

November 7: The Border Security Force has given a list of 97 North-east militant hideouts functioning in Bangladesh to

Bangladesh Rifles, urging them to dismantle the terror infrastructure at the earliest.

November 9: A Metropolitan court in Ahmedabad remanded two SIMI cadres to 14 days in Police custody.

APPENDIX II

PICTORIAL GLIMPSE OF TERROR

26 NOVEMBER

One hundred and sixty Indians and 25 foreigners were killed in an unprecedented terrorist strike in Mumbai from November 26 night to early morning on November 29.

The terrorists, who came by sea, opened fire indiscriminately on passers-by and then occupied two leading hotels and a Jewish religious-cum cultural centre for nearly 48 hours. All of them except one were ultimately killed by the Indian security forces. One person—a Pakistani national reportedly belonging to the Lashkar-e-Toiba, a Pakistan-based terrorist organization—was caught alive and is under interrogation by the Mumbai Police.

PICTURES

NDTV
LIVE
FIRE SPREADING AT TAJ HOTEL

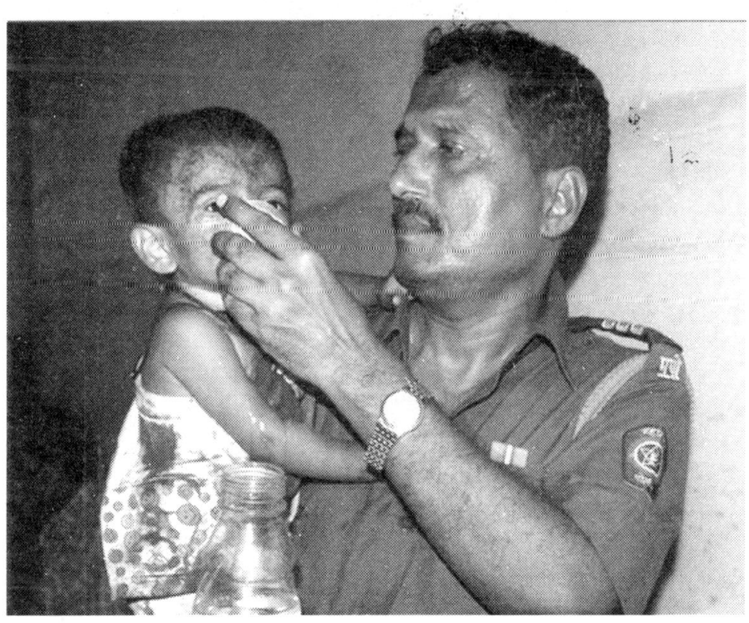

11 SEPTEMBER

World trade centre was one of the wonder of the seven wonders of the world 11th September was the dangerous day for America. 19 students hijacked four U.S.A. planes. At 9:00 A.M. First plane attacked the first tower of world trade centre. 9:15 AM second plane attacked the second tower of word trade centre. Some minutes later third plane attacked pentagon. One pentagon side was damaged. Some minutes later fourth plane damage in alone. An emergency was announced and suddenly white house was also became empties. It was a big Terrorist situation. These was only smoke and snoke at the place of world trade centre. People was falling from windows like hurted pigeons. It was a catastrophic scene. According type terms many people are also ruined their life. 50000 people injured in this attack.

APPENDIX III

COMPARISON OF SALIENT PROVISIONS OF ANTI-TERRORIST LAWS

Sl. No.	*Provision*	*UAPA, 1967*	*TADA, 1987*	*POTA, 2002*
(1)	(2)	(3)	(4)	(5)
1.	Purpose	An Act to provide for the more effective prevention of certain unlawful activities of individuals and associations and for matters connected therewith.	—	The act was the first and only legislative effort by the Union government to define and counter terrorist activities. It was formulated in the back drop of growing terrorist violence in Punjab which had its violent effects in other parts of the country too, including capital New Delhi.
2.	Preample	As Above	An Act to make special provisions for the prevention of, and for coping with, terrorist and disruptive activities and for matters connected therewith or incidental thereto.	An Act to make provisions for the prevention of, and for dealing with, terrorist activities and for matters connected therewith.

(*Contd.*)

APPENDIX (Contd.)

(1)	(2)	(3)	(4)	(5)
3.	Definitions - Unlawful Activity - Disruptive Activity - Terrorist Act - Terrorist	**S/2(f)-"Unlawful activity"**, in relation to an individual or association, means any action taken by such individual or association (whether by committing an act or by words, either spoken or written, or by signs or by visible representation or otherwise),- (i) which is intended, or supports any claim, to bring about, on any ground whatsoever, the cession of a part of the territory of India or the secession of a part of the territory of India from the Union, or which incites any individual or group of individuals to bring about such cession or secession;	**S/2(d)-"Disruptive activity"** has the meaning assigned to it in Section 4, and the expression "disruptionist" shall be construed accordingly; **S/2(h)-"Terrorist act"** has the meaning assigned to it in sub-section (1) of Section 3, and the expression **"Terrorist"** shall be construed accordingly; **S/3-Punishment for terrorist acts**. – (1) Whoever with intent to overawe the Government as by law established or to strike terror in the people or any section of the people or to alienate any section of the people or to adversely affect the harmony amongst different sections of the people does any act or thing by using bombs, dynamite or other explosive substances or inflammable substances or lethal	**S/2(g)- "Terrorist act"** has the meaning assigned to it in sub-section (1) of section 3, and the expression **"Terrorist"** shall be construed accordingly; S/3- 3. Punishment for terrorist acts.- (1) Whoever,— (a) with intent to threaten the unity, integrity, security or sovereignty of India or to strike terror in the people or any section of the people does any act or thing by using bombs, dynamite or other explosive substances or inflammable substances or firearms or other lethal weapons or poisons or noxious gases or other chemicals or by any other substances (whether biological or otherwise) of a hazardous nature or by any other means

1. P	(ii) which disclaims, questions, disrupts or is intended to disrupt the sovereignty and territorial integrity of India.	weapons or poisons or noxious gases or other chemicals or by any other substances (whether biological or otherwise) of a hazardous nature in such a manner as to cause, or as is likely to cause, death of, or injuries to, any person or persons or loss of, or damage to, or destruction of, property or disruption of any supplies or services essential to the life of the community, or detains any person and threatens to kill or injure such person in order to compel the Government or any other person to do or abstain from doing any act, commits a terrorist act. (2) Whoever commits a terrorist act, shall, - (i) if such act has resulted in the death of any person, be punishable with death or imprisonment for life and shall also be liable to fine;	whatsoever, in such a manner as to cause, or likely to cause, death of, or injuries to any person or persons or loss of, or damage to, or destruction of, property or disruption of any supplies or services essential to the life of the community or causes damage or destruction of any property or equipment used or intended to be used for the defense of India or in connection with any other purposes of the Government of India, any State Government or any of their agencies, or detains any person and threatens to kill or injure such person in order to compel the Government or any other person to do or abstain from doing any act; (b) is or continues to be a member of an association declared unlawful under the Unlawful Activities (Prevention) Act, 1967 (37 of 1967), or voluntarily does an act aiding or promoting in any

(Contd.)

APPENDIX (*Contd.*)

(1)	(2)	(3)	(4)	(5)
			(ii) in any other case, be punishable with imprisonment for a term which shall not be less than five years but which may extend to imprisonment for life and shall also be liable to fine. (3) Whoever conspires or attempts to commit, or advocates, abets, advises or incites or knowingly facilitates the commission of, a terrorist act or any act preparatory to a terrorist act, shall be punishable with imprisonment for a term which shall not be less than five years but which may extend to imprisonment for life and shall also be liable to fine. (4) Whoever harbours or conceals, or attempts to harbour or conceal, any terrorist shall be	manner the objects of such association and in either case is in possession of any unlicensed firearms, ammunition, explosive or other instrument or substance capable of causing mass destruction and commits any act resulting in loss of human life or grievous injury to any person or causes significant damage to any property, commits a terrorist act. Explanation.—For the purposes of this sub-section, "a terrorist act" shall include the act of raising funds intended for the purpose of terrorism. (2) Whoever commits a terrorist act, shall,— (a) if such act has resulted in the death of any person, be punishable with death or imprisonment for life and shall

punishable with imprisonment for a term which shall not be less than five years but which may extend to imprisonment for life and shall also be liable to fine. (5) Any person who is a member of a terrorists gang or a terrorist organisation, which is involved in terrorist acts, shall be punishable with imprisonment for a term which shall not be less than five years but which may extend to imprisonment for life and shall also be liable to fine. (6) Whoever holds any property derived or obtained from commission of any terrorist act or has been acquired through the terrorist funds shall be punishable with imprisonment for a term which shall not be less than five years but which may extend to imprisonment for life and shall also be liable to fine.	also be liable to fine; (b) in any other case, be punishable with imprisonment for a term which shall not be less than five years but which may extend to imprisonment for life and shall also be liable to fine. (3) Whoever conspires or attempts to commit, or advocates, abets, advises or incites or knowingly facilitates the commission of, a terrorist act or any act preparatory to a terrorist act, shall be punishable with imprisonment for a term which shall not be less than five years but which may extend to imprisonment for life and shall also be liable to fine. (4) Whoever voluntarily harbors or conceals, or attempts to harbour or conceal any person knowing that such person is a terrorist shall be punishable with imprisonment for a term which

(*Contd.*)

APPENDIX (*Contd.*)

(1)	(2)	(3)	(4)	(5)
			S/4- Punishment for disruptive activities. - (1) Whoever commits or conspires or attempts to commit or abets, advocates, advises, or knowingly facilitates the commission of, any disruptive activity or any act preparatory to a disruptive activity shall be punishable with imprisonment for a term which shall not be less than five years but which may extend to imprisonment for life and shall also be liable to fine. (2) For the purposes of sub-section (1), "disruptive activity" means any action taken, whether by act or by speech or through any other media or in any other manner whatsoever,— (i) which questions, disrupts or is intended to disrupt, whether directly or	shall not be less than three years but which may extend to imprisonment for life and shall also be liable to fine: Provided that this sub-section shall not apply to any case in which the harbour or concealment is by the husband or wife of the offender. (5) Any person who is a member of a terrorist gang or a terrorist organisation, which is involved in terrorist acts, shall be punishable with imprisonment for a term which may extend to imprisonment for life or with fine which may extend to rupees ten lakh or with both. Explanation.—For the purposes of this sub-section, "terrorist organisation" means an organisation which is concerned with or involved in terrorism.

indirectly, the sovereignty and territorial integrity of India; or

(ii) which is intended to bring about or supports any claim, whether directly or indirectly, for the cession of any part of India or the secession of any part of India from the Union.

Explanation – For the purposes of this sub-section, -

(a) "cession" includes the admission of any claim of any foreign country to any part of India, and

(b) "secession" includes the assertion of any claim to determine whether a part of India will remain within the Union.

(3) Without prejudice to the generality of the provisions of sub-section(2), it is hereby

(6) Whoever knowingly holds any property derived or obtained from commission of any terrorist act or has been acquired through the terrorist funds shall be punishable with imprisonment for a term which may extend to imprisonment for life or with fine which may extend to rupees ten lakh or with both.

(7) Whoever threatens any person who is a witness or any other person in whom such witness may be interested, with violence, or wrongfully restrains or confines the witness, or any other person in whom the witness may be interested, or does any other unlawful act with the said intent, shall be punishable with imprisonment which may extend to three years and fine.

(*Contd.*)

APPENDIX (*Contd.*)

(1)	(2)	(3)	(4)	(5)
			declared that any action taken, whether by act or by speech or through any other media or in any other manner whatsoever, which— a. advocates, advises, suggests or incites; or b. predicts, prophesies or pronounces or otherwise expresses, in such manner as to incite, advice, suggest or prompt, the killing or the destruction of any person bound by oath under the constitution to uphold the sovereignty and integrity of India or any public servant shall be deemed to be a disruptive activity within the meaning of this section.	

		(4) Whoever harbours or conceals, or attempts to harbour or conceal, any disruptiionist shall be punishable with imprisonment for a term which shall not be less than five years but which may be extend to imprisonment for life and shall also be liable to fine.	
4. - Organisation - Association - Gang	**S/2(g)-"Unlawful association"** means any association- (i) which has for its object any unlawful activity, or which encourages or aids persons to undertake any unlawful activity, or of which the members undertake such activity; or (ii) which has for its object any activity which is punishable under section 153A or section 153B of the Indian Penal Code (45 of 1860), or which encourages or aids persons to undertake any such activity, or of which the	—	**S/2(5)-** Any person who is a member of a terrorist gang or a terrorist organisation, which is involved in terrorist acts, shall be punishable with imprisonment for a term which may extend to imprisonment for life or with fine which may extend to rupees ten lakh or with both. Explanation.—For the purposes of this sub-section, **"Terrorist organisation"** means an organisation which is concerned with or involved in terrorism.

(*Contd.*)

APPENDIX (*Contd.*)

(1)	(2)	(3)	(4)	(5)
		members undertake any such activity: Provided that nothing contained in sub-clause (ii) shall apply to the State of Jammu and Kashmir.		
5.	Possession of certain unauthorized arms, etc.	—	**S/5- Possession of certain unauthorised arms, etc. in specified areas** – Where any person is in possession of any arms and ammunition specified in Columns 2 and 3 of Category I or Category III (a) of Schedule I to the Arms Rules, 1962, or bombs, dynamite or other explosive substances unauthorisedly in a notified area, he shall, notwithstanding anything contained in any other law for the time being in force, be punishable with imprisonment for a term which shall not be less	**S/4-Possession of certain unauthorized arms, etc.-** Where any person is in unauthorised possession of any— (a) arms or ammunition specified in columns (2) and (3) of Category I or Category III (a) of Schedule I to the Arms Rules, 1962, in a notified area, (b) bombs, dynamite or hazardous explosive substances or other lethal weapons capable of mass destruction or biological or chemical substances of

		than five years but which may extend to imprisonment for life and shall also be liable to fine.	warfare in any area, whether notified or not, he shall be guilty of terrorist act notwithstanding anything contained in any other law for the time being in force, and be punishable with imprisonment for a term which may extend to imprisonment for life or with fine which may extend to rupees ten lakh or with both. Explanation.—In this section, "notified area" means such area as the State Government may, by notification in the Official Gazette, specify.
6. Offence relating to Membership	**S/10-Penalty for being members of an unlawful association-** Whoever is and continues to be a member of an association declared unlawful by a notification issued under section 3 which has become	—	**S/20-Offence relating to membership of a terrorist organization.-** (1) A person commits an offence if he belongs or professes to belong to a terrorist organisation: Provided that this sub-section shall not apply where the person

(Contd.)

APPENDIX (Contd.)

(1)	(2)	(3)	(4)	(5)
		effective under sub-section (3) of that section, or takes part in meetings of any such unlawful association, or contributes to, or receives or solicits any contribution for the purpose of, any such unlawful association, or in any way assists the operations of any such unlawful association, shall be punishable with imprisonment for a term which may extend to two years, and shall also be liable to fine.		charged is able to prove— (a) that the organisation was not declared as a terrorist organisation at the time when he became a member or began to profess to be a member; and (b) that he has not taken part in the activities of the organisation at any time during its inclusion in the Schedule as a terrorist organisation. (2) A person guilty of an offence under this section shall be liable, on conviction, to imprisonment for a term not exceeding ten years or with fine or with both.
7.	Offence relating to Support	**S/13- Punishment for unlawful activities.** (1) Whoever- (a) takes part in or commits, or	—	**S/21-Offence relating to support given to a terrorist organization-** (1) A person commits an offence if—

(b) advocates abets, advises or incites the commission of, any unlawful activity, shall be punishable with imprisonment for a term which may extend to seven years, and shall also be liable to fine.	(a) he invites support for a terrorist organisation, and (b) the support is not, or is not restricted to, the provision of money or other property within the meaning of section 22.
(2) Whoever, in any way, assists any unlawful activity of any	(2) A person commits an offence if he arranges, manages or assists in arranging or managing a meeting which he knows is—
association, declared unlawful under section 3, after the notification	(a) to support a terrorist organisation, or
by which it has been so declared has become effective under subsection	(b) to further the activities of a terrorist organisation, or
(3) of that section, shall be punishable with imprisonment for a term	(c) to be addressed by a person who belongs or professes to belong to a terrorist organisation.
which may extend to five years, or with fine, or with both.	(3) A person commits an offence if he addresses a meeting for the purpose of encouraging support for a terrorist organisation or to further its activities.
(3) Nothing in this section shall apply to any treaty, agreement	
or convention entered into	

(*Contd.*)

APPENDIX (*Contd.*)

(1)	(2)	(3)	(4)	(5)
		between the Government of India and the Government of any other country or to any negotiations therefore carried on by any person authorised in this behalf by the Government of India.		(4) A person guilty of an offence under this section shall be liable on conviction, to imprisonment for a term not exceeding ten years or with fine or with both. Explanation.—For the purposes of this section, the expression "meeting" means a meeting of three or more persons whether or not the public are admitted.
8.	Offence relating to Funding	**S/11-Penalty for dealing with funds of an unlawful association-** If any person on whom a prohibitory order has been served under subsection (1) of section 7 in respect of any moneys, securities or credits pays, delivers, transfers or otherwise deals in any manner whatsoever with the same in	—	**S/22-Fund raising for a terrorist organization to be an offence-** (1) A person commits an offence if he— (a) invites another to provide money or other property, and (b) intends that it should be used, or has reasonable cause to suspect that it may be used, for the purposes of terrorism.

contravention of the prohibitory order, he shall be punishable with imprisonment for a term which may extend to three years, or with fine, or with both, and notwithstanding anything contained in the Code of Criminal Procedure, 1898 (5 of 1898), the court trying such contravention may also impose on the person convicted an additional fine to recover from him the amount of the moneys or credits or the market value of the securities in respect of which the prohibitory order has been contravened or such part thereof as the court may deem fit.	(2) A person commits an offence if he— (a) receives money or other property, and (b) intends that it should be used, or has reasonable cause to suspect that it may be used, for the purposes of terrorism. (3) A person commits an offence if he— (a) provides money or other property, and (b) knows or has reasonable cause to suspect that it will or may be used for the purposes of terrorism. (4) In this section, a reference to the provision of money or other property is a reference to its being given, lent or otherwise made available, whether or not for consideration.

(Contd.)

APPENDIX (Contd.)

(1)	(2)	(3)	(4)	(5)
				(5) A person guilty of an offence under this section shall be liable on conviction, to imprisonment for a term not exceeding fourteen years or with fine or with both.
9.	Power to direct for sample	—	—	**S/27- Power to direct for samples, etc.-** (1) When a police officer investigating a case requests the Court of a Chief Judicial Magistrate or the Court of a Chief Metropolitan Magistrate in writing for obtaining samples of handwriting, finger-prints, foot-prints, photographs, blood, saliva, semen, hair, voice of any accused person, reasonably suspected to be involved in the commission of an offence under this Act, it shall be lawful for the Court of a Chief Judicial

			Magistrate or the Court of a Chief Metropolitan Magistrate to direct that such samples be given by the accused person to the police officer either through a medical practitioner or otherwise, as the case may be. (2) If any accused person refuses to give samples as provided in sub-section (1), the Court shall draw adverse inference against the accused.
10. **Punishment for malicious action for Police officer**	A	—	**S/58-Punishment and compensation for malicious action-** (1) Any police officer who exercises powers corruptly or maliciously, knowing that there are no reasonable grounds for proceeding under this Act, shall be punishable with imprisonment which may extend to two years, or with fine, or with both.

(*Contd.*)

APPENDIX (*Contd.*)

(1)	(2)	(3)	(4)	(5)
				(2) If the Special Court is of the opinion that any person has been corruptly or maliciously proceeded against under this Act, the Court may award such compensation as it deems fit to the person, so proceeded against and it shall be paid by the officer, person, authority or Government, as may be specified in the order.
11.	Admissibility of Confession to Police Officer		**S/15- Certain confessions made to police officers to be taken into consideration-** (1) Nothwithstanding anything in the Code or in the Indian Evidence Act, 1872, but subject to the provisions of this section, a confession made by a person before a police officer not lower in rank than a Superintendent of Police and recorded by such police	**S/32- Certain confessions made to police officers to be taken into consideration-** (1) Notwithstanding anything in the Code or in the Indian Evidence Act, 1872 (1 of 1872), but subject to the provisions of this section, a confession made by a person before a police officer not lower in rank than a Superintendent of Police and

officer either in writing or on any mechanical device like cassettes, tapes or sound tracks from out of which sounds or images can be reproduced, shall be admissible in the trial of such person or co-accused, abettor or conspirator] for an offence under this Act or rules made thereunder: [Provided that co-accused, abettor or conspirator is charged and tried in the same case together with the accused]. (2) The police officer shall, before recording any confession under sub-section (1), explain to the person making it that he is not bound to make a confession and that, if he does so, it may be used as evidence against him and such police officer shall not record any such confession unless upon questioning the person making it, he has reason to believe that it is being made voluntarily.	recorded by such police officer either in writing or on any mechanical or electronic device like cassettes, tapes or sound tracks from out of which sound or images can be reproduced, shall be admissible in the trial of such person for an offence under this Act or the rules made thereunder. (2) A police officer shall, before recording any confession made by a person under sub-section (1), explain to such person in writing that he is not bound to make a confession and that if he does so, it may be used against him: Provided that where such person prefers to remain silent, the police officer shall not compel or induce him to make any confession. (3) The confession shall be recorded in an atmosphere free

(*Contd.*)

APPENDIX (Contd.)

(1)	(2)	(3)	(4)	(5)
				from threat or inducement and shall be in the same language in which the person makes it. (4) The person from whom a confession has been recorded under sub-section (1), shall be produced before the Court of a Chief Metropolitan Magistrate or the Court of a Chief Judicial Magistrate along with the original statement of confession, written or recorded on mechanical or electronic device within forty-eight hours. (5) The Chief Metropolitan Magistrate or the Chief Judicial Magistrate, shall, record the statement, if any, made by the person so produced and get his signature or thumb impression and if there is any complaint of torture, such person shall be directed to be produced for

			medical examination before a Medical Officer not lower in rank than an Assistant Civil Surgeon and thereafter, he shall be sent to judicial custody.
12. Admissibility of evidence collected through Interception of communication	—	—	**S/45-Admissibility of evidence collected through the interception of communications-** Notwithstanding anything in the Code or in any other law for the time being in force, the evidence collected through the interception of wire, electronic or oral communication under this Chapter shall be admissible as evidence against the accused in the Court during the trial of a case: Provided that, the contents of any wire, electronic or oral communication intercepted pursuant to this Chapter or evidence derived therefrom shall

(*Contd.*)

APPENDIX (*Contd.*)

(1)	(2)	(3)	(4)	(5)
				not be received in evidence or otherwise disclosed in any trial, hearing or other proceeding in any court unless each accused has been furnished with a copy of the order of the Competent Authority, and accompanying application, under which the interception was authorised or approved not less than ten days before trial, hearing or proceeding: Provided further that, the period of ten days may be waived by the judge trying the matter, if he comes to the conclusion that it was not possible to furnish the accused with the above information ten days before the trial, hearing or proceeding and that the accused will not be prejudiced by the delay in receiving such information.

13. Bail Provisions	**S/20(8)**-Notwithstanding anything contained in the Code, no person accused of an offence punishable under this Act or any rule made thereunder shall, if in custody, be released on bail or on his own bond unless, – a. the Public Prosecutor has been given an opportunity to oppose the application for such release, and b. where the Public Prosecutor opposes the application, the Court is satisfied that there are reasonable grounds for believing that he is not guilty of such offence and that he is not likely to commit any offence while on bail.	**S/20(6)**- Notwithstanding anything contained in the Code, no person accused of an offence punishable under this Act shall, if in custody, be released on bail or on his own bond unless the Court gives the Public Prosecutor an opportunity of being heard. **S/20(7)**- Where the Public Prosecutor opposes the application of the accused to release on bail, no person accused of an offence punishable under this Act or any rule made thereunder shall be released on bail until the Court is satisfied that there are grounds for believing that he is not guilty of committing such offence: Provided that after the expiry of a period of one year from the date of detention of the accused for an offence under this Act, the provisions of sub-section (6) of this section shall apply.

(*Contd.*)

APPENDIX (Contd.)

(1)	(2)	(3)	(4)	(5)
14.	Presumption as to offence		**S/21-Presumption as to offences under Section 3 –** (1) In a prosecution for an offence under sub-section (1) of Section 3, if it is proved – (a) that the arms or explosives or any other substances specified in Section 3 were recovered from the possession of the accused and there is reason to believe that such arms or explosives or other substances of similar nature, were used in the commission of such offence; or (b) that by the evidence of an expert the fingerprints of the accused were found at the site of the offence or on anything including arms	**S/53-Presumption as to offences under section 3-** (1) In a prosecution for an offence under sub-section (1) of section 3, if it is proved— (a) that the arms or explosives or any other substances specified in section 4 were recovered from the possession of the accused and there is reason to believe that such arms or explosives or other substances of a similar nature, were used in the commission of such offence; or (b) that the finger-prints of the accused were found at the site of the offence or on anything including arms

		and vehicles used in connection with the commission of such offence. (2) In a prosecution for an offence under sub-section 3 of Section 3, if it is proved that the accused rendered any financial assistance to a person accused of, or reasonably suspected of, an offence under that section, the Designated Court shall presume, unless the contrary is proved, that such person has committed the offence under that sub-section.	and vehicles used in connection with the commission of such offence, the Special Court shall draw adverse inference against the accused. (2) In a prosecution for an offence under sub-section (3) of section 3, if it is proved that the accused rendered any financial assistance to a person, having knowledge that such person is accused of, or reasonably suspected of, an offence under that section, the Special Court shall draw adverse inference against the accused.
15. Protection taken in Good-Faith	**S/18-Protection of action taken in good faith-** (1) No suit or other legal proceeding shall lie against the Government in respect of any loss or damage caused or likely to be caused by anything which is in good faith done or intended	**S/26-Protection of action taken under this Act-** No suit, prosecution or other legal proceeding shall lie against the Central Government or State Government or any other authority on whom powers have been conferred under this Act or any rules made thereunder, for	**S/57-Protection of action taken in good faith-** No suit, prosecution or other legal proceeding shall lie against the Central Government or a State Government or any officer or authority of the Central Government or State Government or any other

(Contd.)

APPENDIX (*Contd.*)

(1)	(2)	(3)	(4)	(5)
		to be done in pursuance of this Act or any rules or orders made there under. (2)No suit, prosecution or other legal proceeding shall lie against the District Magistrate or any officer authorised in this behalf by the Government or the District Magistrate in respect of anything which is in good faith done or intended to be done in pursuance of this Act or any rules or orders made there under.	anything which is in good faith done or purported to be done in pursuance of this Act or any rules made thereunder or any order issued under any such rule.	authority on whom powers have been conferred under this Act, for anything which is in good faith done or purported to be done in pursuance of this Act: Provided that no suit, prosecution or other legal proceedings shall lie against any serving member or retired member of the armed forces or other para-military forces in respect of any action taken or purported to be taken by him in good faith, in the course of any operation directed towards combating terrorism.
16.	Obligation to furnish information		—	**S/14-Obligation to furnish information-** (1) Notwithstanding anything contained in any other law, the officer investigating any offence under this Act, with prior

approval in writing of an officer not below the rank of a Superintendent of Police, may require any officer or authority of the Central Government or a State Government or a local authority or a bank, or a company, or a firm or any other institution, establishment, organisation or any individual to furnish information in their possession in relation to such offence, on points or matters, where the investigating officer has reason to believe that such information will be useful for, or relevant to, the purposes of this Act.

(2) Failure to furnish the information called for under sub-section (1), or deliberately furnishing false information shall be punishable with imprisonment for a term which may extend to three years or with fine or with both.

(Contd.)

APPENDIX (Contd.)

(1)	(2)	(3)	(4)	(5)
				(3) Notwithstanding anything contained in the Code, the offence under sub-section (1) shall be tried as a summary case and the procedure prescribed in Chapter XXI of the said Code [except sub-section (2) of section 262] shall be applicable thereto.
17.	Provisions for Custody Period		**S/20- Modified application of certain provisions of the Code-** (1) Nothwithstanding anything contained in the Code or any other law, every offence punishable under this Act or any rule made thereunder shall be deemed to be a cognizable offence within the meaning of clause (c) of Section 2 of the Code, and "cognizable case" as defined in that clause shall be construed accordingly. (2) Section 21 of the Code shall	S/49-Modified application of certain provisions of the Code- (1) Notwithstanding anything contained in the Code or any other law, every offence punishable under this Act shall be deemed to be a cognizable offence within the meaning of clause (c) of section 2 of the Code, and "cognizable case" as defined in that clause shall be construed accordingly. (2) Section 167 of the Code shall apply in relation to a case

apply in relation to a case involving an offence punishable under this Act or any rule made thereunder subject to the modification that the reference to "the State Government" therein shall be construed as a reference to "the Central Government or the State Government".

(3) Section 164 of the Code shall apply in relation to a case involving an offence punishable under this Act or any rule made thereunder, subject to the modification that the reference in subsection (1) thereof to "Metropolitan Magistrate or Judicial Magistrate" shall be construed as a reference to "Metropolitan Magistrate, Judicial Magistrate, Executive Magistrate or Special Executive Magistrate.

(4) Section 167 of the Code shall apply in relation to a case involving an offence punishable under this Act subject to the modification that in sub-section (2),—

(a) the references to "fifteen days", "ninety days" and "sixty days", wherever they occur, shall be construed as references to "thirty days", "ninety days" and "ninety days", respectively; and

(b) after the proviso, the following provisos shall be inserted, namely:—

"Provided further that if it is not possible to complete the investigation within the said period of ninety days, the Special Court shall extend the said period up to one hundred and eighty days, on the report of the Public Prosecutor indicating the progress of the investigation and the specific reasons for the detention of the accused beyond the said period of ninety days:

(Contd.)

APPENDIX (Contd.)

(1)	(2)	(3)	(4)	(5)
			under this Act or any rule made thereunder subject to the modifications that,- a. the reference in sub-section (1) thereof to "Judicial Magistrate" shall be construed as a reference to Judicial Magistrate or Executive Magistrate or Special Executive Magistrate; b. the reference in sub-section (2) thereof to "fifteen days," "ninety days" and "sixty days," wherever they occur, shall be construed as references to "sixty days."[one hundred and eighty days] and [8][one hundred and eighty days], respectively; and (bb)sub-section (2-A) thereof shall be deemed to have been omitted. (bbb) in sub-section (2), after the proviso, the following proviso shall be inserted, namely:-	Provided also that if the police officer making the investigation under this Act, requests, for the purposes of investigation, for police custody from judicial custody of any person from judicial custody, he shall file an affidavit stating the reasons for doing so and shall also explain the delay, if any, for requesting such police custody.". (3) Section 268 of the Code shall apply in relation to a case involving an offence punishable under this Act subject to the modification that— (a) the reference in sub-section (1) thereof— (i) to "the State Government" shall be construed as a reference to "the Central Government or the State Government",

"Provided further that, if it is not possible to complete the investigation within the said period of one hundred and eighty days, the Designated Court shall extend the said period up to one year, on the report of the Public Prosecutor indicating the progress of the investigation and the specific reasons for the detention of the accused beyond the said period of one hundred and eighty days.]

(5) Section 268 of the Code shall apply in relation to a case involving an offence punishable under this Act or any rule made thereunder subject to the modifications that -

a. the reference in sub-section(1) thereof –

(i) to "the State Government" shall be construed as a reference to "the Central Government or the State Government";

(ii) to "order of the State Government" shall be construed as a reference to "order of the Central Government or the State Government, as the case may be"; and

(b) the reference in sub-section (2) thereof, to "the State Government" shall be construed as a reference to "the Central Government or the State Government, as the case may be".

(4) Sections 366, 367 and 371 of the Code shall apply in relation to a case involving an offence triable by a Special Court subject to the modification that the reference to "Court of Session", wherever occurring therein, shall be construed as the reference to "Special Court".

(5) Nothing in section 438 of the Code shall apply in relation to any case involving the arrest of

(Contd.)

APPENDIX (Contd.)

(1)	(2)	(3)	(4)	(5)
			(ii) to "order of the State Government" shall be construed as a reference to "order of the Central Government or the State Government, as the case may be"; or	any person accused of having committed an offence punishable under this Act.
			b. the reference in sub-section (2) thereof, to "State Government" shall be construed as a reference to "Central Government or the State Government, as the case may be".	(6) Notwithstanding anything contained in the Code, no person accused of an offence punishable under this Act shall, if in custody, be released on bail or on his own bond unless the Court gives the Public Prosecutor an opportunity of being heard.
			(6) Sections 366 to 371 and Section 392 of the Code shall apply in relation to a case involving an offence triable by a Designated Court subject to the modifications that the references to "Court of Session" and "High Court", wherever occurring therein, shall be construed as references to "Designated Court" and "Supreme Court", respectively.	(7)Where the Public Prosecutor opposes the application of the accused to release on bail, no person accused of an offence punishable under this Act or any rule made thereunder shall be released on bail until the Court is satisfied that there are grounds for believing that he is not guilty of committing such offence: Provided that after the expiry of

(7) Nothing in Section 438 of the Code shall apply in relation to any case involving the arrest of any person on an accusation of having committed an offence punishable under this act or any rule made thereunder. (8) Notwithstanding anything contained in the Code, no person accused of an offence punishable under this Act or any rule made thereunder shall, if in custody, be released on bail or on his own bond unless, – a. the Public Prosecutor has been given an opportunity to oppose the application for such release, and b. where the Public Prosecutor opposes the application, the Court is satisfied that there are reasonable grounds for believing that he is not guilty of such offence and that he is not likely to commit any offence while on bail.	a period of one year from the date of detention of the accused for an offence under this Act, the provisions of sub-section (6) of this section shall apply. (8) The restrictions on granting of bail specified in sub-sections (6) and (7) are in addition to the restrictions under the Code or any other law for the time being in force on granting of bail. (9) Notwithstanding anything contained in sub-sections (6), (7) and (8), no bail shall be granted to a person accused of an offence punishable under this Act, if he is not an Indian citizen and has entered the country unauthorisedly or illegally except in very exceptional circumstances and for reasons to be recorded in writing.

(*Contd.*)

APPENDIX (*Contd.*)

(1)	(2)	(3)	(4)	(5)
			(9) The limitations on granting of bail specified in sub-section (8) are in addition to the limitations under the Code or any other law for the time being in force on granting of bail.	
18.	Punishment for making demands of radioactive substances, nuclear devices, etc.			
19.	Punishment for organizing of terrorist camps			
20.	Punishment for recruiting for recruiting of any person or persons for terrorist act			

(*Contd.*)

APPENDIX (Contd.)

Sl. No.	Provision	UAPA, 2004	UAPA, 2008
(1)	(2)	(6)	(7)
1.	Purpose	After the Prevention of Terrorism Act, 2002, was repealed through an Ordinance, the President of India, on September 21, 2004, promulgated an Ordinance to amend the Unlawful Activities (Prevention) Act, 1967.	—
2.	Preamble	An Act to provide for the more effective prevention of certain unlawful activities and for dealing with terrorist activities of individuals and associations and for matters connected therewith.	An Act to provide for the more effective prevention of certain unlawful activities and for dealing with terrorist activities of individuals and associations and for matters connected therewith. "Whereas the Security Council of the United Nations in its 4385th meeting adopted Resolution 1373 (2001) on 28th September, 2001, under Chapter VII of the Charter of the United Nations requiring all the States to fake measures to combat international terrorism, And whereas Resolutions 1267 (1999). 1333 (2000), 1363 (2001), 1390 (2002), 1455 (2003), 1526 (2004), 1566 (2004), 1617 (2005), 1735 (2006) and 1322 (2008) of the Security Councilor the united

(Contd.)

APPENDIX (*Contd.*)

(1)	(2)	(6)	(7)
			Nations require the States to take action against certain terrorists and terrorist organisations, to freeze the assets and other economic resources, to prevent the entry into or the transit through their territory, and prevent the direct or indirect supply, sale or transfer of arms and ammunitions to the individuals or entities listed in the Schedule; And whereas the Central Government, in exercise of the powers conferred by section 2 of the United Nations (Security Council) Act, 1947 (43 of 1947.) has made the Prevention and Suppression of Terrorism (Implementation of Security Council Resolutions) Order, 2007; And whereas it is considered necessary to give effect to the said Resolutions and the Order and to make special provisions for the prevention of, and for coping with, terrorist activities and for matters connected therewith or incidental thereto."

3. Definitions - Unlawful Activity - Disruptive Activity - Terrorist Act - Terrorist	**S/2(k)-"Terrorist act"** has the meaning assigned to it in section 15, and the expressions **"Terrorism"** and **"Terrorist"** shall be construed accordingly; **S/2(o)-"Unlawful activity"**, in relation to an individual or association, means any action taken by such individual or association (whether by committing an act or by words, either spoken or written, or by signs or by visible representation or otherwise),- (*i*) which is intended, or supports any claim, to bring about, on any ground whatsoever, the cession of a part of the territory of India or the secession of a part of the territory of India from the Union, or which incites any individual or group of individuals to bring about such cession or secession; or (*ii*) which disclaims, questions, disrupts or is intended to disrupt the sovereignty and territorial integrity of India ; or (*iii*) which causes or is intended to cause disaffection against India; **S/15-Terrorist Act**-Whoever, with intent to threaten the unity, integrity, security or sovereignty of India or to strike terror in the	**S/15-Terrorist Act**-Whoever does any act with intent to threaten or likely to threaten the unity, integrity, security or sovereignty of India or with intent to strike terror or likely to strike terror in the people or any section of the people in India or in any foreign country,— (*a*) by using bombs, dynamite or other explosive substances or inflammable substances or firearms or other lethal weapons or poisonous or noxious gases or other chemicals or by any other substances (whether biological radioactive, nuclear or otherwise) of a hazardous nature or by any other means of whatever nature to cause or likely to cause— (*i*) death of, or injuries to, any person or persons; or (*ii*) loss of, or damage to, or destruction of, property; or (*iii*) disruption of any supplies or services essential to the life of the community in India or in any foreign country; or (*iv*) damage or destruction of any property in India or in a foreign country used or intended to be used for the defence of India or in connection

(*Contd.*)

APPENDIX (*Contd.*)

(1)	(2)	(6)	(7)
		people or any section of the people in India or in any foreign country, does any act by using bombs, dynamite or other explosive substances or inflammable substances or firearms or other lethal weapons or poisons or noxious gases or other chemicals or by any other substances (whether biological or otherwise) of a hazardous nature, in such a manner as to cause, or likely to cause, death of, or injuries to any person or persons or loss of, or damage to, or destruction of, property or disruption of any supplies or services essential to the life of the community in India or in any foreign country or causes damage or destruction of any property or equipment used or intended to be used for the defence of India or in connection with any other purposes of the Government of India, any State Government or any of their agencies, or detains any person and threatens to kill or injure such person in order to compel the Government in India or the Government of a foreign country or any other person to do or abstain from doing any act, commits a terrorist act.	with any other purposes of the Government of India, any State Government or any of their agencies; or (*b*) overawes by means of criminal force or the show of criminal force or attempts to do so or causes death of any public functionary or attempts to cause death of any public functionary; or (*c*) detains, kidnaps or abducts any person and threatens to kill or injure such person or does any other act in order to compel the Government of India, any State Government or the Government of a foreign country or any other person to do or abstain from doing any act, commits a terrorist act. *Explanation*.—For the purpose of this section, public functionary means the constitutional authorities and any other functionary notified in the Official Gazette by the Central Government as a public functionary".

4.	- Organi-sation - Association - Gang	**S/2(l)- "terrorist gang"** means any association, other than terrorist organisation, whether systematic or otherwise, which is concerned with, or involved in, terrorist act; **S/2(m)- "Terrorist organisation"** means an organisation listed in the Schedule or an organisation operating under the same name as an organisation so listed; **S/2(p)-"Unlawful association"** means any association,- (*i*) which has for its object any unlawful activity, or which encourages or aids persons to undertake any unlawful activity, or of which the members undertake such activity; or (*ii*) which has for its object any activity which is punishable under section 153A or section 153B of the Indian Penal Code, or which encourages or aids persons to undertake any such activity, or of which the members undertake any such activity: Provided that nothing contained in sub-clause (*ii*) shall apply to the State of Jammu and Kashmir;	—

(*Contd.*)

APPENDIX (*Contd.*)

(1)	*(2)*	*(6)*	*(7)*
5.	Possession of certain unauthorized arms, etc.	**S/23(1)-Enhanced Penalties-** If any person with intent to aid any terrorist contravenes any provision of, or any rule made under the Explosives Act, 1884 or the Explosive Substances Act, 1908 or the Inflammable Substances Act, 1952 or the Arms Act, 1959, or is in unauthorised possession of any bomb, dynamite or hazardous explosive substance or other lethal weapon or substance capable of mass destruction or biological or chemical substance of warfare, he shall, notwithstanding anything contained in any of the aforesaid Acts or the rules made thereunder, be punishable with imprisonment for a term which shall not be less than five years but which may extend to imprisonment for life, and shall also be liable to fine. (2) Any person who, with intent to aid any terrorist, attempts to contravene or abets, or does any act preparatory to contravention of any provision of any law or rule specified in sub-section (*1*), shall be deemed to have contravened	—

	that provision under sub-section (*1*) and the provisions of that sub-section in relation to such person, have effect subject to the modification that the reference to "imprisonment for life" therein shall be construed as a reference to "imprisonment for ten years".	
6. Offence relating to Membership	**S/10-Penalty for being member of an unlawful association, etc-** Where an association is declared unlawful by a notification issued under section 3 which has become effective under sub-section (*3*) of that section,- (*a*) a person, who- (*i*) is and continues to be a member of such association; or (*ii*) takes part in meetings of such association; or (*iii*) contributes to, or receives or solicits any contri-bution for the purpose of, such association; or (*iv*) in any way assists the operations of such association, shall be punishable with imprisonment for a term which may extend to two years, and shall also be liable to fine; and	—

(*Contd.*)

APPENDIX (*Contd.*)

(1)	(2)	(6)	(7)
		(*b*) a person, who is or continues to be a member of such association, or voluntarily does an act aiding or promoting in any manner the objects of such association and in either case is in possession of any unlicensed firearms, ammunition, explosive or other instrument or substance capable of causing mass destruction and commits any act resulting in loss of human life or grievous injury to any person or causes significant damage to any property,- (*i*) and if such act has resulted in the death of any person, shall be punishable with death or imprisonment for life, and shall also be liable to fine; (*ii*) in any other case, shall be punishable with imprisonment for a term which shall not be less than five years but which may extend to imprisonment for life, and shall also be liable to fine.". S/20-Punishment for being member of terrorist gang or organisation- Any person who is a member of a terrorist gang or	

a terrorist organisation, which is involved in terrorist act, shall be punishable with imprisonment for a term which may extend to imprisonment for life, and shall also be liable to fine.

S/38-Offence relating to membership of a terrorist organization-

(1) A person, who associates himself, or professes to be associated, with a terrorist organisation with intention to further its activities, commits an offence relating to membership of a terrorist organisation:

Provided that this sub-section shall not apply where the person charged is able to prove—

(*a*) that the organisation was not declared as a terrorist organisation at the time when he became a member or began to profess to be a member; and

(*b*) that he has not taken part in the activities of the organisation at any time during its inclusion in the Schedule as a terrorist organisation.

(2) A person, who commits the offence relating to membership of a terrorist organisation under sub-section (1), shall be punishable with imprisonment for a term not exceeding ten years, or with fine, or with both.

(*Contd.*)

APPENDIX (*Contd.*)

(1)	(2)	(6)	(7)
7.	Offence relating to Support	**S/23(2)-Enhanced Penalties-** Any person who, with intent to aid any terrorist, attempts to contravene or abets, or does any act preparatory to contravention of any provision of any law or rule specified in sub-section (*1*), shall be deemed to have contravened that provision under sub-section (*1*) and the provisions of that sub-section in relation to such person, have effect subject to the modification that the reference to "imprisonment for life" therein shall be construed as a reference to "imprisonment for ten years". S/39- Offence relating to support given to a terrorist organization- (1) A person commits the offence relating to support given to a terrorist organisation,- (a) who, with intention to further the activity of a terrorist organisation,- (*i*) invites support for the terrorist organisation, and (*ii*) the support is not or is not restricted to provide money or other property within the	—

<table>
<tr><td></td><td>meaning of section 40; or
(b) who, with intention to further the activity of a terrorist organisation, arranges, manages or assists in arranging or managing a meeting which he knows is-
(i) to support the terrorist organisation, or
(ii) to further the activity of the terrorist organisation, or
(iii) to be addressed by a person who associates or professes to be associated with the terrorist organisation; or
(c) who, with intention to further the activity of a terrorist organisation, addresses a meeting for the purpose of encouraging support for the terrorist organisation or to further its activity.
(2) A person, who commits the offence relating to support given to a terrorist organisation under sub-section (1), shall be punishable with imprisonment for a term not exceeding ten years, or with fine, or with both.</td><td></td></tr>
<tr><td>8. Offence relating to Funding</td><td>S/17- Punishment for raising fund for terrorist act-
Whoever raises fund for the purpose of</td><td>S/17-Punishment for raising funds for terrorist act-
Whoever, in India or in a foreign country, directly</td></tr>
</table>

(*Contd.*)

APPENDIX (*Contd.*)

(1)	(2)	(6)	(7)
		committing a terrorist act shall be punishable with imprisonment for a term which shall not be less than five years but which may extend to imprisonment for life, and shall also be liable to fine. S/40- Offence of raising fund for a terrorist organization- (*1*) A person commits the offence of raising fund for a terrorist organisation, who, with intention to further the activity of a terrorist organisation,- (*a*) invites another person to provide money or other property, and intends that it should be used, or has reasonable cause to suspect that it might be used, for the purposes of terrorism; or (*b*) receives money or other property, and intends that it should be used, or has reasonable cause to suspect that it might be used, for the purposes of terrorism; or (*c*) provides money or other property, and knows, or has reasonable cause to suspect, that it would or might be used for the purposes of terrorism.	or indirectly, raises or collects funds or provides funds to any person or persons or attempts to provide funds to any person or persons, knowing that such funds are likely to be used by such person or persons to commit a terrorist act, notwithstanding whether such funds were actually used or not for commission of such act, shall be punishable with imprisonment for a term which shall not be less than five years but which may extend to imprisonment for life, and shall also be liable to fine.".

	Explanation.- For the purposes of this sub-section, a reference to provide money or other property includes of its being given, lent or otherwise made available, whether or not for consideration. (2) A person, who commits the offence of raising fund for a terrorist organisation under sub-section (*1*), shall be punishable with imprisonment for a term not exceeding fourteen years, or with fine, or with both.	
9. Power to direct for sample	—	—
10. Punishment for malicious action for Police officer	—	—
11. Admissibility of Confession to Police Officer	—	—

(*Contd.*)

APPENDIX (*Contd.*)

(1)	(2)	(6)	(7)
12.	Admissibility of evidence collected through Interception of communication	**S/46-Admissibility of evidence collected through the interception of communications-** Notwithstanding anything contained in the Indian Evidence Act, 1872 or any other law for the time being in force, the evidence collected through the interception of wire, electronic or oral communication under the provisions of the Indian Telegraph Act, 1885 or the Information Technology Act, 2000 or any other law for the time being in force, shall be admissible as evidence against the accused in the court during the trial of a case: Provided that the contents of any wire, electronic or oral communication intercepted or evidence derived therefrom shall not be received in evidence or otherwise disclosed in any trial, hearing or other proceeding in any court unless each accused has been furnished with a copy of the order of the competent authority under the aforesaid law, under which the interception was directed, not less than ten days before trial, hearing or proceeding:	—

	Provided further that the period of ten days may be waived by the judge trying the matter, if he comes to the conclusion that it was not possible to furnish the accused with such order ten days before the trial, hearing or proceeding and that the accused shall not be prejudiced by the delay in receiving such order.	
13. Bail Provisions	—	**S/43D(5)-**Notwithstanding anything contained in the Code, no person accused of an offence punishable under Chapters IV and VI of this Act shall, if in custody, be released on bail or on his own bond unless the Public Prosecutor has been given an opportunity of being heard on the application for such release: Provided that such accused person shall not be released on bail or on his own bond if the Court, on a perusal of the case diary or the report made under section 173 of the Code is of the opinion that there are reasonable grounds for believing that the accusation against such person is prima facie true.
14. Presumption as to offence	—	**S/43E- Presumption as to offence under section 15-** In a prosecution for an offence under section 15, if it is proved —

(*Contd.*)

APPENDIX (*Contd.*)

(1)	(2)	(6)	(7)
			(*a*) that the arms or explosives or any other substances specified in the said section were recovered from the possession of the accused and there is reason to believe that such arms or explosives or other substances of a similar nature were used in the commission of such offence; or (*b*) that by the evidence of the expert the finger-prints of the accused or any other definitive evidence suggesting the involvement of the accused in the offence were found at the site of the offence or on anything including arms and vehicles used in connection with the commission of such offence, the Court shall presume, unless the contrary is shown, that the accused has committed such offence.
15.	Protection taken in Good-Faith	**S/49-Protection of action taken in good faith-** No suit, prosecution or other legal proceeding shall lie against- (*a*) the Central Government or a State Government or any officer or authority of the Central Government or State Government or	—

	District Magistrate or any officer authorised in this behalf by the Government or the District Magistrate or any other authority on whom powers have been conferred under this Act, for anything which is in good faith done or purported to be done in pursuance of this Act or any rule or order made thereunder; and (*b*) any serving or retired member of the armed forces or para-military forces in respect of any action taken or purported to be taken by him in good faith, in the course of any operation directed towards combating terrorism.	
16. Obligation to furnish information	—	**S/43F-Obligation to furnish information-** (*1*) Notwithstanding anything contained in any other law, the officer investigating any offence under this Act, with the prior approval in writing of an officer not below the rank of a Superintendent of Police, may require any officer or authority of the Central Government or a State Government or a local authority or a bank, or a company, or a firm or any other institution, establishment, organisation or any individual to furnish information in his or its possession in relation to such offence, on points or matters, where the investigating officer has reason to

(*Contd.*)

Appendix (*Contd.*)

(1)	(2)	(6)	(7)
			believe that such information will be useful for, or relevant to, the purposes of this Act. (2) The failure to furnish the information called for under sub-section (*1*), or deliberately furnishing false information shall be punishable with imprisonment for a term which may extend to three years or with fine or with both. (3) Notwithstanding anything contained in the Code, an offence under sub-section (2) shall be tried as a summary case and the procedure prescribed in Chapter XXI of the said Code [except sub-section (2) of section 262] shall be applicable thereto.'.
17.	Provisions for Custody Period	—	**S/43D(2)- Modified application of certain provisions of the Code-** (*1*) Notwithstanding anything contained in the Code or any other law, every offence punishable under this Act shall be deemed to be a cognizable offence within the meaning of clause (*c*) of section 2 of the Code, and "cognizable case" as defined in that clause shall be construed accordingly.

(2) Section 167 of the Code shall apply in relation to a case involving an offence punishable under this Act subject to the modification that in sub-section (2),—

(*a*) the references to "fifteen days", "ninety days" and "sixty days", wherever they occur, shall be construed as references to "thirty days", "ninety days" and "ninety days" respectively; and

(*b*) after the proviso, the following provisos shall be inserted, namely:—

"Provided further that if it is not possible to complete the investigation within the said period of ninety days, the Court may if it is satisfied with the report of the Public Prosecutor indicating the progress of the investigation and the specific reasons for the detention of the accused beyond the said period of ninety days, extend the said period*up to one hundred and eighty days:

Provided also that if the police officer making the investigation under this Act, requests, for the purposes of investigation, for police custody from judicial custody of any person in judicial custody, he shall file an affidavit stating the reasons for doing so and shall also explain the delay, if any, for requesting such police custody".

(*Contd.*)

APPENDIX (*Contd.*)

(1)	(2)	(6)	(7)
			(3) Section 268 of the Code shall apply in relation to a case involving an offence punishable under this Act subject to the modification that— (*a*) the reference in sub-section (*1*) thereof— (*i*) to "the State Government" shall be construed as a reference to "the Central Government or the State Government."; (*ii*) to "order of the State Government" shall be construed as a reference to "order of the Central Government or the State Government, as the case may be"; and (*b*) the reference in sub-section (2) thereof, to "the State Government" shall be construed as a reference to "the Central Government or the State Government, as the case may be". (*4*) Nothing in section 438 of the Code shall apply in relation to any case involving the arrest of any person accused of having committed an offence punishable under this Act. (*5*) Notwithstanding anything contained in the Code, no person accused of an offence punishable

under Chapters IV and VI of this Act shall, if in custody, be released on bail or on his own bond unless the Public Prosecutor has been given an opportunity of being heard on the application for such release:

Provided that such accused person shall not be released on bail or on his own bond if the Court, on a perusal of the case diary or the report made under section 173 of the Code is of the opinion that there are reasonable grounds for believing that the accusation against such person is prima facie true.

(*6*) The restrictions on granting of bail specified in sub-section (*5*) is in addition to the restrictions under the Code or any other law for the time being in force on granting of bail.

(*7*) Notwithstanding anything contained in sub-sections (*5*) and (*6*), no bail shall be granted to a person accused of an offence punishable under this Act, if he is not an Indian citizen and has entered the country unauthorisedly or illegally except in very exceptional circumstances and for reasons to be recorded in writing.

(Contd.)

APPENDIX (*Contd.*)

(1)	(2)	(6)	(7)
18.	Punishment for making demands of radioactive substances, nuclear devices, etc.	—	**S/16A-** Whoever intentionally, by use offence or threat of use of force or by any other means, demands any bomb, dynamite or other explosive substance or inflammable substances or fire arms or other lethal weapons or poisonous or noxious or other chemicals or any biological, radiological, nuclear material or device, with the intention of aiding, abetting or committing a terrorist act, shall be punishable with imprisonment for a term which may extend to ten years, and shall also be liable to fine.".
19.	Punishment for organizing of terrorist camps	—	**S/18A-** Whoever organises or causes to be organised any camp or camps for imparting training in terrorism shall be punishable with imprisonment for a term which shall not be less than five years but which may extend to imprisonment for life, and shall also be liable to fine.
20.	Punishment for recruiting for recruiting of any person or persons for terrorist act	—	**S/18B-** Whoever recruits or causes to be recruited any person or persons for commission of a terrorist act shall be punishable with imprisonment for a term which shall not be less than five years but which may extend to imprisonment for life, and shall also be liable to fine.

Bibliography

Books and Commentaries

Trilok Nath, National Security.

Sadhan Mukherjee, Trrerism and Antonov case.

Raju, K. Thomas, Indian Security Policy.

Ravi Nair, "Comporting the violence commuted by armed position groups."

Usha Rama Nathan, Extra ordinary laws and Human.

H.M. Raj Shekhar, The Nature of Indian Federalism.

U.S. Bajpai, Indian Security.

Bary Buzan, People States and Fear.

Bimal Prasad, International Studies.

Zalmy Khalilzad, Security in Asia.

J.C. Johri, Indian Government and Politics.

David Arnold, "Police power and Demise of British Rule in India."

M.P. Jain, Constitutional law of India.

K. Subramanium, Indian Security Perspectives.

H.M. Seirvai, Constitutional law of India.

W. Freidamann, Laws in changing society.

Nagendra Singh, Human Rights International Co- operation.

J.A. Andrews, Human Rights in International law.

I. Menon (ed.), Human Rights in International Law.

A.B. Robertson (ed.), Human Rights in national and International Law.

Upendra Baxi, Human Rights, Accountability and development Indian journal of international Law.
M.J. Akbar, Riots After Riots.
U. Baxi, the crisis of the Indian Legal System.
H. Beddard, Human Rights Europe.
Moskowitz, Human rights and world order.
G.O. Koppall, the emergency, the court, and Indian Democracy.

Index